THE ITINERANT ECONOMIST

THE ITINERANT ECONOMIST
MEMOIRS OF A DISMAL SCIENTIST

RUSSELL JONES

LONDON PUBLISHING PARTNERSHIP

Published by London Publishing Partnership
www.londonpublishingpartnership.co.uk

ISBN: 978-1-907994-32-6 (pbk)

A catalogue record for this book is
available from the British Library

This book has been composed in Clavo

Copy-edited and typeset by
T&T Productions Ltd, London
www.tandtproductions.com

Cover design: www.ngicreative.com
Cover images: Shutterstock, iStockphoto

Printed and bound in
Great Britain by Page Bros

*For Mick and the girls, and
all the time I wasn't there*

Economics is a very dangerous science.

— John Maynard Keynes, *Essays in Biography*

If you don't know where you're going, you might end up some place else.

— Yogi Berra

CONTENTS

FOREWORD

It was Lehman Brothers that first brought Russell Jones and me together. I had just been appointed Chief Economist Europe and Russell had been brought in as Chief Economist Japan. En route to Tokyo, Russell spent several weeks in our London Office at Broadgate while awaiting his visa, and I took an instant liking to this intelligent, well-spoken, experienced market economist with his love of economics, economic history and economic policy, with his warm manner, good pen and irreverent sense of humour.

Unlike some in the economics team at the time – and many in the firm – Russell already understood the basic implications of the fact that the world had globalised: that it meant not just having an office in every region but the need to understand each country's asset prices, financial flows and broader economic developments as part of a linked, if not always coherent, international system.

A year or so later, when I became Global Chief Economist, it was possible both to round out the team with a Chief Economist in the US who took the point and to promote Russell to Chief Economist Asia. He flourished. That experience, which was Russell's second tour in the region, did much to shape him. He gained managerial experience, he met many senior policymakers, his views were sought, he featured frequently in the media – he became a name. Later he was to bring that experience back to London, thereafter to the Gulf, and then to Sydney.

As honest as he is emotional and intelligent – and he is all three, in spades – Russell tells it all as he saw it from the vantage point of some of the world's biggest investment banks. Traders who range from the highly intelligent to the idiotic. Bankers who range from the imaginative through to the plain dull. Managers who range from skilful, modest and honest to incompetent, arrogant and dissembling. It is like that in all big institutions, of course; but in the investment banks, particularly during that period, the colours were brighter, the characters larger. No wonder the decisions they took ranged from the bold and prescient to the ridiculous and catastrophic.

Interwoven with such intrinsically domestic detail is a critical discussion of each of the main economic and financial events of the past quarter-century. This was a period of great change, with episodes of considerable turbulence, including, of course, the biggest financial crash and economic recession since the Great Depression. Russell chronicles it all.

Throughout the book, Russell spares no one, and least of all himself. He tells what he got wrong in just the same way as he explains what he got right. And he has the gift – and the honesty – to look at most issues from the other person's point of view. Particularly intriguing is the tussle that, as a man politically somewhat to the left of centre, Russell had with his conscience in this industry in which political inclinations are skewed to the right.

In short, this is not the book of a whistle-blower: the world is more complicated than most writers on this subject acknowledge. And fascinatingly, Russell's story is more moving, more telling, and more convincing than many others written in a spirit of shock-horror.

JOHN LLEWELLYN

PREFACE

A number of books have been written by people who have enjoyed lengthy careers in the financial markets, and they usually fall into one of two categories. They are either dry scholarly tomes that focus on the economic experience of some particular country, period or crisis, or they are deliberately titillating page turners that dwell on one or other of the excesses for which the financial industry has become notorious. This book does not drop neatly into either of these boxes, although it no doubt contains elements of both. The danger with it, therefore, is that it falls between two stools: those looking for scandal and grist to the mill of banker-bashing and economist-baiting might find it unfulfilling, while the academic community may well see it as lightweight and lacking in rigour.

To those that find this to be the case, I apologise, but I suggest that such judgements would largely miss the point. My desire has been to produce something altogether more personal, humble and unpretentious than a guide to City hedonism or the definitive judgement on the vicissitudes of successive business cycles.

This book traces my story over a period that began before the 'Big Bang' of 1986 and continued after the Global Financial Crisis of 2008. I was an economist employed by some of the financial world's most influential firms, based in a number of the world's major financial hubs, and during an epoch when the markets came to dominate so much of everyone's lives. I would never claim to have become part of the profession's feted glitterati, but over time I came to occupy increasingly senior positions, and this offered me unique insights into both the sector's unremitting ebbs and flows and some of the most important macroeconomic events of a unique era. The fact is that I saw a lot, and I believe the story of what I saw, and how I saw it, is worth telling.

What I therefore present is an account of what it was like to be tasked with what was, for much of the time, an extraordinarily exciting and challenging job. I also try to shine some light, as honestly as possible, on what people like me did and how we did it. For example, how did my role evolve over the years? What were the pitfalls of the job? What was it like to lead such a peripatetic and, on occasion, glamorous life? What was it like to deal with the alpha males and prima donnas with which the industry is associated? What are the issues that dominated my days and why? What did I and my contemporaries get right and what did we get wrong – and again, why? What did I make of the policymakers and other power brokers whom I met? And what lessons can I draw from my experiences for the future of the global economy and the financial industry?

In discussing all this, I must stress that my career, such as it was, would never have gone anywhere without the sponsorship and encouragement of my parents, the love and indulgence of my endlessly put-upon wife and children, the intellectual prowess and generosity of those who taught me, and the support of many of those who worked for and alongside me over the years. So to all of you, my heartfelt thanks.

As far as the layout of the book is concerned, it is presented largely in chronological order, rather than thematically. For the most part, each chapter mixes descriptions of the institutions and places I worked in, and the people I worked alongside, with the issues that confronted me as an economist and manager. After an introduction aimed at providing an explanation of what someone with my job description actually does, the narrative begins in the late seventies with my initial academic struggles and a description of my formative influences. It then moves on to the start of my career in the markets, which coincided with the initial liberalisation of the UK's financial sector in the mid eighties and the era of what became known as Thatcherism.

Subsequent chapters cover my two extended spells in Japan in the nineties, during which time the deflation of the 'Bubble Economy' turned into a generation-long economic nightmare; a brief interregnum back in the UK at the giant global investment bank UBS; my extended employment by the now-defunct Lehman Brothers; and two interludes on the buy side of the business in the mid noughties at a hedge fund and at the giant sovereign wealth fund that is the Abu Dhabi Investment Authority. The narrative culminates with my experiences at Royal Bank of Canada and

Westpac during the Global Financial Crisis and its aftermath, and a final chapter offers some concluding observations.

I have tried, where possible, to verify the dates, time lines and events alluded to. But as the book relates to an extended personal journey, I have no doubt that it is unavoidably prone to selective memory and a certain subjectivity. Needless to say, the responsibility for any factual errors remains with the author.

Acknowledgements

This book is to a large extent my wife's responsibility. When I downed tools at my last job in the financial markets in Australia in December 2012, I was faced with three months off before taking up the reins at Llewellyn Consulting in early April 2013. Frankly, I was looking forward to doing little beyond reading, keeping fit, watching some sport, enjoying Sydney's wonderful beaches and, if the opportunity presented itself, exploring a little of the outback. My wife, however, had other ideas, saying that the last thing she wanted was for me to be hanging around the house getting under her feet all day. I needed to find an outlet. 'Right', I said, 'I am going to write a book about my career', something that I had been threatening to do for a couple of years. I sat down in my office that very day and began, and what you are holding is the result.

That said, many people have helped me during the process, and, of course, there would have been no book at all without all those individuals who I have worked with during the course of my career.

Particular thanks must go to John Llewellyn, Paul Chertkow, David McWilliams, Jim O'Neill, Bill Keegan, Gavyn Davies and Jamil Baz, all of whom read the manuscript and provided vital input and direction.

My family also looked over the early drafts and made sure that I retained a sense of perspective, eschewed much of the trivial, the irrelevant and the bitchy, and generally avoided many of the sour and self-serving pitfalls that so many memoirs fall prey to. They deserve enormous credit for putting up with both my mood swings and my physical absences while I wrote the book.

Finally, I must thank my publishers, London Publishing Partnership, and in particular Sam Clark and Richard Baggaley. They were a pleasure to work with and did a wonderful job in turning my verbal meanderings into something worthy of release to the outside world.

THE ITINERANT ECONOMIST

CHAPTER 1

A RANDOM WALK

My career as a financial markets economist has spanned more than a generation: the period from the euphoria of the City of London's 'Big Bang' in 1986 until the trials, tribulations and recriminations of recent years, when we have been reminded just how much everyone loves a morality tale. Over that time I have been employed by a number of famous (some would say infamous) banks and other institutions and have, at different times, been based in several of the world's financial hubs.

It was a period during which the financial services industry expanded dramatically and exerted a disproportionate influence, for good or ill, on the lives of almost everyone on the planet, from senior politicians and policymakers to the humblest bank depositor and beyond. With this 'age of finance' came successive booms and busts and ultimately a calamitous economic crisis, the likes of which had not been seen since the thirties. It was a time of enormous flux and upheaval in the balance of global political and economic power. It was an era during which any number of fortunes were made and lost; while some accumulated obscene amounts of wealth, others languished in abject poverty. Individuals and institutions, even countries, that had once seemed unassailable suffered precipitate and ignominious falls from grace. It was a period of innovation and discovery, of arrogance and hubris, of elation and despair, of fundamental lessons forgotten and painfully relearned.

Despite one or two moments in the sun, my own direct role in all this has, in truth, been little more than a walk-on part. Indeed, looking back, in many ways my career has been somewhat random and chequered, if not one of less than heroic failure. But I have worked with some truly exceptional people. I had a ringside seat for a lot of extraordinary events. I saw and experienced at first hand the seemingly arbitrary absurdities of how financial firms were managed: all the egotism, the overconfidence, the bizarre mergers and acquisitions, the haphazard changes of strategy, the nepotism, the brazen dispensation of personal patronage, and the downright stupidity for which the industry is renowned. I witnessed some of the individual excesses that have on occasion driven the tabloid press into a frenzy and given the industry such a bad reputation with the general public. I saw my company's US headquarters destroyed on 9/11. I met some of the world's foremost movers and shakers. I travelled the world from Bogotá to Reykjavik and from Oman to Windhoek, and in between I was able to explore many of the most exciting and exotic cities on the planet. And, unlike many others who beat a similar path, I have managed to survive and exit of my own volition, at the time of my choosing, with my health and reputation intact. The fact is that I know any number of people who were less fortunate: people who lost wives, lost careers, lost fortunes, lost the plot, lost their sanity – some who even lost their lives.

In this sense I have been lucky. Lucky to earn the comfortable living I have for the length of time I have. Lucky to enjoy the luxury and pampering that have often gone with it. Lucky, for the most part, to be able to gloss over my own intellectual (and other) shortcomings. Lucky to do a job where no two days were the same and where boredom was rarely a factor. Lucky never to be sacked (although I came desperately close on more than one occasion). Lucky to have had a stable and happy family life that kept my feet on the ground and reminded me of life's more enduring values and rewards.

I worked in an industry that can in many ways be compared to the human body's cardiovascular system. Just as the heart and lungs enable the body to function, so the financial sector allows the economy to function and grow. When the financial sector works well, it exerts vital discipline on governments and companies. It facilitates sound investments (not least in infrastructure), encourages innovation and entrepreneurship, enables retirement planning and home ownership, and even broadens further education. However, if it works poorly it is degenerative. When it breaks down altogether, the effects are, as we have been reminded in recent years, catastrophic.

The financial system is an extraordinarily complex beast, and the motivations and objectives of the myriad savers and investors that underlie it are constantly adapting and evolving as society itself progresses. There is therefore a fundamental requirement for continuous interpretation of how this process is developing and will continue to develop. That is where people like me come in.

Putting things in more practical terms, my job amounted to the application of macroeconomic analysis and forecasting to financial markets with a view, in particular, to predicting how different classes of investment would perform over future periods. Over the years I have at one stage or another focused on all the major financial markets: bonds, equities and foreign exchange. The forecasts that are made can be very narrow and apply to a single piece of high-frequency economic data (such as industrial production or consumer price inflation) and its potential impact, or they can be very broad, stretching out to several years (or even longer) and encompassing any number of aspects of an economy's performance and the various markets that will be influenced by that performance. A key element of this process involves trying to understand the future direction of economic policy. Economic policy has three components: fiscal – what the government spends, what it raises in taxes and what it borrows; monetary – the level of interest rates, the growth of the money supply and credit aggregates, and the attitude towards the exchange rate; and the supply side – the evolution of an economy's basic institutions, its regulatory environment and its incentive structure.

Understanding the future direction of economic policy in turn requires knowledge of the latest theoretical debates among academic economists and an understanding of the social, cultural and political environment within which a country or countries may be operating. This knowledge requires a strong sense of historical context. History may not often repeat itself, but it certainly resonates, and I would assert that it is all too often an underweighted, if not ignored, consideration in my profession. This is especially so among the young and inexperienced, but also more widely, including among those who should know better – not least the policymakers themselves. My view has long been that economics students would do well to learn more history and politics and less mathematics.

However, the job is not just about assembling a series of projections of questionable value for different macroeconomic indicators and investment vehicles. What one cannot afford to be is some wonkish back-office computer nerd intermittently sending out into the ether one's latest set of unexplained numbers. The job has a much more wide-ranging, practical and human element. Indeed, in many ways it is about communication.

As a financial markets economist, you are required to gather and process an extraordinarily large, and ever-expanding, portfolio of information. You never quite know what the markets and those functioning in them will focus on next and what will therefore become pertinent. It might be an obscure monetary aggregate, the offshore ownership structure of a country's government bond market, demographic profiles over the next fifty years, the potential make-up of a new government, the voting record of a particular member of a central bank policy committee, the regional breakdown of a set of unemployment statistics, or the response to an economic crisis that happened eighty years ago. I was even once asked what the average number of electric power sockets in a recently built Chinese home was. Don't ask why.

One is also a summariser, an interpreter and a conduit for the transmission of that information. This role applies first to the traders (those individuals who actively deal in certain financial assets), the salespeople (those who act as intermediaries between the firm's ultimate clients and the traders), the risk managers (those who try to ensure that the firm's exposure to different asset markets is sensibly controlled), the investment bankers (those who advise the firm's clients on their financing options) and the senior management of one's own firm. But it also applies to the firm's client base, both big and small, at home and abroad. In fulfilling this second role, one may be addressing that client's own economists or other researchers, its asset allocators, its portfolio managers or its management.

Furthermore, you are encouraged to play a public relations role for your firm, speaking at conferences and appearing in the media. All of this means that not only are you constantly developing and refining your ideas, but you must also be able to articulate those ideas in one forum or another. You have to be able to communicate coherently, both verbally and in print, quickly and concisely.

The pieces that you write may be an assessment of a fragment of high-frequency data, they may be an essay on the outcome of a future event, or they may be long and detailed reports on some important aspect of the macroeconomic or financial landscape. There is an audience for all of these variations, but I have found that there is nothing better for establishing your credibility than writing the definitive study of a critical question. A huge premium is also attached to an ability to offer a succinct and insightful analysis of a particularly complex issue.

This is an extensive job description and no one could possibly master this kind of comprehensive remit overnight. Indeed, to be an economist in the financial markets is to occupy a completely thankless position. After all, if explaining the past and understanding the present are difficult enough – and an awful lot of the job is spent trying to do just that – then predicting the future with any consistent degree of accuracy is harder still. However, forecasters do not make life easy for themselves. They repeatedly fall into the same methodological and presentational traps, while there are other unavoidable considerations that render difficult the precise judgement of how good a forecast actually was. A fascinating analysis of macroeconomic forecasting conducted by the OECD just before I began my career drew the following broad conclusions, which remain pretty apposite.[1]

- Single-country forecasts frequently contain implicit inconsistencies. For example, the sum of individual-country forecasts of exports often exceeds the sum of forecasts of imports – which is logically impossible at the level of the world economy and imparts an upward bias to single-economy forecasts. Inflation forecasts often suffer similarly.

- The variance of forecasts is typically less than that of the outcomes, i.e. forecasters tend to shave the tops and bottoms off their forecasts.

- Forecasters tend to 'cluster', or to group around one another, presumably for fear of looking unwarrantedly extreme.

- There is size-of-organisation bias. 'Clustering' tends to be an inverse function of the size of the institution making the forecast. Forecasters in small organisations tend to be more outlandish. If they are wrong, few people notice, whereas if they are right, they gain publicity.

- It is difficult to assess how accurate economic forecasts have been. A year-ahead forecast may change fundamentally following a budget or a development such as a major increase in oil prices. Forecasts made a few days apart may therefore differ substantially for good reason.

- Economic forecasts are less accurate than is implied by the way in which they are presented. Forecasting to within a tenth of a percentage point for GDP growth, which is often the habit among financial market economists, is absurdly precise given the uncertainties involved.

The attitudes that prevail across financial market firms towards forecasts and economists are not exactly forgiving, and in saying this I would most definitely extend the judgement to my fellow workers. Part of the problem is that because the vicissitudes of the business cycle and the economy constantly affect the entire population, 'everyone is an economist'. Or at least everyone considers themselves qualified to opine on economics in a way that a layman would never do in relation to, say, physics or chemistry. Something else that has revealed itself over the years is that externally generated forecasts and views seem to enjoy a greater degree of initial credibility than those produced in-house. Familiarity, or proximity, tend to breed contempt.

When you are wrong – and you will be wrong an awful lot of the time – at best you are likely to be the butt of one of the numerous jokes about economists of which one's colleagues never tire (believe me, I have heard them all). Alternatively, you may be subject to derision, if not the sort of verbal tirade associated with Malcolm Tucker, the wonderfully Machiavellian character of TV's *The Thick of It*. At worst, you may see whatever credibility you had with your colleagues and with the firm's counterparties evaporate and the exit door swing open.

On the other hand, when you are right, it's considered to be down to luck (which, sadly, is often true!). But it's your job to be right and any plaudits, however enthusiastic, never last long. The attention spans of traders, salespeople and fund managers are notoriously short and their capacity for compassion and generosity of spirit is in similarly limited supply. There is always another forecast to get wrong or event to misdiagnose just around the corner.

Admittedly, part of the problem lies with some of the economists themselves. You need a certain amount of ego, if not machismo, to function in the markets. It is not an environment for shrinking violets. But some economists have long displayed a tendency to confuse this with the abandonment of any notion of humility. They are only too happy to extol the virtues of their methods (however run-of-the-mill) and to trumpet their successes (such as they are) while studiously forgetting their failures (which are usually many). Selective memory is a common trait in my profession. But a trader, a salesman or a portfolio manager who took your advice to heart, acted on it and suffered financially as a result is unlikely to be forgiving.

Marketing to clients is one of the most important aspects of the job. My particular definition of this part of the role is that one is there to offer a coherent interpretation of events. This means putting events into historical and comparative context, while presenting a series of alternative views of future developments. You provide your best estimate of the events that are most likely to come to fruition, and how the various scenarios might affect the asset class in which the client is interested.

Taking this a step further, the process has two key elements. First, there is a requirement to identify where the centre of gravity of market sentiment might be misaligned with the underlying fundamental macroeconomic forces. In other words, you need to be able to spot instances where others may have lost the plot. This may originate from poor analytics or intellectual myopia and it is perhaps best summed up in the notion that sometimes the markets just ask the wrong question. For example, they might neglect to adjust recent developments to reflect the prevailing stage of the business cycle; they might struggle to separate the cyclical from the structural, or fail to sufficiently consider the broader trade and financial linkages affecting an economy. Second, there is a requirement to identify events that will perforce have to happen. This relates in the main to the unavoidable correction of fundamental macroeconomic disequilibria and therefore to recognising that policymakers will at some stage have to face the inevitable. Part and parcel of this element of the job is a need to identify 'watch fors', such as potential future policy adjustments that offer insights into when it is appropriate to acquiesce in, or go against, the prevailing trend.

Furthermore, and perhaps self-servingly, I took the view that my value lay not so much in whether I was ultimately proved right or wrong in my 'best guess', or for that matter in my interpretation of what was going on, but rather in whether the information and signposts I provided helped the client to make an informed and rational investment decision. Obviously, having a thorough piece of research to back all this up was helpful.

Of course, some did judge you on the narrow veracity of your views and could be extremely critical of those who made a bad call. Furthermore, one certainly did not want to get a reputation for being consistently 'wrong', although precisely what 'wrong' or 'right' meant could be pretty nebulous. On the other hand, sad to say, I know of some economists who are regularly sought out for just that reason: they are viewed as reliable contra-indicators, and if their views, however misguided, enable the client to make money, then all well and good! To my knowledge, such a judgement was never applied to me, although I imagine I would be the last one to know if it had been.

At the outset of my career, in giving presentations I would borrow heavily from my senior colleagues. But what also became clear at an early stage was that you had to prepare thoroughly for these events. Just turning up and winging it was very dangerous, especially if you didn't know the client. For my part, I adopted what I called the 12:1 approach. For every hour I spoke, I tried to put in about twelve hours of preparation. Even allowing for the fact that many presentations are quite similar, over the course of my career that is an awful lot of preparation. In 2008, which was admittedly an intense year, I undertook more than 250 face-to-face presentations with clients, while there were also any number of conference calls and internal meetings.

The typical meeting would last up to an hour. It could be one-to-one in nature, or one could be confronted with a group, and sometimes a very large group, whose individual knowledge of what you were going to talk about could vary enormously. You might therefore find yourself at a loss to know at what technical level to pitch things. Are you dealing with a room full of people with doctorates in economics or a group of laymen? And how much English do they understand? You get some clues – central bankers will tend to be very technically and linguistically proficient, for example. And you rapidly learn to ask the salesperson accompanying you to brief you about the audience. But you can still judge it poorly, which is acutely embarrassing and can in extremis irreparably damage a relationship and your reputation.

Some economists like to go page by page through a formally structured presentation built around a series of slides that could be put up on a screen or put in a pack to be passed round the attending participants. In this way, the economist sets the agenda and can steer the presentation towards his preferred topics. Indeed, I worked with one very highly regarded UK economist who would keep to a script *verbatim* and practice his precise delivery for hours at a time in front of a mirror. Moreover, he hated any interruption to the extent that it could completely knock him off track. Naturally, his colleagues would take great delight in disrupting his solitary training sessions as often as possible.

I always thought that this sort of approach had the tendency to become unduly formulaic after a few iterations, inducing narcolepsy. It could also make one lazy and narrow in outlook. I much preferred to ask the client at the outset of the meeting what he or she wanted to talk about. This meant I would be addressing their particular concerns, while the tone and format of their questions would also help me to understand at what level I should pitch things. This could be much more challenging, in that one could be detached from one's comfort zone, but it was typically more interesting for all concerned. It offered the chance for real dialogue, and I often learned more this way. This approach worked for me throughout my career and ultimately helped me to earn a reputation as a thoughtful and interesting presenter. On the other hand, it meant that my preparation had to be much broader.

Of course, a lot of clients, and especially those who were young or unsure of themselves, just threw the ball straight back to you and said, 'you start off and we will interrupt where we see fit', although the fact is that the ones that took this line rarely interjected. They just let you spoon-feed them. I thought this was lazy. When, for a period in my career, I went on the 'buy side' of the business and was therefore on the receiving end of presentations, I always tried to give the presenter some inkling of what I was most interested in.

If you have to give five or more presentations in a day, as I frequently had to do, client passivity can become a nightmare. On an extended marketing trip – and they could last for a fortnight – the last thing I wanted was to be faced with the prospect of offering more or less the same presentation over and over again for hour after hour, day after day. The danger was that you switched to autopilot to the extent that it could become akin to an out-of-body experience. Alternatively, you could completely forget where you were in a presentation and find yourself wondering if you had made a certain point already or even whether you made it at the previous meeting!

If the clients wouldn't play ball, to maintain one's sanity one was faced with changing the content, the order or even the very conclusions of the presentation. Indeed, once, at the end of a long marketing trip in Asia, and when the client was unfamiliar with us all, two Lehman Brothers colleagues and I swapped identities and presentations – and no one noticed. After all, we had heard each other give them enough times. The 12:1 rule had been met several times over.

Generally, I encouraged interruptions. As long as they were constructive, they helped to develop one's thoughts and made the meeting richer. That said, if they were not constructive, if they were ill-informed, rambling or tangential to the points you were trying to make, they could be a problem. And the fact is that some people just liked to gun for you. This might be to stress-test your arguments. It might be to defend an alternative view in front of their subordinates. Or it might just be because a particular individual liked the sound of his or her own voice. You just had to manage such occasions by staying calm and reasonable. Over time you became less disturbed by the difficult or impolite people you encountered, although a nasty egotistical client always gets my blood pressure up – and I rarely forgot them.

The one thing that you literally *never* forget is the first time that a presentation goes horribly wrong. It is a searing experience from which some struggle to entirely recover. The first occasion that I crashed and burned was when, a year or so into my career, my boss asked me to stand in for him at the last minute. The problem was that he didn't brief me about the client. As it turned out, he was a chief economist for a major asset manager, he had a PhD and he was very market savvy. He rapidly exposed my market inexperience and the holes in my technical tool kit. It was a very long and chastening hour. But I remember ploughing on, concluding that I had no choice, and hoping that my ums and errs and dissembling did not appear quite as appalling to him as they felt to me. And I am glad to say that I did present to him again. He didn't refuse to see me, although whether that was out of human decency or because he wanted some amusement, I never found out.

This episode brought home not just that you need to 'know your client': it also taught me that you need to know your limitations. There is nothing wrong in saying that you don't know much about a topic or that you don't have a strong opinion on something. That is much better than pretending that you do and then being found out. Bullshitting is one of the most difficult arts to perform successfully, and it has a huge downside.

I hate to stereotype individuals or groups, but certain types of client displayed consistent behaviour and would therefore encourage a particular type of preparation on my part. The most polite, most diverse in gender terms (the markets have remained something of a boys' club throughout my career), and often the most well-informed and balanced in outlook were almost always the central bankers, government officials and international civil servants, such as those that populated the IMF, the OECD and the BIS. The Japanese were usually the most passive and were reluctant to take issue with you during presentations. The blue-blooded Brits were the haughtiest and invariably the most anti-European. The Aussies and Kiwis were the most relaxed and friendly, although that did not mean that they were necessarily lacking in smarts. The most intense were often from the Indian subcontinent or elsewhere in Asia. And the toughest, most impatient and rudest were the hedge fund managers, and especially those in the US, with New Yorkers top of the pile.

Indeed, hedge fund managers often appeared to believe that their particular status meant that the normal rules of human relationships could be suspended. The typical meeting with a hedge fund manager – and with very few exceptions they were male – would start late, as they would almost always keep you waiting, and would begin with the statement that they could only give you a few minutes (even when you had flown halfway around the world and bent over backwards to turn up at the time they specified) because they were 'in the middle of a trade'. You might also immediately be confronted with the dreaded 'just give me your three best trade ideas', a request that was rather at variance with an economist's skill set and almost certainly deliberately designed to put you on the back foot. Even if you had prepared yourself for this kind of minimalist approach to investment advice (and one learned to have such responses in reserve), the three ideas you offered would invariably be exactly what the person in front of you was not doing and would be shot down in flames or just instantly dismissed as 'consensus views', and therefore of no value.

Other common hedge fund 'tricks' include being told on arrival that the designated host of your meeting was out of the country and hadn't bothered to tell you; the senior fund manager who joins the meeting late and makes you start again; the attendee who spends the entire meeting ignoring you and playing with their Blackberry; the person who turns to the back of your presentation and interrupts you to ask a question about a chart you had not planned to focus on for another ten minutes, if at all; and the guy (it was always a guy) who walks out of the meeting with no explanation and never returns. And what you rarely, if ever, received was an apology.

Then there is the bigoted client. These came in various categories, shapes and sizes, but they were invariably male and often had no formal training in economics. There was the political bigot – always right wing and often American or British. There was the know-it-all: 'it's so easy; everyone else is stupid, especially those making policy; why can't everyone see it as clearly as I do?' There was the conspiracy theorist, who was convinced that all official statistics, but especially the inflation numbers, were either deliberately manipulated or completely fabricated. There was the 'gold bug', who thought everything that central banks and governments could and would do was going to be inflationary and that all we needed to do was to return to 'sound money', and in particular the Gold Standard. And, of course, there was just the narrow-minded fool.

Here is a selection of things I have heard from clients over the years:

- 'I think we should just build a wall around Japan and sink it – it's toxic';

- 'the French are all communists';

- 'Gordon Brown is a communist';

- 'the Bundesbank/ECB/BOJ/BOE is just so fucking stupid';

- 'how can inflation only be 2% when the price of everything I buy is going up';

- 'why would the UK even consider something as dumb as to join the Euro';

- 'I think we should just nuke 'em [Iraqis]';

- 'these countries are all fucked up because they have Labour governments';

- 'to understand that all Chinese are crooks, you just have to look at their statistics';
- 'the Fed is destroying American democracy by debasing our currency'.

I could go on.

Even though most reasonable people would want to take the other side of these views, one could simply not afford to react, or at least one had to react carefully and moderately. For a start, there would generally be a salesperson present, whose very professional life depended on their relationship with this client. But there was a bigger picture too. The client in question might be very important to the firm as a whole. Hence, you just had to humour people like this or try to change the subject. You get better at dealing with them over time, but many were the occasions on which I wanted to walk out of a meeting or tell someone just how sad, small-minded and pathetic they were.

Another regular source of frustration was the salesperson who chaperoned you to client meetings. Over the years I have worked with some fantastic salespeople: totally professional and good to be around. In general, though, I have found financial market salespeople to be a particular breed. They would often bury their true personalities very deeply. The side that I usually saw was selfish, blinkered, fragile, paranoid, devious and stressed. Their relationships with their clients are everything to them, to the extent that anything, and anybody, else becomes secondary. You, the economist, and the views you bring, are merely a means to an end and that end is their commission on trades.

Some salespeople would come across as incredibly protective of their clients, others would pretty much worship the ground their clients walked on. They would quote at length what the client said, the successful trades they had done and the money they had made, and they'd regale you with wide-eyed and avaricious stories of their much-sought-after lifestyles. This was especially the case with hedge fund managers, who, of course, could dispense financial patronage on a massive scale. To be a trusted salesperson to a Soros or a Moore Capital could be a ticket to financial security for life. But the cost in terms of their personality was frequently terminal.

All this meant that the salesperson would want you to tell the client what the client wanted to hear. You might have a PhD, you might have decades of experience, but you would be briefed in minute detail about what to say and what to avoid saying. You would sit and watch the extraordinary fawning and sycophancy that some salespeople indulged in, and you would be amazed by how deluded some of these people were to imagine that the client liked them for themselves, rather than as someone who, like many others, provided a service and could be depended on for tickets to this concert or that sporting event, or who would pick up the tab at this bar or that five-star restaurant. I never ceased to be surprised by how much some of these people were willing to prostitute themselves, or for that matter how much their jobs consumed them.

Then, of course, there was the salesperson who thought that the meeting was about him rather than about delivering the economist to the client. In this spirit he would interrupt your presentation with his own observations, which might be inconsistent with what you were saying, or just gobbledegook (remember: everyone's an economist), or to curry favour he might side with the client in a debate. This sort of behaviour used to drive me mad and was also common among senior managers who might accompany you to a meeting. They could rarely bear to be silent or to be out of the spotlight for long. Indeed, as recently as last year I went to visit a major European central bank and over lunch with the head of its reserve management department found myself constantly being interrupted by my boss. After the fourth or fifth such episode there was a pregnant pause, after which the client just said, 'now Russell, where were we before we were side-tracked'. Such victories were rare, though – and he still didn't shut up.

Traders would rarely come on marketing trips or attend client meetings, although when they did I often found their different slant on things fascinating. It is easy to characterise the trader as one of life's risk takers, if not its gamblers, with an attention span that rarely extends beyond the most recent flow that has moved the market up or down. And yes, many were just like that. If they had to attend a meeting with you, these guys would be like caged tigers, unable to keep still, forever fingering their Blackberries like small boys playing with their privates, and they would rarely see the event through. But some of the better traders I knew were incredibly well informed and would love to debate with economists. They actively studied the macro landscape and anything else, from psychology to the theory of numbers, if it would give them an edge. Having them around in a meeting could really add something to the discussion, not least because it might help a client to turn my economic analysis into a specific asset allocation decision that could make him money. It might also allow me to switch off and take a breather for a few moments.

Over the years, marketing trips were perhaps the best source of amusing stories; some that relate to myself and some that relate to others and have become market legends. Perhaps my favourite is that of the economist who fell asleep in his own presentation. Jet lag and fatigue have been occupational hazards over the course of my career. Indeed, it is hard to describe quite how difficult it could be giving your sixth presentation of the day to a key client who expects you to treat him as the most important person in the world when you are nine time zones away from home and when you were staring at the ceiling of your hotel room from 3:30 am that morning. I once flew from London to Wellington, New Zealand, and back in the space of four days for the sake of a single meeting, and on another occasion did four one-hour presentations in four different US cities (Dallas, Kansas City, Milwaukee and Chicago) in a single day! But at least I managed to stay awake in each one.

This could not be said for a certain ageing economist working for a UK stockbroker in Japan in the eighties. A long way from home, he was sitting beside his salesman on a comfortable sofa conducting the day's last meeting at the end of a series of trying days. Halfway through his spiel, the client interrupted him to ask a long and convoluted question. His flow interrupted, the exhausted economist just couldn't keep his eyes open and almost instantaneously nodded off. The salesman noticed that his colleague's eyes were shut and tried to wake him up by gently jiggling up and down as the client, oblivious, droned on. But the economist had 'gone' in the way that only chronic jet lag can encourage and the salesman only succeeded in causing him to tip sideways off the edge of the sofa! There but for the grace of God...

Another abiding memory is of a lunch I had with the governor of an Asian central bank some fifteen years ago. I was at Lehman Brothers at the time and my colleague (and US chief economist) Steve Slifer had known this particular senior policymaker for many years; certainly for some time before he was elevated to run the bank. Steve and I were invited to eat at the governor's favourite restaurant and were treated to an extended feast of largely unrecognisable and, at least to this particular Westerner, less-than-appetising delicacies. What is more, by the side of each place was a cut-glass jug of what I at first took to be iced tea but which I soon discovered was a brand of domestically manufactured whisky. Finest single malt this was not. Each of the ten courses was washed down with a toast of this firewater, so that by the end of the meal (during which we occasionally discussed the world economy), Steve and I were hopelessly drunk.

The governor, who clearly had considerably more experience of this hooch than us, was still on sparkling form however, and as we still had three hours before our flight to Tokyo, he invited us back to the bank to give an impromptu presentation to its economics department. This was hardly something we could refuse and Steve and I were duly ferried back with him in his chauffeur-driven limousine and gave a barely coherent thirty-minute talk to a room full of economists, of whom only a few could speak English. Talk about a theatre of the absurd! The hangover I suffered on the flight back to Japan was nothing short of epic, but the client and the attendant salesman were happy and that is what mattered.

A third story worth recounting is that of a particularly gregarious US economist who when invited into the office of the client he was visiting managed to trip on the carpet and fall headlong into a glass coffee table, cutting his forehead open in the process. He insisted on carrying on with his presentation, nevertheless, while the client and accompanying salesman intermittently passed him paper towels to staunch the flow of blood. When these ran out the meeting was adjourned and the economist was taken to hospital to get stitched up. Now that is what I call going above and beyond the call of duty.

So why do we do this job? Well someone has to. We all need aspects of the context in which we operate explained to us and we all – individuals, companies and governments – look and plan ahead all the time. We all forecast constantly. We all have in our head a base case or best case of how the future will play out and some notion of less positive outcomes. It might only apply to what will happen when we cross the road. It might not be that scientifically based. It might be coloured by wishful thinking or some other bias. But these projections of the future will be based on a set of assumptions and we use them to work out contingency plans. Much of the time our internal dialogue is saying, 'if things don't work out the way I would like or the way I think most probable, then I will have understood to some extent why and will respond in this way or that'.

All that economists are doing is using such additional expertise and knowledge as they might possess above and beyond that of the layman to generate a projection of a reasonable economic outcome, and the skew of risks around that outcome, for a particular event or set of events. Yes, as most of us are often privy to roughly the same information set, we frequently reach similar conclusions: the market consensus if you like. But not always. Accumulated experience and a particular skill set can encourage different conclusions. Nor is the consensus view without value. It is generally better than naive forecasts such as might be generated by just using the outcome in the previous period or the average of some previous set of periods. Moreover, as I hinted earlier, it is often the analytical approach taken and the assessment of risks around your central case that can be most useful. I always thought that one of the smarter questions I used to get asked was, 'if you are wrong with your base case view, in which direction do you think you will be wrong, and why?'

The fact is that financial market firms cannot function without economists. A thought experiment I often ran (especially around bonus time) was what would happen if my team just walked off the job and there was no macro research input? For all their proclivity to opine on the subject, the traders and salespeople were often not formally trained in economics. Hence, the traders would struggle to understand and interpret markets. The salespeople would have little of substance to sell. Their clients would ridicule, or even abandon, them. Without our constant drip-feed of analytical commentary, they would be rudderless, or at least fenced in by their own narrow prejudices. Every day was a round of 'Russ, this means x doesn't it?' 'Russ, that Chinese number was good, right?'; 'Russ, what do you know about this new central banker?'; 'Russ, my client wants to know what happened the last time the Fed did this?'; 'Russ, why is the market ignoring that and dwelling on this?' Spoon feed me. Make me sound smart. Make me some money.

Yet at the end of the year, we would often find ourselves well down the compensation pecking order and our bonus pool would invariably be whittled down so that those of others might be inflated. The loss of a successful trader or salesperson was invariably seen as a bigger problem than the loss of a good economist. Of course, some of the firms I worked for had a more enlightened view of research than others, but achieving something akin to the financial and broader recognition that I feel we deserved was a huge challenge. Indeed, no matter how persuasive or politically astute one might be, one often had to resort to veiled or unveiled threats to obtain something close to what one thought fair. The problem was that when it came to blackmail and extortion, my professional peer group just couldn't compete with the rest of the firm, where the art of pursuing financial self-interest had generally been taken to stratospheric levels.

The bonus culture is one of the most widely publicised and criticised aspects of the financial world, the public perception being that vast sums are handed out at the end of each year to people who have done little or nothing to earn that money, or who have only generated profits for their firm through the provision of misinformation, sleight of hand or some nefarious act or other. It is impossible in the light of recent events and the numerous high-profile cases of financial subterfuge on the part of certain individuals to deny that the industry is culpable of such behaviour. Nor would I want to do so. I cannot defend the indefensible. The financial sector has long acted as a magnet for the greedy, the selfish and the thoughtless, and some of the things that have been perpetrated over the last two and a half decades, not least in the area of employee compensation, have been little short of obscene.

But performance-related pay isn't necessarily a bad thing. If appropriately framed, it can provide the impetus for productivity enhancement. The real issue, therefore, is the precise manner in which this approach to pay has been employed by financial firms.

Part of the problem was that bonuses were calculated in a way that was too arbitrary and lacking in transparency, and the process was captured by too many who saw such payments as a right. The real underlying issue is one of perverse incentives. Once those incentives were embedded, there was little or no desire within firms to change them. Indeed, efforts in this direction were likely to make it very difficult to retain or recruit staff.

With basic pay in the industry often not as extravagant as it is sometimes portrayed (it was bonuses that really drove remuneration into the stratosphere), and with no threat (until the last few post-crisis years) that bonus payments could be 'clawed back' in the event of poor performance, traders, who were in any case some of life's chancers, were incentivised to roll the dice and take excessive risks. What is more, the senior management of financial market firms tended to be dominated by previously successful traders. They often saw the establishment of a forceful proprietary trading team – a group set up to trade using the firm's own cash – as a top priority, with little thought paid to the expense. Senior management would also hanker after the buzz of their old jobs. They wanted to continue to trade even though their other responsibilities might blunt the edge that brought about their original elevation to the upper echelons of the bank. But a more fundamental problem was that a residual love of risk would affect other decisions they made; decisions that they took within the context of a further layer of misaligned and malign incentives. After all, the company's shareholders could largely be depended on to carry the can for any errors they made. And unfortunately, such attitudes would cascade down through the firm to all levels.

The fact is that overall salaries became too skewed towards bonuses. This was particularly the case at the large investment banks, where, until 2007, base salaries typically accounted for only a minor proportion of total compensation. Indeed, I was subject to just such a regime during my time at Lehman Brothers and Royal Bank of Canada. In an industry that attracts more than its fair share of strong characters and big egos, and where the attitude of 'you get nothing unless you fight for it' is actively cultivated, this was asking for trouble, especially as many of the people I worked with over the years enjoyed lifestyles that could certainly not be described as frugal.

Bonus time itself was a horrible period, when the worst elements of human nature went on display. Despite endless efforts by HR departments to present it in a different light and apply formal 'bonus calculation rules', decision making on the size and allocation of the pot was a secretive and highly subjective process during which divisional and personal feuds would be settled, senior management made sure they feathered their nests, the biggest egos would threaten to resign if they were not paid a certain (grossly inflated and unwarranted) amount, certain individuals, for whatever reasons, would be identified as being too important to the business to upset (read lose), and people at the lower end of the food chain could be treated as an afterthought. On the other hand, most employees would believe that what they had done over the previous twelve months should make them immune to the broader financial situation of the firm or the division or department in which they worked.

In the end, it was a recipe for an orgy of petty politics, nepotism, posturing, greed and self-aggrandisement. Both as a manager and as a recipient, I used to hate the whole process. I therefore greeted the rebalancing of compensation packages away from bonuses that began in 2009 with relief, although this is not to pretend that the issues around remuneration in the industry – particularly the attitudes of many individuals – have been fully addressed: they certainly have not.

The challenge that we economists had to overcome in the bonus debate was the unfortunate fact that, as far as management and much of the rest of the firm were concerned, we were a necessary but unfortunate *cost*. It was difficult to definitively demonstrate your contribution to the bottom line. A trader can always point to their profit and loss (P&L) account; a salesman to commission earned; an investment banker to the deals brokered and the fees brought in; a manager to his or her division's P&L or their strategic importance to the firm's business plan. But an economist? Our value was much harder to establish. It was a decidedly grey area. Yes, if the firm's traders and a client or two backed your non-consensus call on a central bank interest rate decision and things went your way, you could point to an obvious financial win. But how can you quantify the benefits of an accurate inflation forecast made two years ago, a beautifully written analysis of a structural change in the world economy that will play out over several decades, the sagacity of your comments at morning meetings, a particularly clear client presentation, or a perfectly pitched soundbite on live television news? It's much tougher.

Over the years, various management teams I dealt with would, on occasion, seek to apply more rigid metrics to the performance of people like myself and to force us through a similar evaluation process to everyone else. The '360 degree' internal and external surveys I could accept, although these were also subject to biases, not least those related to personality and sample size, and the external ones could easily be manipulated by the larger financial institutions. But some of the other measures I found ridiculous, if not outright Stalinist in nature, and I fought tooth and nail against them. For example, I have been confronted with proposals to judge economists' performance on the basis of the number of research notes published (no mention of quality, length or accuracy); on how many clients were visited (little interest in their relative importance or how the meeting went); on the number of phone calls made to clients (no interest in the length of call, the topic of conversation or the client response); on how many TV/

radio/newspaper appearances were made (even though few in the audience would have any contact with your particular financial institution); and the one that irked me most of all: on the notional P&L on the trade recommendations we were forced to attach to the end of our research articles. In addition to writing original, thought-provoking and prescient research, then, we were asked to produce the relative value calls that salespeople could sell and traders could trade! We were in short being asked to do everyone else's job for them and if we didn't do it very well, we lost out financially to their gain!

Given all this, I always tended to conclude that economists as a group were underappreciated and (relatively) underpaid. The bottom line for management seemed to be that as you can't measure the contribution of research accurately, you can screw them. My own view was more akin to that of Albert Einstein, who is reputed to have said: 'What counts can't always be measured and what can be measured doesn't always count.' Not that this will encourage many from outside the business reading this to shed too many tears on my behalf. No doubt they will conclude that I am just displaying the same self-centred attitudes as everyone else in finance. You see: we can't win!

Politically speaking, the markets are not quite the hive of free market fundamentalism that you might expect. Yes, those of the political right tend to predominate, but there are fewer true believers than is commonly supposed. It could also be argued that in many instances a form of inverted 'classism' exists. In London, the most outspoken Tories often tend to be those from the poorest backgrounds – the archetypal East End barrow boy traders were generally Mrs Thatcher's biggest fans. The middle- and upper-class employees tended to be 'wetter', although this was rarely the case on the vexed issue of Europe, where the 'Little Englander' mentality was supremely dominant. I wish I had five pounds for every time someone had said to me: 'I love France but...'. It was (and is) the financial markets equivalent of the ever-odious, 'I am not a racist, but...'.

I can also honestly say that political moderation was perhaps most in evidence in economics and research departments. The majority of those I worked with, and certainly my more experienced colleagues, leant towards the 'soft centre'. If they voted Conservative, it was typically without much ideological fervour. If they voted Labour, they were the mildest of social democrats. Certainly, my own centre-left politics (one Tory colleague christened me a 'Bordeaux Socialist' because of my penchant for red wine) were no rarity. Indeed, some of the more reputable City economists, not least Gavyn Davies of Goldman Sachs fame, were left-leaning, and any number have over the years offered their support to the left-wing and centrist parties of British politics. This was also a tendency that I encountered in Europe, Australia and New Zealand.

It's also fair to say that the ribbing one took from one's colleagues as a liberal/leftie diminished over time. Back in the mid-eighties heyday of Thatcher and Reagan, when the British Labour Movement appeared to be so anachronistic and out of touch, I seemed to be under remorseless attack. Latterly, when my politics came up in a work setting at all, I was confident enough to joke that I was in reality a Communist and had been trying to bring down the capitalist system from the inside for more than twenty-five years, adding that in 2008 I and my other clandestine comrades nearly succeeded. Another line I liked to employ was borrowed from an Australian Labor Party MP, who when accused of enjoying the trappings of his elevated public position more than his politics suggested he should responded that 'there is nothing in socialist doctrine that says that one should impoverish oneself during the capitalist phase of development'. However, this joke tended to go over a lot of people's heads.

What have changed rather less over time, however, are the assumptions that people outside the business make about one's political leanings. I have lost count of the times I have been at some social gathering and found myself talking to someone who, because of what I do for a living, assumed I must be a Tory. But you can't win. If the person you were chatting to was of that ilk and you tried to put them right about your views, they would see you as a traitor and/or a hypocrite. And it wasn't much better if the person was of the left. I have also lost count of the number of times that I have been accused of selling my soul to the investment banking devil.

I can't deny that, given my political leanings, there is some element of hypocrisy in what I have done over the last twenty-six years. But frankly, I was doing the only job for which I showed any innate talent in the only environment where I saw the realistic possibility of earning a decent living from it. Moreover, such political purity as I ever aspired to in my youth has been progressively diluted over the years as the world has moved on, my family responsibilities have multiplied (parenthood is probably the most powerful source of conservatism) and the cynicisms of middle age have overtaken me. I have also seen so many left-of-centre governments disappoint. But I have always resented the fact that people would presume to know my personal moral and ethical values, how I voted and perhaps even how I behaved merely from being told of the industry in which I worked.

All of which brings me to the issue of the widespread external perception of the financial world's unbridled excess and debauchery. It would be foolish to deny the egotism, the selfishness, the avarice and the acquisitive nature of many with whom I worked, nor indeed the bending and breaking of the law that has been so much in evidence over my time in the industry, and not least in the last decade. Similarly, I cannot deny the culture of alcohol abuse with which the industry is associated. This too is a fact of life, although it typically applies to a minority and I often wonder quite how much worse it is than in other professions and industries.

When I first began my career, binge-drinking certainly appeared to be more prevalent than it is today, and it seemed more deliberately conspicuous in nature. For example, at one company I worked for in the late eighties, the gilt trading desk's idea of a Friday afternoon postprandial digestif was to consume a pint of port each, with the obvious catastrophic consequences for productivity and office harmony when the guilty parties belatedly found their way back to work. On the other hand, I would never want to understate the 'heroic' capacity of my Australian colleagues at the last firm I worked for to consume beer until the early hours and then turn up on time for work the next day.

Turning to sex, well I suppose that there were as many instances of office romances, affairs and trysts in the financial world as in any other industry. On the other hand, I will admit that over the years I occasionally became aware of the provision of sexual favours in the hope that it would facilitate future business, both directly by saleswomen and indirectly through the arrangement of prostitutes. What is more, what was often expected of secretaries, and for that matter by secretaries, during my time in Japan went rather beyond the typical Western job description. Indeed, I also have it on excellent authority that one senior (non-Japanese) economist working for a Japanese bank was effectively offered the use of a 'concubine' as part of his contract – I should add that he turned the offer down. As for homosexuality, it was very much the love that could not speak its name. I got to know a number of gay people well during the course of my career, but most went out of their way to hide their sexual orientation and it was hard to gain their confidence. In the financial world, 'coming out' was, until the greater focus on diversity of recent years, seen neither as a positive career move nor as something that was conducive to a quiet life in what was an environment frequently characterised by testosterone, machismo and myopia.

As for drugs, well I won't deny they were occasionally around and in close proximity to the dealing floor, although rather less than is generally perceived, not least because many banks began drug testing employees in the late nineties. But I knew one senior City economist who enjoyed a long and successful career whose breakfast each day consisted of a cup of black coffee and a large joint of finest Moroccan hashish, after which he would happily go on to address the trading floor about the economic events ahead. He would also regularly partake of a top-up during his lunch break, but it never seemed to affect his performance and no one ever suspected what he was up to. I have to say that, rather than frowning upon such behaviour, I am in awe of it. Such indulgences would leave most human beings an incoherent wreck, if not comatose, but in his case it merely elicited a sort of Zen-like calm.

There was a period in the early noughties when on a Thursday or Friday night the trained eye could spot the drug dealers arriving on their mopeds to deliver their powders and potions to their City customers in Broadgate Circus. I also know one or two salesmen and traders who succumbed to serious cocaine habits, although I would stress that on each occasion that I came across this, the company in question not only kept it quiet but assisted them in getting help.

Perhaps the most gratuitous episodes of excess that I witnessed were bound up with client entertainment, particularly when hedge fund managers were being taken out. On such occasions it was common for contests to develop to order the most expensive round of cocktails or bottles of fine wine, with senior management insisting that they, rather than the client, won. The smart client would put up a good show of competing and then gracefully accept defeat once the stakes had been bid up to absurd levels. This meant that over the course of the evening one could end up sampling, if not drowning in, some of the finest alcoholic beverages known to man. There was also the odd episode of a more sordid nature, it is true – such as when a senior hedge fund manager was wined, dined and whored across Tokyo in a (successful) attempt to convince him to use the firm I was working for at the time as his prime broker.

If I was witness or party to alcoholic excess over the years, the same could be said of food. I have been lucky to sample some of the world's finest cuisine, served in some of the world's finest restaurants, with perhaps the only downside being that I have often been 'singing for my supper' while doing so. When you are sitting there gathering your thoughts for a presentation or a discussion where you will be the focus of attention and have to be on your toes, the delights of the food on offer tend to pass you by. Indeed, if you are actually charged with giving a formal speech over lunch or dinner, the food will *literally* pass you by. Your untouched plate will be removed before you have had a chance to sample it, and you are beholden to some sympathetic waiter to take pity on you and save you something that you can consume in an obscene rush when the event is over.

Plying my trade across numerous foreign lands has also meant trying things that are, to say the least, different: foods for which the term 'acquired taste' was invented. Over the years I have been confronted by deer penis in Singapore (I thought it was a sausage); a spicy chicken dish in Beijing that encourages your mouth to go numb, rather as it would at the dentist, with distinctly embarrassing results over the course of the rest of the meal; blow fish sashimi (the one that can kill you if the chef gets it wrong) and whale blubber (I initially thought it was tofu) in Tokyo; and the spinal cord of a cow in Abu Dhabi (think BSE!).

But the weirdest thing I ever ate was in Iceland. After a speech I had made to the Icelandic banking community in Reykjavik in the mid nineties, there was a dinner, the first course of which was a small, silvery-whitish cube presented on a square plate. This cube gave off a smell that was unspeakable. When, with the encouragement of my hosts, I put it in my mouth, it was as if all the fish I had ever eaten in my life had been concentrated into a single lump and mixed with household bleach. The net result was that fluid flowed from every orifice in my head. To help me swallow it, and believe me I didn't want to, I was then instructed to shotgun the small glass of clear liquor that was provided by the side of the plate. This did the trick but only tended to aggravate the entire reaction where the bodily fluids were concerned.

CHAPTER 1

I had just eaten hákarl: a Greenland shark that is buried in the ground with its innards still in situ for six to twelve weeks before being hung out to dry in the Arctic wind for several months. I kept it down, but I swear that if I concentrate I can still taste the taste and smell the smell.

This episode could be considered a metaphor for my whole financial career.

CHAPTER 2

INITIAL
STIRRINGS

So how did this career, with all its twists, turns and adventures, come about? Well in many ways it was an accident. My calling was not the result of some grand plan hatched as an adolescent or foisted on me by authoritarian parents. Nor was it the result of familial patronage, or some greedy individualistic desire to get rich, at least not in the sense that it was for so many of those who I found myself working with. My background was middle class out of working class. My father, ultimately one of Britain's foremost hoteliers, was born into relative poverty in Liverpool and was forced to leave school at 14 when his father died. Thanks to his hard work and diligence, I was the first of my family to attend a fee-paying school and the first to have the chance to attend university. I like to think that I inherited at least some of my father's strong work ethic and, under the tutelage of two excellent schoolmasters, I developed a passion for economics in my mid teens.

This was the mid seventies. Britain's post-war boom was over and many illusions – political, social and economic – were being shattered. As practised, the Keynesian conventional policymaking wisdom of the fifties and sixties had fallen prey to hubris, and was proving inadequate to meet the challenges of the first oil shock, exchange rate instability and the disturbingly high inflation that followed. Social and political unrest was rife in the UK and elsewhere.[2] Notwithstanding the fact that parts of the fabric of society appeared to be unravelling, I found it fascinating, especially the policymaking angle.

I did well in my A levels and an economics degree seemed to be the logical next step. The problem was that I was poor at maths.

Indeed, I had developed something of a phobia about it; a phobia that lasts to this day. Yet economics was becoming more and more mathematics and model based. The seventies saw a growing tendency within academia (only recently partially reversed) to view the subject as a pure science, complete with the sort of natural laws one associates with physics, for example.[3] Too many economists were seeing reality through the lenses of their models, and mathematical beauty was being confused with reality, which was unfortunately a lot messier. Any interactions between economics and history, politics, psychology, anthropology and philosophy – the elements that I found so fascinating and which must necessarily colour the way that economies are in practice run – were being assumed away as either dangerous or irrelevant.[4]

The net result of my mathematical shortcomings and the rise of the economic puritans was that I was denied a place at Cambridge and instead found myself taking a joint honours degree in economics and economic history at Bristol. As it turned out, this proved to be a stroke of luck. The course was overwhelmingly qualitative rather than quantitative. Not only that, but I became fascinated by twentieth-century economic history, and in particular the era of the Great Depression. I have been living off the knowledge of that period that I accumulated at that time for much of the past two and a half decades.

Although I largely escaped ordeal by equation, both at school and at university, the overwhelming majority of those who taught me were Friedmanite monetarists, if not disciples of the 'new classical' school of economics. In their wonderful world, individuals pursued 'maximising' behaviour, preferences were stable, expectations were wholly 'rational' and markets were 'efficient'. Every piece of new information was processed immediately and correctly by economic agents. Prices reacted instantaneously and appropriately to any relevant news, but didn't react to irrelevancies. Hence, the world tended towards harmony, stability and predictability, such that asset bubbles, financial crises and major recessions were largely beyond the ken of these economists. They preached the absence of a long-term trade-off between growth or employment and inflation, the primacy of monetary policy, and that fiscal activism was at best a cumbersome tool for demand management and at worst something that could both exaggerate the amplitude of business cycles and undermine the flexibility and dynamism of an economy. Some even went so far as to suggest that business cycles largely reflected random fluctuations in productivity growth: so-called real business cycle theory.[5]

Their policy mantras were the maintenance of 'sound money' and fiscal discipline in the macroeconomy and the paring back of regulatory interference in the microeconomy. Over time, the task of government should be confined to the rule of law, defence and addressing the relatively few market failures that they could accept as insurmountable. In their eyes economics became almost an adjunct of moral philosophy. It was that simple. Or so they said.[6]

I saw all this as just a mathematically super-charged version of the old 'classical' orthodoxy that Keynes and others had seemingly overthrown in the thirties.[7] However elegant to behold as a system of equations, such theories held very little intuitive appeal. Indeed, I found them abstract, oversimplistic and detached from the practicalities of the real world, where preferences were unstable, people were often 'satisfisers' rather than 'maximisers', information was frequently imperfect and the future impossible to predict with any confidence. In short, the assumptions of the 'new classicists' were nothing short of Panglossian and I am glad to say that over recent years work in the field of behavioural economics has tended to confirm that people are, in reality, rather more fair-minded and moral and less calculating than many of the new classical textbooks would suggest. While the immediate post-war generation of economists seemed sensibly to use maths in a limited fashion to add some element of precision to their insights, the newer generation were hell bent on creating an axiomatic system, the virtue of which seemed to accrue from its very detachment from reality.

Of course, one's philosophies tend to evolve and become more nuanced with age and experience, but I have retained a predominantly Keynesian approach to economics throughout my career, albeit progressively embellished with a greater understanding of the importance of the supply side. Indeed, if anything, the events of the past five years or so have only served to make me more convinced than ever of the fundamental truths of Keynes's methodological framework. Two of these truths, in particular, seem to have lasted the test of time.

First, there is the distinction between risk that is measurable in probabilistic terms and uncertainty that is not. And second, there is the related fact that confidence (in effect the inverse of uncertainty) needs to be nurtured rather than neutered. Once lost, it can be devilishly difficult to re-establish. In its absence, an economy can become effectively marooned well away from full employment. Alternatively, the 'natural' processes by which that economy re-equilibrates after a severe downswing can prove so hesitant and tortuous that they prove to be inconsistent with social and political stability. Such risks are likely to be particularly to the fore when balance-sheet adjustments – the desire to scale down debt burdens – have left the economy in question in a 'liquidity trap', with the entire nominal interest rate structure anchored close to the zero bound. In these circumstances, notwithstanding resort to the unwieldy and unfortunately rather feeble option of quantitative easing, fiscal expansion comes into its own.[8]

Back in the early eighties I was lucky enough to encounter two remarkable exceptions to the monetarist majority who helped me to put my scepticism about the conventional wisdom into a more coherent framework and who managed to capture my imagination.

My economic history tutor, Dr George Peden, was an acknowledged expert on the thirties, and in particular on British rearmament and the original economics of Keynes rather than the bastardised version that came to dominate much Anglo-Saxon policymaking after 1945. His courses and published research were perhaps the most powerful catalyst for my becoming a disciple of Britain's – and, I believe, the world's – foremost macroeconomist. Under George's excellent, if occasionally pedantic, guidance (George had previously been a copy editor on a Scottish newspaper, and was as a result a stickler for correct grammar and linguistic coherence) I became fascinated by the man who in many ways invented modern macroeconomics. Keynes's fertility of mind, intellectual sweep, clarity of exposition and desire to turn innovative thinking into practical solutions for everyday problems was, and is, unique.[9]

Keynes was very much a Renaissance man. He did it all. He had been a Cambridge don (first in mathematics and then in economics), a writer of major books on macroeconomic theory, a Treasury mandarin during both world wars and in peacetime, a member of the Court of the Bank of England, an external advisor to both prime ministers and chancellors of the exchequer, a journalist, a fund manager (both on his own account and on that of his Cambridge college and a major insurance company), and one of the key designers of the world's post-war economic and financial architecture. He also found time to make friends with most of the great and the good of the worlds of politics and aesthetics; he helped to set up the Arts Council of Great Britain; and he enjoyed a rather unconventional sex life, ultimately marrying and living happily ever after with an exiled Russian ballerina. I had found my intellectual hero and ploughed through his voluminous writings, often venturing some way off-piste from my designated courses.

I was also lucky enough in my final undergraduate year to be taught by Professor Willem Buiter. He too was a disciple of Keynes, but on an altogether different level to myself. A student of Nobel Laureate James Tobin in the US, he was, at a ridiculously young age, taking international macroeconomic theory into new directions and fighting an intellectual rearguard action against the monetarists, 'new classicists' and free market fundamentalists. What is more, he was doing it on their territory, using modelling techniques and underlying assumptions that had much in common with theirs. There was no textbook for his third-year course. He was literally making it up as he went along, and it was spellbinding. Meanwhile, Professor Buiter was often to be seen driving around the Georgian terraces of the Clifton area of Bristol in a convertible MGB with a delectable blonde in the passenger seat. I lapped all this up and had found another intellectual hero, whose utterances on the global economy I follow to this day. Indeed, over recent years he too (as chief economist at Citibank) has entered the financial world, and our paths have crossed again. But more of that later.

Anyway, intellectually energised by my two mentors, despite my lack of mathematical prowess, my first degree was sufficiently good to warrant an invitation to do a postgrad course. The problem was that in 1981, at the onset of the Thatcherite Revolution in the UK, precious little public funding for postgraduate research was available, especially for an economic historian whose ideas ran against the grain of the dominant consensus. Thankfully, however, the small sum of money that I had recently inherited from my maternal grandfather was enough to pay my fees and keep me in beer and cigarettes for another year. This meant that I had to complete my master's degree in half the usual time, but I was more than happy to attempt to do so.

I stayed at Bristol under George Peden's wing, choosing to write my thesis on the integration of Keynes's views on the interaction of high levels of employment and wage inflation into the UK policymaking community.[10] It meant that I spent hundreds of hours trawling through the government papers released to the National Archives (then known as the Public Record Office) in Kew under the (then) thirty-year release ruling. I also had to interview an array of former academics, retired civil servants and politicians who had served in Whitehall in the forties and fifties. The list represented a collection of the finest brains of that era, including Nobel Laureate James Meade, Sir Austin Robinson, Professor Joan Robinson, Lord Croham, Lord Franks, Lord Plowden, Sir Donald McDougall, Sir Richard Stone (another Nobel Laureate), Lord Roberthall and Lord Kahn. They all gave generously of their time and my abiding memory of them was their extraordinary politeness towards me and their enthusiasm for what I was doing.

This was particularly the case with Lord Roberthall, the Australian-born economist who advised successive British governments from the war until 1961, and who was, by the time I got to know him, into his 80s. I would spend hour after hour at his flat in Pimlico drinking the tea regularly supplied by his kindly artist wife, listening to his remarkably candid and detailed reminiscences (which he would often supplement by referring to his own handwritten diaries[11]), and passive smoking the endless stream of Player's Number Six cigarettes that he consumed every day.

I was also lucky enough, with George's help, to convince Sir Alec Cairncross (then Master of St Peter's College, Oxford) to be my external examiner. Sir Alex was a contemporary of Keynes at Cambridge and in 1961 had filled Lord Roberthall's shoes as Chief Economic Advisor to the UK government. Although well into his 70s by the time I knew him, he was as sharp as a tack and was intent on writing his own histories of various aspects of the UK's post-war economic travails.[12] My research therefore dovetailed nicely with his own. Like Lord Roberthall, he was supremely generous with his time and hospitality, often inviting me to his home in Oxford to chat, while his matronly wife would stuff me full of home-made shortbread and cream cakes.

I was always amazed at the extraordinary breadth of his knowledge of economics, from the most obscure theory to the practical detail of the government's latest policy initiative. He was a veritable walking talking encyclopaedia of economic policy, from which I was determined to extract as much information as I possibly could.

I found my postgraduate degree utterly fascinating. Indeed it was one of the happiest years of my life, and I had few problems finishing the project within the truncated time span available. Having completed my 70,000-word thesis, the question was what to do next. In contrast to much of today's generation of students, career planning was not something that I had ever expended much energy on. Academia was attractive, but the economic history departments of UK universities were not exactly a growth industry at the time. I did not possess a doctorate, although Sir Alec suggested that my master's thesis could be turned into one easily enough and was willing to continue to oversee my research. But money was short.

In the end, after a pretty cursory perusal of the *Financial Times* jobs pages, I applied for a job at a Japanese multinational company's London headquarters and was accepted. I stayed there for two uneventful years, helping to research the economic, political and even legal issues involved in the assembly of tenders for large infrastructure project contracts in Europe, Africa and the Middle East. The money was good for someone of my age (22/23) – I could afford to rent a basement flat in trendy Notting Hill and I travelled to some exotic places – and along the way I learned a little about the Japanese way of doing business: lessons that stood me in good stead in later years. I also had enough spare time on my hands to take up an offer from Allen & Unwin to extend my master's thesis into a book.[13] But just in case there is anyone out there foolish enough to think that the production of obscure academic tomes can offer an easy path to fortune and fame, the total income from the racily titled *Wages and Employment Policy, 1936–1985* was about £500. This works out at less than ten pence per hour for the time spent writing and researching the book.

What the writing of the book did do, however, was convince me that I owed it to myself to try to somehow make a career out of economics. So in 1984 I accepted an offer from Lord Plowden (brokered in part by Sir Alec) to help him write the memoirs of his time as a post-war policymaker at the Treasury.[14]

A successful businessman in the thirties and an advisor to the Ministry of Aircraft Production during the war, in March 1947 Lord Plowden was appointed Chief Planning Officer. In this guise he acted as an independent (i.e. non-civil service and external) advisor to a succession of chancellors of the exchequer in both the Attlee and Churchill governments, working closely with career civil servants such as Lord Roberthall. Although not a trained economist, he helped to navigate Britain's rather fraught post-1945 transition from an all-out war footing to a more market-orientated peacetime economy. This meant that his purview stretched beyond macro demand management to the details of domestic resource allocation and into international economic diplomacy. His job involved almost as much liaison with the prime minister and foreign secretary as with the chancellor of the exchequer. It meant that he was in regular contact with similarly senior officials in the US and across Europe. He was intricately involved in landmark events such as the Convertibility Crisis of 1947, the devaluation of sterling in 1949, the organisation and distribution of Marshall Aid, and the decision of Britain in 1950 to eschew the Schuman Coal and Steel Plan that effectively kick-started the process of European economic and political integration. Later he was also intricately involved in the vexed issue of financing Britain's military contribution to the Korean War.

Lord Plowden wanted someone to extract the Treasury and other government papers relating to the key episodes in his post-war Whitehall career; someone to interview his surviving contemporaries to tease out their recollections of key incidents; someone to ask him the right questions to jog his own rather patchy memory; and someone to write the first draft of the book. And for the better part of the next two years, working from home and again at the National Archives in Kew, as well as for a period at the US National Archives in Washington, that is what I did. It was a little like going to economic finishing school. I had a reasonable grasp of the relevant economic theory, I was familiar with the particular economic, social and political circumstances prevailing at the time, and I knew what the ultimate policy decisions were – but what this project really gave me was an insight into how those decisions were actually reached, how different options were (or were not) weighed up, and how the various characters involved interacted with one another to make those decisions.

Lord Plowden might not have been quite the academic genius that Sir Alec was, but he was a man of great professional courage and integrity. He was the consummate Whitehall political operator and facilitator within government. His particular skill was to 'work between the lines' and to get the things done that had to be done. Needless to say, he also had some wonderful stories to tell, many of them on the most human of levels, and not least about how great political figures such as Churchill, Attlee and Truman would conduct themselves in private: their personal habits and quirks, their likes and dislikes, and how they liked to work with their civil servants and advisors. I emerged from the project with a much clearer understanding of how economic policy was made: the fudges, the compromises, the subservience to narrow political interests, and the vulnerability to random events over which governments exert little or no control. If it didn't quite turn me into a cynic, the experience certainly made me more of a realist about how and why governments do what they do. My former boss at Lehman Brothers (and now my business partner), John Llewellyn, once summed this issue up perfectly when, in the introduction to a speech, he told of hearing Robert Solow saying: 'There are two things that it is wise to avoid seeing being made: economic policy decisions and sausages.'

In 1986 – while Lord Plowden's book, *An Industrialist in the Treasury*, went through its extended editing process and the publishing machine – I was once again confronted with the need to find a career. Although opportunities within academia remained limited and poorly paid, I was confident that what I had achieved with my postgrad work and with Lord Plowden would stand me in good stead. I was accepted for a range of economist jobs: from the Government Economic Service to the Confederation of British Industry, the latter rather cutting across my political leanings. But despite my first-hand training in the black arts of policymaking, what really interested me was the City.

After the largely traumatic years of the mid to late seventies, London's financial markets had regained their confidence and were booming as Mrs Thatcher's government abandoned exchange controls, deregulated important parts of the domestic economy, privatised the nationalised industries, encouraged home ownership, eased the tax burden on higher earners, and generally pandered much more than had previous post-war governments to capital over labour. The enduring process of globalisation was enjoying a new lease of life, and just as the reactionary trade union behemoths were in headlong retreat in the mid eighties, the banks and the stockbroking community were on a roll. What is more, there were plans afoot to sweep away the remaining restrictive practices in the banking industry and allow London to fully embrace the financial revolution that was spreading from the US across the world. Big Bang was imminent.[15]

As the financial sector was encouraged to blossom and assumed greater and greater importance in the eyes of the media and the country as a whole, economists became some of the most visual spokespeople for the industry. I found all of this very exciting. Although I thought some of the politics associated with the process rather crass and unsavoury, and many of the views being expressed wide of the mark, I decided that this was where I wanted to be. Here was the opportunity of a well-paid career doing something for which I believed I had at least some sort of talent.

I went to a number of interviews with banks and brokers, blowing one because I admitted to being a member of the Labour Party. I vividly remember being asked by the long-forgotten chief economist of the now long-defunct firm in question how 'someone like me' would respond when (as he suggested they regularly did) some of those working on the floor of the London Stock Exchange cheered when an increase in the unemployment rate was announced? Without being rude – and it was difficult not to tell this arrogant little man to stick his job where the sun didn't shine – I was reduced to swallowing my pride and mouthing some platitudes about being professional and taking a lead from civil servants, who are meant to be non-partisan in any advice they might give their minister, whatever the social context. Anyway, thankfully, the other firms I contacted had broader minds and were more interested in my abilities as an economist than my politics.

In the end I was offered a position by the Hong Kong Bank's International Treasury Management Division (ITM), which advised companies both in Britain and around the world on how to manage their foreign exchange exposure. I was to work as the assistant to their Head of Currency Economics, Dr Paul Chertkow, and my career in the markets began on 4 June 1986.

CHAPTER 3

A FALSE START

Paul, an easy-going, LSE-educated Canadian, was a well-known name in the markets and a regular talking head on BBC TV and radio, where it was not just his views on the foreign exchange markets that were highly sought after. He was a valued commentator on all things macroeconomic. Indeed, my first exposures to him were hearing him on BBC Radio 4's *Today* programme and seeing his name quoted in the *Financial Times*.

My role at ITM was to replace someone who went on to become one of the most famous City economists of all: Dr Jim O'Neill. Jim, who already enjoyed an excellent reputation, had just moved to the US to work at the bank's New York operation. But before 'crossing the pond', Paul and Jim had effectively pioneered currency economics in the London market. I had some big shoes to fill, then, and some big expectations to meet, although I should add that, from the outset, Jim was a great support, and we have remained in intermittent touch over the years as his career has extended into the stratosphere and mine has meandered along its erratic path.

Back then we used to talk a couple of times a week by phone and, as a novice, I would eagerly soak up his ideas on the foreign exchange markets and try to assimilate them into my own gradually evolving framework of thought. He has probably forgotten this now (an example perhaps of economists' selective memory), but as a fan of Liverpool FC, I remember regularly trying to cheer him up about Manchester United's then somewhat second-rate status in English and European football! Obviously, such opportunities were in rather shorter supply over the next twenty-five years.

The ITM headquarters were at the eastern edge of the City, just off Bishopsgate, in Devonshire Square. The building had once been one of a series of warehouses belonging to the East India Company. Completely renovated in the early eighties, it was a state-of-the-art

office development housing numerous other financial institutions, and its cafés, restaurants, bars and subterranean gym were
all symbols of the City's renewed vibrancy and success. At lunchtime and in the early evening the square's central courtyard was
flooded with well-dressed people strutting around like peacocks
and conspicuously consuming their new-found (or inherited)
wealth.

This was all very exciting. Indeed, it was impossible not to be
caught up, at least to some extent, in the burgeoning zeitgeist. On
the other hand, from day one of the job, it dawned on me that I
was poorly equipped for my new vocation. Yes, my research had
taught me a lot about the plumbing of macro policymaking. Yes,
I had learned my international economics theory from one of the
brightest and best, in the form of Willem Buiter. And yes, I had
a better grasp of the historical context in which the day's events
were taking place than most. But my knowledge, such as it was,
largely related to the UK economy, and my job involved analysing
all the major currencies. And in the mid eighties there were a lot
more of these than there are today. The moniker did not just apply
to the US dollar, the Deutschmark, the Japanese yen, the Swiss
franc and sterling. This was the pre-euro era and a good deal of
what Paul and I had to pass judgement on therefore related to the
performance of the French franc, the Dutch guilder, the Spanish
peseta and the other European legacy currencies that operated
within the framework of the Exchange Rate Mechanism (ERM) of
the European Monetary System. There were numerous other currencies to cover, including the Finnish markka (if I remember correctly: I am not even sure I knew what the Finnish currency was
called before 1986), the Hong Kong dollar, the Singapore dollar and
the Australian and New Zealand dollars. What is more, this was
a period when there was much greater variation and volatility in
interest rates, and when capital controls and other idiosyncratic
policy weapons to restrict currency variability were much more
common than is the case today. There was so much to learn about
so many different economies.

Then there were the other financial markets that exerted such
a huge influence on currency dynamics. Having a decent grasp
of the mechanics of spot foreign exchange was only part of the
story. To really understand what was going on in the trading room
and more broadly, and to be able to have an informed conversation with ITM's clients, I needed to rapidly come to terms with the

complexities of bonds, equities, forward rate agreements, interest rate and cross currency swaps, options and other more esoteric financial derivatives. I had a massive amount to assimilate and a lot of it was very mathematical in nature.

Paul's approach to my financial markets education was anything but formal. It was basically to drop me in at the deep end and let me get on with it. It was a case of 'learning by doing', if not 'ordeal by fire'. I could ask whatever I wanted, whenever I wanted (although I tended to do less of this than I might have in an effort to hide my near-universal ignorance), and I was lucky in that part of what ITM did was to advise clients about the technicalities of financial risk management. This meant that there were lots of Paul's own presentations on file to fall back on, but basically I was left alone to teach myself the nuts and bolts of the job. From the word go Paul had no qualms whatsoever about putting me on the phone to clients, asking me to address the trading floor, or even encouraging me to give a set-piece presentation. This was a leap of faith on his part for which I am eternally grateful. It could so easily have backfired on him.

The basic economics of the various countries we focused on I picked up quickly enough, although I necessarily had to prioritise and focus on one or two key aspects of each one. As Professor Buiter would have recommended, I found myself dwelling more than anything else on their monetary and fiscal policy mixes. In fact, I found the requirement to learn about different economies and their policy frameworks fascinating. The financial market angle was altogether more challenging, though, especially given my phobia of maths. At weekends and after work I was often to be found furtively browsing in the finance section at LSE's Economists' Bookshop, searching for tomes that put some of the more complex products into layman's language and which I could keep for reference.

Overall, I embraced the initial challenges, appreciated Paul's (essentially blind) confidence in me, and took the view that by sounding enthusiastic and confident – and concentrating as far as possible on the areas I knew, or at least understood – I could survive, if not thrive. I was also helped by two other considerations.

First, while Paul's understanding of the foreign exchange and other financial markets was absolutely first rate, he was largely a qualitative analyst rather than a quantitative one. He was, at heart, like me: a practitioner of the art of political economy.

Although extremely numerate, he didn't rely heavily on formal mathematical models. Instead, he backed his own judgement and experience. He had a decent grasp of history, recognised the importance of political and other trade-offs and, above all, the nebulous, but absolutely vital, concepts of 'confidence' and 'credibility' in determining how markets would react to policy. And again like me, he saw the economic and political world in terms of its imperfections and shades of grey, rather than seeing it as black and white.

Second, there was my ability to speak and write concisely and coherently. This has stood me in good stead throughout my career. People are more likely to give you the benefit of any doubt they might have about you when you deliver a clear message. Indeed, passing on some of George Peden's attention to linguistic detail is something that I have consistently tried to drum into those that have worked for me over the years. No doubt I have bored some of my teams to death with one of my mantras:

> People are busy and are bombarded with a massive amount of information. They are looking for reasons not to have to read or listen to things. If they can't understand what you are saying, they will ignore you. So, keep it brief, clear and offer a bottom line.

Meanwhile, as I desperately tried to come to terms with my new professional responsibilities, I was exposed to my first experience of trading-room culture.

For someone arriving in the City from academia, or from another industry, the first shock to the system is perhaps the early starts. By the mid eighties, the days when a stockbroker would swan into the office at 10 a.m., make a few phone calls, go to lunch with a client at noon, make a few more phone calls in the middle of the afternoon and be on the train home to Weybridge by 5 p.m. were over. I had to be in the ITM office by about 7.30 a.m., with a view to being at least cursorily prepared for the morning meeting, which the entire trading room would attend at 7.45 a.m. After all, I might have to play a supporting part to Paul, who set the scene, outlining what had happened overnight in the US and Asia and previewing the key events on the calendar for the day ahead. Living as I did at the time in west London, this meant that I had to be up by 6.10 a.m. and on my way to work soon after 6.30 a.m. That hurt.

In fact, though, by the standards of most of the rest of my career this represented a lie-in. Indeed, with a hiatus or two, I found myself arriving at work earlier and earlier as time went on. In recent years, 5.30 a.m. starts were not uncommon, and an arrival in the office before 7 a.m. was typical. In a British winter this can be pretty brutal, although it has meant that throughout my career I have missed the rush hour in whatever city I have been working. On the other hand, it has meant that my working days would rarely fall short of eleven hours and that my evenings have been truncated, often to the deep chagrin of my wife and friends. Lights out at 10.30 or 11 p.m. therefore became the norm.

The other consideration that immediately struck me was all the technology on show: the clocks that showed the time in all the world's major financial hubs, the screens of constantly updating prices, the myriad phone handsets (and, yes, people did often have two or three of these under their chins at once), the intercom systems that allowed traders and brokers to communicate with, or abuse, one another, the vast number of computers, the word-processors (which I remember at the time were vast free-standing affairs), the special bond price calculators, and the terminals that the traders used to price complex option and swap deals. It all fed the 'buzz': the noise and sense of dynamism and hyperactivity that infected what was actually, by most standards, a small trading floor.

In today's terms, the technology in 1986 was little short of antediluvian. There was no email, no Bloomberg terminals, no flat screens, no online trading platforms, no remote cameras to stream an economist's on-the-spot commentary into a far-removed TV studio. And a vast ocean of paper forms still had to be manually processed before trades could be confirmed. What is more, a good deal of financial market trading at that time was still conducted by 'open outcry' at London's various physical exchanges. Today, they scarcely exist.

The systems used were also unbelievably unwieldy compared with what is now largely taken for granted, and, as a very small team, we could not rely on some junior gofer to help us out. If anything, I was the gofer. Time series of economic and financial data were available with a lag from a specialised provider, but they had to be downloaded in raw form using a complex system of numerical codes from a special terminal, manipulated by a further confusing system of numerical and alphabetical codes, and they were often out of date and peppered with errors that had to be painstakingly weeded out.

Hard copies of the latest UK data releases, complete with the numerous official revisions that characterise almost every official time series, had to be picked up in person from the Treasury or what was then called the Central Statistical Office. The key details were then phoned in to the trading floor using the office mobile, which was the size and weight of a brick and completely unreliable, so that one was often to be found queuing up outside one of London's red public phone boxes in order to give one's anxiously waiting colleagues the information they required.

For US data, the newswires did a pretty good job, but with the information being delivered by junior journalists rather than trained economists, some of the nuances of the figures could get lost. For the myriad other overseas countries we covered, the newswires' service was patchier and we were beholden to the various publications that their domestic statistical offices (sometimes not in English) or the IMF or OECD sent out on a monthly basis. Paul's office was packed to the rafters with back copies of these tomes, and I would often find myself searching for hours for some obscure number in a booklet released years ago and now probably out of date.

Our own production methods were similarly antiquated. For example, ITM sent out a weekly telex to clients on a Friday afternoon summarising our views. Neither was there any desktop publishing available to smarten up our more formal weekly and monthly documents. These were produced with the help of a printing company situated a couple of miles away and were posted out via the Royal Mail in the often-vain hope that they might arrive on a client's desk early the following week. We would draft the text and set up the tables and charts painstakingly on our huge clunky word processors, collate the output on a couple of floppy disks and then walk (or sometimes run or taxi) the reports around to the printers and oversee their typesetting and assembly into publishable form. The process was like pulling teeth and invariably something would go awry, meaning that one of us might be there until late at night or publication was postponed. It also meant that Paul had to spend a good deal of his time and the company's money wining and dining the unbelievably dull and reactionary owner of said printing firm to make sure that we were treated as priority clients.

Social attitudes in the eighties were different from those today. There was much less political correctness, and HR departments' codes of behaviour were less in evidence and were taken less seriously. The language used on the trading floor was frequently agricultural. Sexism was rife, and there was also an undercurrent of soft racism that on occasion reared its ugly head more explicitly. Meanwhile, as I mentioned earlier, the predominant shade of politics was blue, with those on the left being figures of fun or abuse.

This was the period when Margaret Thatcher was at the height of her powers. On the world stage she was lionised by Ronald Reagan and Mikhail Gorbachev alike, while domestically – thanks to council house sales, privatisation, the taming of the unions and increasing inflows of foreign direct investment into UK industry – popular capitalism was rampant. A third election victory seemed inevitable. Questioning any of this was unlikely to get you very far. I learned to keep my mouth shut.

The first thing that struck me about my new colleagues was their apparent confidence in what they were doing. Subsequently, I came to realise that much of this was a sham and that they were as insecure as I was, if not more so, but at the time the certainty and volume with which views on the markets were expressed – and with which colleagues, counterparties, policymakers, football teams or even restaurants were ridiculed or praised – seemed remarkable. What was also clear was that these views could be rapidly reversed and the opposite position taken with barely a hint of guilt or embarrassment. There was more than an element of juvenile bullying in all of this banter.

Another immediate observation was how self-absorbed most of these people were. They were a remarkable cocktail of the acquisitive and the avaricious. Young women were brazenly ogled and, if especially attractive, pursued remorselessly. Money, or what it could buy, was discussed and flaunted constantly. Bonus projections (always stratospheric), house prices (always rising rapidly), cars (always German) and holiday destinations (always exotic) were favourite topics of conversation. The latest gadgets were paraded. I have an abiding memory of a senior bond salesman proudly strolling into the office with his mistress (who was another bond salesperson) on one arm and a portable CD player on the other. This was extraordinary on two counts. First, office romances struck me as inherently unstable, and actively showing off your infidelity to one's colleagues was both incredibly arrogant and a recipe for personal and professional disaster. Second, the word unwieldy was invented for this CD player. It was clearly extremely heavy, the size of the sort of voluminous handbag favoured by Mrs Thatcher, and it had a thick leather shoulder strap. In any case, at that time, I think there were only about ten CDs available and five of those were by Dire Straits.

The City's booze culture was something else that I encountered from day one. Business lunches were rarely dry, or at least those that Paul put on for clients weren't. Going out for a bottle of wine or a couple of pints at lunchtime was commonplace, as indeed was having a drink to 'decompress' after work. Thursday nights and Friday lunchtimes were typically the biggest occasions. I can well remember being sent back to the office from ITM's favourite wine bar on London Wall at 1.30 p.m. on Fridays to make sure that the US economic data released at that time was not going to do too much damage to the traders' P&Ls. If all was well, then few of those involved would return to the office, although Paul and I always had to make sure that the Friday afternoon telex went out.

For many of my colleagues, getting drunk seemed to be an end in itself and was often combined with a pee-high competition to see who could order the most impressively expensive things to drink and run up the largest bill. Personally, I found this kind of behaviour childish and unprofessional. I would much rather spend an hour in the gym at lunchtime than an hour in the pub. And in the evenings I was keener on getting home to my then fiancée and to my existing friends, most of whom worked in very different environments. The downside of this attitude was that it marked me out as a bore and a killjoy, but I could live with that.

Looking back at that era, it was another world professionally. We often focused on a very different set of indicators and many of the dominant themes of the day would be alien to today's economists and market professionals. The eighties was a period when, after the monetary and fiscal errors and supply shocks of the previous decade, the overwhelming policy priorities were disinflation and reducing the influence of the public sector.

'Policy rules' increasingly came to dominate 'discretion', and, beyond the operation of 'automatic stabilisers', the use of fiscal policy to manage demand was largely eschewed, although government debt ratios were slow to decline and governments at times fell over themselves to offer any number of spurious rationales to support the case for tax cuts. The trials and tribulations of the seventies had given Keynesianism, as it had been practised during that period, a bad name. As hinted in the introduction, my own sense was that the criticism was overdone. Fiscal policy was not merely about social policy, income distribution and incentives, as many conservative economists believed. If sensibly applied, it retained the ability to smooth the business cycle. Infrastructure investment could exert a significant positive effect on growth potential and would always require public sponsorship because of numerous market failures. Meanwhile, policymakers ignored the mix of fiscal and monetary policy at their peril, not least because of its influence on the exchange rate. For evidence of this, one only has to examine the extraordinary swings in the US dollar during the era of Reaganomics (when the US combined loose fiscal policy with high real policy rates) and its aftermath. Furthermore, I retained a strong belief (which proved correct in the aftermath of the 2008 financial crisis) that, if the world was ever again threatened by a catastrophic downturn and interest rates approached the zero bound, monetary policy would lose its bite and fiscal policy and the economics of Keynes would come into their own.

Despite the primacy attached to the objective of price stability, the abandonment of fiscal activism and a growing onus on supply-side reform, the policy frameworks of the late eighties varied enormously and were adjusted with greater frequency than is now the case. Few central banks enjoyed the sort of operational independence that is today the general rule. Germany's Bundesbank and Switzerland's National Bank were perhaps the most obvious exceptions, and the Fed under Paul Volcker also operated with considerable de facto autonomy, but formal inflation targeting, with its supporting information (such as regular Inflation Reports), had not yet arrived. New Zealand was to pioneer this in the modern era in 1989 and it would subsequently be copied by a range of economies in both the developed and emerging worlds over the following two decades.

Monetary targets still occupied a significant place in the policymaking process in Germany and Switzerland, and, despite the enormous difficulties encountered in adhering to them in the early eighties, the US and the UK still paid some degree of lip service to such 'nominal anchors'. The Bank of Japan also published, and made regular reference to, money supply growth targets. In the EU the primary policy anchor was the Exchange Rate Mechanism and the conservative German monetary policy that lay at its core but, at least in 1986, this was still a relatively loose system of currency pegs to the Deutschmark. Since its inception in 1979, realignments had proved all too common and some countries were still perceived as 'serial devaluers', not least France, which had undergone a series of destabilising parity adjustments in the initial years of the Mitterrand presidency.

But perhaps the most striking contrast with today was the lack of central bank transparency. Fed Chairman Paul Volcker was a market hero because he was seen as having broken the back of US inflation in the early eighties, but the Fed did little to help one understand what it was up to. A twice-yearly Congressional testimony by the Fed chairman began in 1975, semi-annual macro projections were released from 1979, and the 'Beige Book' on regional economic conditions was first published in 1983. But the US central bank largely let its actions speak for themselves. There were no immediate formal policy announcements from the Federal Open Markets Committee (FOMC). These arrived on a regular basis only in 1995 and, when I began my career, FOMC minutes were released with a six-week (rather than today's three-week) lag and were rather more limited in scope than they are now. Determining for certain that there had been an adjustment in the federal funds rate required detailed analysis of the short-term supply and demand for funds in the US money markets in the days around a meeting. Amazingly, it was not uncommon for experienced Fed watchers for a time to actually reach different conclusions about the central bank's intentions with regard to its policy rate. Needless to say, this could be a recipe for unnecessary volatility in asset prices and uncertainty in the broader economy.

Elsewhere, the Bundesbank sometimes appeared to take a sadistic pleasure in wrong-footing the markets with a policy surprise, while in general central bankers of that time would have been horrified to see the sort of openness and forward policy guidance that is now so commonplace. John Plender of the *Financial Times* perhaps came up with the most succinct summation of the prevailing attitude of that time when he recalled once overhearing the head of public relations at the Bank of England describing his job as that of keeping in regular contact with the media while making sure that he conveyed nothing of significance to them.[16]

Official interest rate moves tended to be more common, and larger, than they are now, although this is hardly surprising given that so many central banks are today operating at or around the zero bound. Today's customary 25 basis points or quarter-point adjustments were a rarity then. Indeed, such moves would be dismissed by the markets as largely meaningless. Adjustments of 50 or 100 basis points were more common, and on occasion changes could be larger still.

In fixed-income markets, the US 30-year bond (also known as the 'Long Bond') was as much the global benchmark as the 10-year Treasury bond, while in the foreign exchange markets, the US trade statistics were the most important release of the month. Over recent years, though, it is hard to remember a time when a set of US trade numbers caused any market reaction whatsoever. The US employment report, just as is the case now, was the most closely watched piece of data of all, but I don't remember hearing much about the ISM (or the NAPM business confidence survey as it was then known) until 1987 or later. And government statistical offices were in those days still reporting GNP, which incorporates net factor incomes from abroad, rather than GDP, which does not.

As far as discussion of the issues of the day was concerned, there was so much less commentary available than there is today. We had the *Financial Times* and the *Wall Street Journal* and the *Economist*, all of which were as much required reading then as they are now and usually provided one with the bulk of what was required to sound authoritative at morning meetings. But the blogosphere was just unimaginable at the time. Academic economists had little or no outlet in the press, although the evergreen Milton Friedman and J. K. Galbraith were exceptions. For in-depth analysis I fell back heavily onto the IMF and OECD's regular Economic Outlook publications and the latter's annual surveys of individual economies, which were (and still are) a mine of useful data. Central bank bulletins also provide interesting material but tend to be very backward looking. The market commentators who set the agenda of the time were Henry Kaufman at Salomon Brothers, Gordon Pepper at Greenwells, Gavyn Davies and David Morrison at Simon & Coates (later Goldman Sachs), and Bill Martin at Phillips & Drew.

Aside from Bank Credit Analyst and one or two expensive consultancies, independent commentators were extremely rare. It is also worth remembering that there were only a handful of terrestrial TV stations in the UK at the time, and while they were increasingly looking at the markets in greater detail and with greater expertise than had hitherto been the case (much of this expertise co-opted in from the financial sector), there was nothing like the depth of analysis seen today. The BBC had an economics editor who would regularly comment on key developments on the evening news and its *Money Programme* (on which I would in due course appear) was required viewing every week. CNBC and Bloomberg TV were still merely twinkles in the eyes of their founders.

The predominant economic issues affecting market sentiment when I began my career were 'Reaganomics'; the Plaza Accord on exchange rates, and how much lower it would drive the dollar; the ERM and whether we were moving into an environment of less frequent parity adjustments; disinflation in the context of slumping oil prices; and the debate over whether the UK's 'Thatcherite Revolution' would result in a sustained improvement in economic performance.

My own views on most of these matters were less than fully formed, and my default option was frequently to follow Paul's more studied lead. Nevertheless, I can remember being more bearish on the dollar than he was (which was the right call), at least until the Louvre Accord of 1987. On the ERM, I was sceptical that much was changing, which was the wrong call. I didn't realise it, but the increasing reluctance to sanction currency realignments within the system at the time represented a slight quickening of the pace towards European monetary union.

While I was desperately trying to make some sense of all these matters, Paul went away on holiday in late August and was happy to leave me in charge of things economic in the office while he was away. But if I found that difficult to comprehend, his announcement immediately on his return that he was leaving the firm came as a much bigger shock. I had been there only three months and suddenly it looked like my City career might be over! What sort of madness was this?

What I had yet fully to grasp was that the imminent arrival of Big Bang was generating an extraordinary amount of uncertainty and change in the City. The process of financial sector reform that had begun in earnest with the arrival of the Conservative government in 1979 was accelerating to meet the challenges of what promised to be a huge increase in competition. While some firms were disintegrating, others were expanding or coalescing into entirely new entities. Players which had hitherto occupied one niche or another were seeking partners to allow them to occupy other niches, while the large international banks were desperate to get a bigger slice of the London market and in the process were keen to embrace whatever talent they could get their hands on, either by buying smaller specialised operations outright or by offering prized individuals deals that they found hard to refuse.

With the industry's tectonic plates fusing and shifting in this way, the headhunting community was having a field day and almost anyone who was anyone was being courted for some position or other. People had dollar signs in their eyes as salaries were remorselessly bid up. Although I was little more than a virgin in terms of my professional experience at this time, even I found myself the object of a number of enquiries as to my skillset and availability. This was ridiculous: I knew next to nothing!

What I learned from Paul was that a decision had been taken to withdraw ITM's business back into the main entity of Hong Kong Bank, and Paul, who was being actively wooed by several other firms, decided that he no longer wanted to be part of it. He had decided to take up a generous offer to bring his international economics and currency expertise to Hoare Govett.

Hoare Govett was one of the bluest of blue-blooded City firms and part of the elite of UK corporate stockbroking. However, in keeping with the financial sector's 'spin the bottle' experimentation of the time, the firm had in 1984 embarked on a marriage of (in)convenience with the US west coast commercial bank Security Pacific. On paper, Security Pacific Hoare Govett (SPHG) certainly had some financial clout, but whether the resultant juxtaposition of singularly different businesses and corporate cultures could ever gel and weather the storms that were bound to lie ahead was a different matter altogether.

As it transpired, my own position was less grim than I initially feared. Paul, sympathetic to my situation, had lined me up a position with James Capel, the research-based stockbroking firm that Hong Kong Bank had itself recently taken over, while also promising to see if he could convince SPHG of the need for him to have an assistant.

My own preference was to follow Paul. Capel's economics department was substantial and extremely highly regarded, but I would effectively be the most junior member of a ten-man team. This would mean that the opportunities to be much more than a dogsbody would be limited and yet the pressures to prove my worth enormous. I still knew little about the markets and felt intellectually intimidated by the technical skills of the more senior members of the group. Furthermore, Capel's chief economist had seemed less than enthused by my prospective arrival and was barely older than me! In short, I just didn't think I would survive for very long.

I was incredibly relieved, therefore, when Paul called to say that he had secured a role for me at his new shop. Even though my remit was to be broader than just being his backup, I could continue to rely on him acting as a sympathetic mentor and something of a shield to hide my numerous shortcomings. So, at the end of my first summer in the City I began my second job. Just a few weeks before Big Bang was due to become a reality, on 27 October 1986, I duly delivered myself to SPHG's rather cramped and dowdy head-quarters close to Chancery Lane tube station on High Holborn.

CHAPTER 4

A MARRIAGE OF INCONVENIENCE

In the late seventies, the role of the City of London was largely confined to mobilising funds for investment and providing access to payment services. But the focus on these dull, if worthy, priorities meant that it was becoming increasingly uncompetitive. It was a club that largely excluded foreigners and operated in an ancient – even anachronistic – way. In global terms, it was becoming a backwater, especially when compared with New York which, since the collapse of the Bretton Woods monetary system in the early seventies, had embarked on a period of increasingly innovative growth, embracing securitisation, a welter of mechanisms to raise capital that were cheaper than bank loans, and new risk management products such as interest rate and currency swaps.

Things began to change in London after the election of Mrs Thatcher in 1979, but it was Big Bang in the autumn of 1986 that really sparked a revolution in City modi operandi. Indeed, the reforms associated with it continued to reverberate around the Square Mile and beyond for years to come. At a stroke, the stock exchange outlawed fixed commissions for trades and abolished the 'single capacity rule' with its traditional distinctions between 'jobbers', who traded on the floor of the exchange, and 'brokers', who acted on behalf of investors, while at the same time opening the London markets to foreign companies. The net result was a typhoon of what economists would call creative destruction. Old constraints on doing business were swept away and a new era of more intense competition, the search for economies of scale, rapid innovation and huge investment in technology began. Nothing was ever the same again.

What is more, the industry's long-standing reliance on well-to-do public schoolboys was loosened, and recruitment became more open and meritocratic. The best talent from the finest universities and business schools was sought after, and a career in finance increasingly became the flavour of the month for the global student population, not least because of the impressive pecuniary rewards on offer. But the net was also cast wider closer to home, in that there were suddenly more opportunities for anyone who could demonstrate that his or her drive, if not ruthlessness, could be put to good use. Essex and the eastern suburbs of London, from where many of Mrs Thatcher's new breed of working class Conservatives originated, became a secondary recruiting ground for traders and salespeople. This is not to deny that there had long been a (limited) conduit for working class talent to make a name for itself in the City, but Big Bang opened the floodgates for 'Basildon Man' in a way that would have been unthinkable a decade or two earlier.

As a result of the release of these dynamic forces, the City was not simply saved from irrelevance but, over a short period of time, was transformed back into the world's major financial centre for the first time since 1914. What is more, it increasingly came to be seen as a substantial direct contributor to the UK's economic growth: a consideration that increased the financial industry's influence over successive British governments and encouraged many of the regulatory shortcomings in areas such as capital adequacy, liquidity and risk concentration that came to light later. As it subsequently transpired, Big Bang proved to be a recipe for the triumph of large, multifaceted, mainly US, international conglomerates or 'securities houses' that could more readily benefit from the broader eradication of the world's financial boundaries. Virtually none of the City's old indigenous firms were to survive, although we weren't to know that this would be the case in the autumn of 1986. At that time, (often blind) optimism was the name of the game.

SPHG was a much bigger and more extensive operation than ITM. In the UK the firm boasted a huge equity research capability to back up both its new market-making capacity and its extensive corporate finance business, but it also had fingers in many of the world's other major equity markets, not least those in Asia. Furthermore, it was a big player in the gilt and other European fixed-income markets while, courtesy of Security Pacific, also being a primary dealer in the US Treasury market (meaning it was one of a select band of firms responsible for the dissemination of US government debt into the broader financial market place) and active in Japanese government bonds.

Then there was foreign exchange, where Paul's (and supposedly my) expertise was to come into play. SecPac, as it was known within the firm, already had an important hub in Los Angeles, where, remarkably, because of the vagaries of international time zones the working day would begin at 4 a.m. and traders would routinely set their alarm clocks for 2.45 a.m. My one and only visit to SecPac's downtown LA office left me in a state of total mental and physical discombobulation, although some of the people I met there claimed to love their schedules, which allowed them to leave the office at 2 p.m., play a round of golf, have an early dinner with their wives and children, and still be in bed in good time to get more than six hours of sleep. I was not convinced, and I remember at the time vowing never to complain again about my own pre-dawn alarm call.

Initially, I was rather overawed by the scale of SPHG, and once again the confidence of those I encountered took me aback. I was also now in a somewhat larger, if rather disparate, team of economists. What rapidly became clear was that there were too many chiefs and not enough Indians, and no universally acknowledged pyramid of command. As was to become an unfortunate rule over the course of my career, management proved incapable of making the difficult decisions that were necessary to put in place a coherent and sustainable structure for macroeconomic research. They preferred instead to fight their own personal turf battles through the patronage they bestowed upon competing individuals, who typically had a very high regard for their own abilities, were convinced of their divine right to run the show, and often were less than effusive in their praise for their peers. The result was an atmosphere somewhere between creative tension and utter chaos. When Paul and I joined SPHG, there were there already two foreign-exchange-focused economists, one in London and one in LA, whose influence we would somehow have to supplant (and, in short order, we did). But there were also two other senior economists in London and they were barely on speaking terms with each other and pursued different agendas and applied different methods. With Paul also very much a political animal and keen to stamp his authority on the firm, it was clear to me from the outset that this situation was unlikely to play out smoothly.

Roger Nightingale looked after the equity client base and Richard Jeffrey looked after the fixed-income client base. Roger had built his reputation on the fact that in the seventies he was the first City economist to recognise the importance of North Sea oil to the UK economy. He wanted to be a one-man band and was resistant to outside interference, in the sense that he largely ignored it. Something of a throwback to the City's previous era, he was a consummate and relaxed communicator who liked nothing better than to wax lyrical on the UK and the world over an extended, usually liquid, lunch. He was a monetarist, a Thatcherite and an excellent drafter of highly entertaining and approachable pieces of research. The clients and much of the salesforce loved him and I have to say that, despite looking at the world through a rather different lens, I couldn't help but like him too. He was always jolly and polite, if a little reclusive. He wanted to plough his own furrow and obey his own rules, and that is what he did.

Richard was a different animal. We had briefly crossed paths at Bristol, although he was a couple of years ahead of me and he had studied single-honours economics. He was much more technical in his approach to the job than I was, and he was of the monetarist and rational expectations mindset. In that sense, he had accepted the conventional wisdom both at Bristol and beyond. He was tremendously hard working, rarely putting in sub-twelve-hour days or taking a holiday, and he had rapidly built up an encyclopaedic knowledge of the UK monetary system and the gilt market. And, in contrast to Roger, he was ambitious managerially. But where he differed most from Roger was in terms of style. Although kind, generous and entertaining away from the office, Richard could be dry and overbearing in presentation, and his 'bedside manner' could jar both with those who worked with him and those he was advising. Sometimes he seemed unable to grasp the notion that his view was just one of a number of possible futures or indeed that his faith in the New Classical school of economics just might be misplaced.

While I was convinced that the personality traits of these individuals were bound to bubble to the surface and cause problems in due course, I could hardly dwell on them as the pressure was on to prove my worth immediately. I found that what allowed me to gain some initial traction at SPHG was that, despite my inexperience, my communication skills and the fact that I was willing to stand up and express a clear view (even when less than fully informed) were appreciated. These traits stood me in good stead relative to the other junior members of the team, who were more shy and retiring. Moreover, one of them was female and found it impossible to stop her feminist leanings on occasion shining through in her dealings with her male colleagues. Sadly, this did not endear her to some, who were quick to brand her difficult and lacking in (their definition of) humour. I hate to admit that I was content to pay lip service to some of the male chauvinist and juvenile banter that circulated around the trading floor, and this afforded me a certain amount of acceptance, while she found herself out of the loop, despite being a technically more gifted economist. Sad to say, her City career never quite developed as it might have done.

I was initially given some responsibility for monitoring the economies of Germany, Holland and France, although my role as Paul's alternate meant that I also had to keep my eye on other countries, and where possible I tried to demonstrate to Richard (to little avail) that I might have something of interest to say about the UK. About the only time that I would get the chance to put my name to anything significant relating to my home country was at Budget time, which was a huge occasion for the economics departments of UK banks and brokers despite the fact that we were told by the government that fiscal policy's role was now very much secondary to that of monetary policy. We would listen to the chancellor's speech live from the House of Commons on the radio (the budget was not yet televised) and then, on receipt of the mountain of official documentation that accompanied it, wade through the fine detail and sit down as a group and write an entire booklet, often running to fifty pages or more, about its implications for everything from official interest rates and the exchange rate to gilt issuance and the outlook for UK exporters. This was a task that would extend deep into the night. Our draft would then be sent to the printers while we retired to one of the pubs in Smithfield meat market, which were open from the early hours, for a pint or two of Guinness and a full English breakfast, sometimes bumping into competitors following the same well-worn routine. First thing in the morning, on receipt of the completed document, and having perhaps snatched an hour's sleep in the office, we would present our judgement to the traders and salespeople and any clients that were interested and then struggle to stay awake for the rest of the day. Nothing like the same fuss is made over the Budget now, although this in part reflects the fact that so much of the information in it is disseminated in advance, both officially and unofficially.

I was soon sent on a fact-finding trip to Frankfurt to expand my knowledge of the German economy. Jim O'Neill kindly put me in touch with a couple of economists he knew there and Richard set up some other meetings. I remember being put up at the Frankfurter Hof and eating in the restaurant and consuming an entire bottle of red wine on my own on my first night there, with the result that I was pretty hungover when I began my fact finding. I also recall that at my first meeting I was offered a cognac to go with my coffee at 9 a.m. in the morning. These were still very different days.

My other memory of that trip is going in to meet the entire economics team at Dresdner Bank. This was populated by a number of rather austere German gentlemen in their forties, all of whom seemed to possess PhDs, and giving them an hour-long lecture on the outlook for the global economy, including my own rather pessimistic read on Germany's prospects. I think it was nerves. I just started talking and didn't stop. God knows what they must have thought of me, although they were studiously polite.

The revolution in the way the City operated was matched by a revolution in the way the City looked. For example, the 'inside out' Lloyd's Building was completed in 1986. The old Billingsgate Fish Market down by the Thames was converted into the home of one of the new financial conglomerates (although the story, perhaps apocryphal, was that the whiff of fish took many years to finally disappear), and Broad Street station was demolished in order to allow the construction of Broadgate, into which SPHG moved early in 1987. Instead of the dark and dingy sixties-built rabbit warren that was Holborn, the firm now had its own purpose-built offices in one of the most sought-after addresses in the City.

There were two huge trading floors: one for debt and foreign exchange and one for equities. Research also had its own massive open-plan floor, with us economists occupying one corner. Needless to say, the investment bankers had their own palatial quarters suitably divorced from the rest of us mere mortals, and there were myriad meeting rooms and an entire level of dining and presentation suites as well. And all of this was constructed around a vast atrium bedecked with exotic plants – all in all, a massive waste of both space and money.

Broadgate was opened by no less a figure than Mrs Thatcher herself and, on completion, it was the biggest office complex in Europe. It was seen as a powerful symbol of the City's renaissance and it was certainly suitably brash for the time. SPHG shared it with a number of other large financial institutions, including Warburgs, UBS and Lehman Brothers, the latter two of which I would go on to work for in later years. Indeed, I spent a total of more than eight years of my career in one part of Broadgate or another.

In between various corporate headquarters there was a vast piazza, festooned with cafes, bars, sandwich shops and restaurants. At its centre there was a circular space that in the winter months became a public ice rink and around and above which there was a large semicircular bar, part open to the elements. Here, over many years, the workers of Broadgate came to blow millions and millions of pounds of their hard-earned (or not-so-hard-earned) cash on overpriced champagne, vintage wines, designer beers and exotic cocktails. It was almost never quiet, and on a Thursday and Friday night it was a zoo. I couldn't stand the place, but some of the people I worked with seemed to spend much of their leisure time there.

In early 1987 the City of London, like Britain as a whole, was booming, basking in its renewed importance and believing much of its own publicity. The inevitable and, for some firms and individuals, devastating fallout from Big Bang had yet to begin in earnest. Salaries were still being bid up to dizzying heights. The media loved to dwell on the successes and excesses of City life. Glossy magazine features about it were common. TV and film companies made (absurd) dramas about the lives of those working there. But most of the hype passed me by. I was about to get married and buy my first apartment. After a twelve-hour day that began just before 6 a.m., I just didn't have the energy to party much even if I had wanted to. And I didn't. The thought of bar-hopping and cavorting with the nouveau riche, or for that matter with the old money, left me cold. I avoided the bleating champagne Charlies like the plague and continued to develop a reputation as something of a loner, if not a bit of a wonk and a bore.

At SPHG I began to see clients face to face more regularly, but I remained something of an understudy to Paul and Richard, and, initially at least, I was not trusted to market on my own. On the other hand, I was encouraged to address the morning meetings that took place every day on the two trading floors, and which the more senior economists found a bit of a chore.

My time at SPHG also saw my initial media exposure. Indeed, my first radio interview was with a very young and dishevelled-looking Richard Quest in his pre-CNN, BBC Business days. My overriding memory is of him feeding me lines to fit his story and my stumbling over them. We must have done a dozen takes before he had anything remotely acceptable on tape. I rapidly improved, though, not least because I stopped trying to give a pre-rehearsed monologue. Indeed, I was soon quite a regular on the various Breakfast TV business slots and once or twice found myself appearing on the main BBC evening news. I would stress, however, that this was not a way to significantly supplement one's income. The only time I was ever paid was when I appeared on Radio Scotland, from whom I received a couple of cheques for £20. Given this, I will have no truck with stereotyping the Scots as unduly parsimonious.

I still try to mentally prepare a few sound bites and one-liners for TV and radio interviews, but apart from that I trust myself to deal with whatever question comes my way off the cuff. Moreover, what a close friend calls 'the voice' helps. I just seem to have the sort of voice that works. Of course, the reality is that you can never know precisely where one of these events is going to go, not least given that the journalist interviewing you may have only the most tenuous grasp of the subject in question. And this can be particularly disconcerting if it is going out live. But over time, one also learns how to duck difficult or irrelevant questions and recalibrate the interview to match your own agenda.

Generally speaking, I tend not to get nervous while I am doing these things, although a certain level of tension can be a good thing: it seems to concentrate the mind. However, the one time I did almost allow my nerves to overwhelm me was when I was invited on to the CNN morning business show in New York in the mid nineties. The host was a fellow Brit called Stuart Varney who I liked a lot. Despite the ungodly hour at which he had to broadcast he was invariably chirpy, while also retaining a very English sense of humour. As the producer was counting us both down, he said: 'Nothing to worry about: there are only about 300 million people watching worldwide.' Cosseted in the studio and with an immediate audience of a couple of uninterested cameramen and Stuart's makeup girl, I hadn't thought about that.

The stresses and strains in Hoare Govett's marriage of inconvenience with Security Pacific had already been building for some time when the stock market crash of October 1987 dealt the firm a blow from which it never really recovered. However, this was perhaps the one keynote market event of the last thirty years that I missed completely. I was on my honeymoon in Mexico at the time and this was the era before the 24-hour media cycle, or for that matter the Blackberry, had arrived. Indeed, the first time I came across CNN's global news coverage was on a trip to Tokyo in the spring of the following year. It was certainly not in evidence on the tropical paradise of Isla Mujeres off the coast of the Yucatán, or for that matter deep in the jungle on the Guatamalan border, where we spent much of our time.

My first inkling of what had happened came when we reached Mexico City at the end of our trip. Walking around the financial district on the evening of our arrival, I remember remarking to my wife how miserable everyone looked. What I subsequently found out was that the Mexican stock market had fallen by more than just about any other during the crisis. Later that night, sitting in the bar of our hotel, I picked up an English-language newspaper and was confronted with the full details of the momentous events of 19 October. Then, a little later, my wife and I struck up a conversation with an American, who duly informed us that not only had London been caught up in a financial hurricane, it had suffered a real one. Not to put too fine a point on it, we both thought that he was taking the piss.

It was only when I got back to the office the following week that I realised how bad things had been at SPHG. It had been carnage. Traders and salespeople had been locking themselves into toilets, refusing to answer phones, or just walking out of the building. But it was not just the young foot soldiers in the trenches who had panicked. No one in a position of authority had any experience of this kind of thing, and there was little leadership or guidance. Moreover, both the firm's equity book and its fixed income book were poorly positioned for such an event.

The sudden collapse in stock prices also came as a complete shock to my economist colleagues and the vast majority of the profession as a whole, although the fact is that the timing of such events simply cannot be predicted. You can perhaps identify unsustainable macro and market disequilibria and imbalances, you can sometimes point out policy errors and you can specify risks, but the gut-wrenching loss of confidence and rationality that characterises a market crash is impossible to foretell.

CHAPTER 4

Looking back from 2013, the period around the crash of '87 is perhaps the part of my formative years in the markets that is most worth dwelling on. And notwithstanding my three-week absence in the middle of it, it is certainly the time that made the deepest impression on me, not least because the country I was focusing on most intently featured heavily in it, and because developments in the foreign exchange markets played a key role.

In hindsight, the crash of October 1987 reflected the unintended consequences of a number of misdirected policy initiatives. The events surrounding it also provided defining moments for certain institutions and individuals.

By early 1987 it was increasingly clear that by completely changing the perceived balance of risk and reward in the market, the G5's Plaza Accord of September 1985 had overachieved in its stated aim of driving down the US dollar. By that stage the US currency had fallen by some 60% in trade-weighted terms and the issue for policymakers had in fact become how to arrest its decline. This was generating consternation in Japan, which had been forced to embark on an aggressive round of monetary and fiscal reflation (Japan was one of the few countries that retained an affinity for old-style Keynesian methods in the eighties) in an effort to stave off a recession focused on its hard-pressed tradable-goods sector. Moreover, by sparking huge inflows into the Deutschmark, it was encouraging tensions within the ERM. These were especially unwelcome in France, which had abandoned the disastrous 'Socialism in one Country' strategy that characterised the early years of the Mitterrand Presidency and was trying to slough off its reputation as a serial depreciator of its currency and establish what would in future become described as 'Le Franc Fort'. Nevertheless, with the Bundesbank unwilling to cut official interest rates from their already historically low levels to ease the pressures on the weaker currencies, France, among others, was reluctantly forced to devalue once again.

All this led in the following month to the Louvre Accord: a coordinated effort by the major economic powers – by then the G7 (although Italy actually refused to sign the final agreement) – to seek to stabilise the dollar against the yen and the Deutschmark through a combination of direct foreign exchange intervention to sustain certain unpublished target zones and the establishment of sympathetic policy priorities among the various signatories. Hence, in the summer of 1987 the Federal Reserve placed the dollar at the top of its list of factors driving monetary policy for the first time since the breakdown of Bretton Woods some fifteen years earlier. The Bundesbank, however, was a more reluctant participant in this process. Keen to reassert the primacy of domestic monetary developments in policy formulation, in October 1987 it raised interest rates for the first time since 1981, with the specific aim of bringing wayward money supply growth to heel. A huge row with US Treasury Secretary James Baker then spilled out into the open and, with fears gathering of an extended period of higher interest rates and international policy dysfunction, stock market investors voted with their feet. Indeed, such was the panic that the US financial system was for a short period threatened with complete meltdown.

The Fed was forced to ride to the rescue, acting in time-honoured fashion as lender of last resort and providing the necessary liquidity to stave off catastrophe. Alan Greenspan had recently taken over the reins from Paul Volcker, who had effectively been shown the door by the Reagan White House, and his management of the crisis did much to underpin his credibility in the eyes of the market and set the stage for his long career as the most important central banker in the world. On the other hand, the Louvre Accord was abandoned and the dollar dropped, both on the foreign exchanges and down the Fed's list of priorities. Pressure on the franc soon reasserted itself, and the Bundesbank was forced to follow the example of the Fed and other central banks and ease. But what was particularly interesting was that the Bank of France bucked the international trend and tightened.

This was the moment when the policy of Le Franc Fort became reality, and it ushered in a period when interest rate changes rather than parity changes became the default policy management option for ERM members. The system had changed fundamentally.

The next few years also saw efforts to accelerate the movement towards European monetary union, with the French government very much setting the agenda. The feeling in Paris was that Germany's monetary supremacy within Europe had to be addressed, and the best way to achieve this was to push ahead with the creation of a single currency and of a central bank that would serve Europe as a whole rather than just its strongest economy.

Another aspect of the crisis is that it sounded the death knell for broader efforts to manage the constellation of international exchange rates. Governments and central banks from around the world talk to each other and exchange ideas regularly at any number of official and unofficial forums, and this is undoubtedly a good thing: but the Plaza and Louvre Accords were the high-water marks of global currency management. The consensus now is that they almost certainly generated more costs than benefits. G7 meetings continue, and have intermittently caught the imagination of the currency markets and the press, but what they have achieved since in the area of foreign exchange has been modest.

All of which leaves the issues of why the outcome of the 1987 Crash was so different from the outcomes of those in 1929 and 2008?

The first issue I addressed in a paper that I hurriedly wrote for SPHG clients at the time. This did much to establish my credibility both within the firm and outside it, and it concentrated on the particularly unhealthy circumstances that led up to the Wall Street Crash and the horrendous policy errors that subsequently turned things from bad to catastrophic. In this sense, Black Monday (as the crash of '87 had become known) had one silver lining on a personal level. The points I emphasised then, and which I believe still make a good deal of sense, are as follows.

- In 1929 macroeconomics was in its infancy. There were few data and certainly no national income statistics. There was little understanding of the notion of effective demand or of how fiscal and monetary policy might be used to sustain it. Theories of stabilisation policy were being developed, but they were incomplete and often treated as heretical by those in positions of power. The conventional wisdom was that economies would rapidly adjust to negative shocks and that the government should leave well alone, focusing exclusively on 'sound finance'.

- Monetary policy was constrained for at least the first two years of the downturn (and for longer in the US and much of Europe) by adherence to the Gold Standard, or at least a bastardised version of the pre-war system, where few played by the rules, and which, rather than operating as a stabilising force as it did before World War I, in the twenties did the opposite. Because of the Gold Standard, real interest rates remained punishingly high, and many exchange rates became so at variance with internal or external balance that they were swept aside by speculative panics.

- There was no obvious international agency to coordinate policy and through which to channel emergency aid and funding.

- There was no single global hegemon to drive a coordinated approach to policy. Britain was a busted flush, while the US showed little desire to pick up the mantle.

- The twenties were characterised by structural capital flow imbalances and distortions generated by war loans and reparations, and by a rising tide of protectionism. This developed into a trade war when the US introduced the Smoot–Hawley tariff in 1930 and Britain constructed a formal system of imperial trade preference after 1932.

- The cyclical upswing of the twenties was regionally imbalanced and characterised by underlying vulnerabilities. Prices had generally been falling or were at depressed levels. Germany, weighed down by onerous post-war reparation payments and dependent on a consistent inflow of foreign capital, was an exception, sinking into a quagmire first of hyperinflation and then of political instability, while in the East, Japan was beset by what to recent observers will appear a familiar series of financial crises.

- The Great Depression was greatly exacerbated by banking sector fragilities. Too many banking systems around the world were fragmented, inadequately serviced by the central bank as lender of last resort, and exposed by poor systems of deposit insurance, regulation and prudential management. In the four years of depression, over 9,000 US banks (40% of the total) failed or were amalgamated with others. The net result was a significant loss of deposits, the blocking of many accounts and a deep-seated unwillingness to lend, all of which delivered a crushing blow to confidence. Similar circumstances were observable elsewhere.

- Automatic fiscal stabilisers were chronically underdeveloped. Government shares in GDP in the major economies were much smaller than they have been over recent decades. In 1930, central government typically accounted for less than 20% of GDP and the figure was as low as 5% in the US. Of total government disbursements, the amount allocated to unemployment insurance and relief was minimal (1% of the total in the US).

- Fiscal activism, meanwhile, was rare. Japan indulged in it, and it was successful, at least initially, but it was an exception. Even in the US, and despite the New Deal, fiscal policy lacked coherence and never exerted a sustained and unambiguously expansionary impact on the economy until rearmament kicked in the late thirties.[17]

- A final characteristic of the pre-1929 period was the scale of the speculative frenzy in the stock market, the accumulation of personal sector debt, and the extent of the build-up in low-return investment in the US. These were just off the scale relative to the eighties and, when they started to unwind, the resultant balance sheet adjustment was ferocious.

There was nothing comparable to all this in the eighties. I therefore concluded that, provided policymakers responded rationally, the crash of '87 would be more a correction and a temporary constraint on growth than a harbinger of depression.

As it happened, even my relatively sanguine view of the post-crash conjuncture proved overly pessimistic, and any cyclical pause was hard to discern. Recession did follow in the US and then elsewhere a couple of years later, but it was shallow by post-war standards and it eventuated only after rising inflation had caused central banks to reverse the easing measures introduced in late 1987 and early 1988 and take monetary policy into restrictive territory.

Twenty years later, when conducting a similar audit of the prevailing macro backdrop, I came to some rather more disturbing conclusions. In 2007, what struck me were the similarities with the twenties in terms of asset price and private-sector balance sheet excess, the perversity of capital flows, currency manipulation, and the fragilities of banking sectors in the context of poor regulation and prudential management. These were the factors that were to push the global economy to the brink, even in the face of macroeconomic policy responses that were for the most part more timely and aggressive.

Both the equity and debt divisions of SPHG suffered huge losses at this time. Even though the markets and the major economies soon shook off the shock, the company did not. It was holed below the water line, although it took some time to sink. In the meantime, a succession of managerial changes rapidly followed and I found myself suddenly tasked with looking at Japan, and single-handedly (I kid you not), when I had some time, the rest of Asia.

In retrospect, this looks like an extraordinary decision, although ultimately, after a few bumps, it probably made my career. Apart from having spent a short time working for a Japanese company and therefore knowing a little about how the Japanese approached business and having some insights into their psyche, I knew little about the place. I had never been there. I spoke a handful of words of the language and, beyond some familiarity with the broader issues influencing the yen's relationship with the dollar, I was a novice when it came to looking at their economy. What is more, SPHG already had an economist looking at Japan – an experienced and knowledgeable one too. Unfortunately for him, however, he had three problems as far as the firm's management was concerned: he was an unexciting communicator, he could not keep to deadlines, and he was reluctant to commit himself to a view, which was suicidal in his position. And so it proved.

I was delighted with the shift of focus. I had my own economy to analyse for the first time (and which no one else in the firm knew much about) and so could begin to retreat from Paul's influence. I had my own captive audience in the form of SPHG's Japanese equity and debt sales groups, who were desperate for someone who would provide them with a steady stream of pertinent output and who they could confidently put in front of clients. And I was encouraged to travel to Japan and Asia at regular intervals but not asked to live there. SPHG, unlike most UK banks and securities houses, was quite happy for its Japan economist to remain on the other side of the world most of the time. This reflected cost issues and the preferences of my predecessor. I was soon to learn that it both made the job harder to do and to some extent undermined my credibility with clients. Misguided though this all was, I was initially quite happy to accept it. After all, I was newly married and trying to persuade my wife to move to Tokyo was not something I wanted to consider at the time.

I must also admit that I have little memory of feeling any sense of sympathy for my predecessor, despite the fact that he was middle aged, married and had young children. So I can only conclude that although I always claim to have risen above the worst aspects of the City's law of the jungle, I had in reality rapidly taken on some of its traits. In retrospect I am ashamed. He must have been devastated. I certainly would have been had I been in his shoes.

I soon found myself desperately trying to learn about Japan's extraordinary economy, which, as amazing as this may seem today, was then held up as a role model for the rest of the OECD. It enjoyed rapid growth, full employment, relative price stability, a structural external surplus, a strong currency, placid industrial relations, a stock market that had been rising consistently through the eighties (and proved remarkably resilient to the '87 Crash), and it boasted some of the most innovative companies in the world. Its apparent vibrancy and persistent outperformance were the very antithesis of Britain's extended period of relative decline, whatever the claims of Mrs Thatcher and her supporters. In 1988, its great period of asset price appreciation – subsequently termed the 'Bubble Economy' – was approaching its zenith. Indeed, I well remember the introductory paragraph of some competitor research that fell on my desk at the time. It said: 'Japan's economic and financial situation can be summed up in three words: Boom! Boom! Boom!' But more of this later.

As has been the case throughout my career, finding the time to undertake the necessary research to do my job was difficult and, as has proved all too typical, I found myself dumped into the deep end with precious little preparation. However much I felt that I could fall back on the basic building blocks of macroeconomic analysis, it rapidly became clear that I was once again going to have to live on my wits and bluff my way through for some time to come.

I was almost immediately sent on a fact-finding trip to Singapore, Hong Kong, Taiwan, Seoul and Tokyo. This was combined with a round of client presentations in each of these centres, where I had to demonstrate that, young and relatively inexperienced though I was, I was a step up from my predecessor. Looking back, this was ridiculous. I could have done irreparable damage to my own career and to SPHG's reputation, although by that stage the latter was already self-destructing without any obvious contribution from yours truly. Did I demur? Of course not. Did anyone in a position of power suggest this was a risk? Not within my earshot. In my later, more sensible and senior, incarnations it is something that I would never have dreamed of imposing on myself, or on anyone else. But in the late eighties it was what was done, and what you did.

My initial venture to the Far East was an eye opener in so many ways. I was amazed by the vibrancy and modernity of the economies I visited and by the brashness of the expatriates I encountered. The cities were hives of activity that rarely seemed to slow down, even after midnight. A powerful entrepreneurial spirit and single-mindedness was much in evidence. People wanted to get rich, and expectations ran high. The hotels were palatial, the restaurants wonderful, and the service superior to anything you could find at home. It all made Britain, booming or not, look sad and old.

Hong Kong exhibited colonial atmospherics that, unsurprisingly, it struggles to retain today, some seventeen years after the handover to China. The people I encountered, including those who worked for SPHG, were Brits. They were a confident and boozy crowd that dominated the local financial industry. They were happy to escape the UK's high taxes and economic trials and enjoy the trappings of their assumed superiority over the locals and over a mainland economy whose journey away from communism was still at a relatively early stage. Life seemed pretty sweet for them and they let you know it.

A similar sense of self-belief was on show among the expats in Singapore. The city was more modern to look at than Hong Kong and the local population more earnest and less fun. Indeed, the word 'sterile' might have been invented for it. However, my clearest memory about the place on that first trip was when, in answer to my question about his outlook for the city state, a local economist informed me that he rarely went on record about the future in any great detail as the authorities didn't encourage any views that might be at variance with their own! Sadly, for all its economic success, nothing much has changed.

Nevertheless, despite its government's paranoia, Singapore at that time at least made a show of democracy and pretended not to be a one-party state. Neither South Korea nor Taiwan had yet made that jump, although in both cases it was not far off. Indeed, while I was in Seoul I was caught up on the fringes of a democracy demonstration and had my one and only encounter with tear gas. It was horrific and I was still dealing with the physical effects twenty-four hours later. With both these nations forged out of painful Japanese colonial occupations and bloody civil wars, they retained more than a whiff of the dictatorships that had underpinned their development. Their respective capital cities, despite their sheen of modernity, had a flavour of Eastern Europe. The ranks of identical numbered concrete apartment blocks along the banks of the Seoul's Han River would not have been out of place in Moscow or Kiev, or for that matter in George Orwell's *Nineteen Eighty-Four*. The English language was also much less in evidence, and the two cities felt more alien and oppressive than Hong Kong or Singapore. They were huge, chaotic and rather less developed. Furthermore, both shared a similar smell: a combination of petrol fumes, raw sewage, garlic and some undefined sweetness that I have never been able to nail down.

Taipei remains the one Asian city that I have never learned to love. Indeed, as one American colleague of mine once commented: if the world needed an enema, God would administer it via Taipei. Seoul I was more attracted to, despite or perhaps because of its edginess and the sense that it is situated on the edge of civilisation (the North Korean border is only about twenty-five miles away), and I have always found the earthiness and bluntness of the Koreans refreshing.

That first trip to Seoul also saw an episode that speaks to the temptations of international business travel and my own naivety. On my first evening there I retired to the Irish bar in the Westin Hotel, the wonderfully named O'Kim's, for a nightcap and to go through my notes for the next day's meetings. After a few minutes, I looked up to see that sitting next to me was a very attractive young Korean girl, who smiled engagingly and asked me if I was alone and would like some company. 'That's very kind, but I have some work to do', I replied. She was gone in a flash and I turned around to see a phalanx of scantily clad girls sitting on stools against the wall, at which point the cogs in my brain began to turn. So much for the seasoned traveller.

Tokyo was the last stop on that first Asian tour and it was worth waiting for. I was not the first of my family to visit Japan. My father had been there in 1945, when as a nineteen-year-old able seaman he was on the first British naval ship to enter Tokyo Bay after the Japanese laid down their arms. A few days later he and the rest of the crew on the battleship HMS *King George V* were witness to Japan's formal surrender and the final act of World War II. Needless to say, my father's experiences of the country were rather different from mine. His abiding memories are of the almost complete devastation of Tokyo and Yokohama, of the desperate lice-infested poverty and starvation of those who survived, and of the unspeakable physical condition of the Allied prisoners of war whom he helped to liberate from the camps. Such horrors were not in evidence in 1988.

I had been told a lot about modern-day Tokyo by my London colleagues, but nothing could have prepared me for its scale, its energy, its contrasts and its unique eccentricities. My initial reaction was that it oozed wealth and self-assurance. It felt and behaved like the capital city of the most successful economy in the world. Much of the downtown skyline was like something out of sixties TV cartoon series *The Jetsons*. There was neon everywhere. Consistent with the notion that Japan's 'bubble' was more than anything else a business investment bubble, there were state-of-the-art corporate headquarters punching skywards on almost every city centre block. The roads were incredibly busy, even late at night, and especially in the areas like Roppongi and Shinjuku where people congregated to enjoy the city's raucous nightlife. Most of the cars seemed to be the latest models. One was constantly struck by the density of people on the main streets and by how many were in uniform of one sort or another: guarding, guiding, advising or just hanging around for no apparent reason. The subway system was like an ants' nest and yet, in stark contrast to London's creaking, unreliable, largely Victorian tube system, it functioned with clockwork efficiency. The main stations such as Shinjuku, Shibuya and Tokyo station itself were themselves cities in microcosm, populated by any number of small stores and restaurants, some specialising in fast food, others serving top-quality sushi, and through which rivers of people flooded. Three million people passed through Shinjuku station every day.

The restaurant I ate in at my five-star hotel on the first night offered French food as good as anything I had eaten in Europe. The service was impeccable and the prices mind boggling. It was only the overseas visitors such as me who seemed to have to worry whether their expense accounts would stretch far enough. Yet this was a city of enormous contrasts. On my second night I sat on a rough wooden bench eating chicken yakitori skewers and drinking beer out of a bottle in one of the many makeshift restaurants underneath Tokyo Station, and that was equally enjoyable. You could also turn off any main thoroughfare and immediately find yourself in the quietest of residential neighbourhoods or in a tiny perfectly manicured park. For all the opulence of the headquarters of the major corporations and for all the vast verdant splendour of the Imperial Palace gardens, much of the housing stock was modest in the extreme. Downtown living space came at an extraordinary premium and people lived cheek by jowl in a manner that most Westerners would consider beneath their dignity. All that most people could afford was a tiny flimsy-walled apartment in a block of other tiny flimsy-walled apartments. If you hankered after something slightly grander, then you were consigned to at least a ninety-minute commute, during which you would probably have to stand – in both directions. Of course, there were many beautifully stocked department stores selling ridiculously priced designer goods, but the number of tiny specialist mom and pop retail outlets was what really attracted one's attention. Napoleon said that Britain was a nation of shopkeepers. He never got to Japan.

I was greeted with enthusiasm by my colleagues both at HG's small but well-appointed office overlooking the Imperial Palace gardens (which were at the time valued more highly than the entire state of California) and at the larger space occupied by SecPac, high in the huge, foreign-dominated, Ark Hills complex a little way across town. They chaperoned me to various client meetings at which I managed to avoid embarrassing myself, and they also took great delight in showing me some of the delights and idiosyncrasies of this stupendous metropolis.

The other key element of the trip was to make contact with some policymakers, and in particular officials at the Ministry of Finance (MOF) and Bank of Japan (BOJ), the departments that dominate Japanese economic policymaking and indeed domestic policymaking full stop. Of the two, the MOF was the more important and was typically the chosen destination for the best and brightest from Japan's education system. The headquarters of both the BOJ and the MOF are relatively old, having somehow managed to survive the Allied bombing of Tokyo. The BOJ, with its classic Japanese architectural style, was, externally at least, by far the more impressive. Indeed, on seeing the MOF building for the first time I thought it more appropriate to a third-world nation than to one of the most powerful countries on the planet. Such an impression was only confirmed on entering its labyrinthine, dingy, inadequately air-conditioned corridors and cramped offices, where exhausted-looking officials seemed to be consumed by a chaotic sprawl of files and documents. Yet these people were the praetorian guard of the Japanese civil service!

Despite their appalling working conditions – which, I was told, were deliberately left this way as a means to assuage public criticism of their privileged position within society – the people I met at the MOF and BOJ were only too keen to hear my still partially formed views, and in general they responded politely, if guardedly, to my questions of them. What is more, I made some contacts on that first trip that I have sustained throughout by entire career – contacts who proved invaluable in broadening my understanding of Japan. This applied to one gentleman in particular: Akinari Horii.

At the time I first met Horii-san he was a senior economist in the BOJ's research and statistics department and he was used as the primary contact with foreign visitors. His English was near-perfect, which was rare among the Japanese, and it was not American-accented but British. He was also, I soon realised, smart as a tack, having received an MBA with distinction from the Wharton School and worked for a period at the Bank for International Settlements in Basel. Over the next twenty-five years, as he rose through the ranks to be effectively Head of Economic Research, Yokohama branch manager, Liaison Officer with the Japanese Diet, the BOJ's representative in New York and Assistant Governor with Responsibility for International Activities, he would always find time to talk. His views might not always give you the correct steer about BOJ or government policy but they would offer fascinating insights into the nature of the debate at the Japanese central bank and beyond. I owe him a lot.

I fell for Tokyo from the word go. I can't have spent more than four or five days there on that first trip, but it was enough to get me hooked for life. It was, and remains, a unique city. Vast. Boiling. Fascinating. Charming. Vexing.

Over the next year or so I took several more trips to Japan and Asia and built up my knowledge of the region. I was also sent on my first business trip to the US, where I saw some thirty clients over five exhausting but enjoyable days. I was really embracing the role and felt that, although I was for the most part geographically displaced from Asia, I was coming to terms with my responsibilities and starting to actually have some sensible things to say. But as is typical in the markets, things rarely remain stable for long.

In the middle of 1988 the decision was taken in London to close HG's Japanese equity business, while SecPac's Japanese debt operation was also downsized and a number of key personnel let go. The firm's Tokyo operations were always hugely expensive to run, and at a time when the company as a whole was under intense stress, it was an obvious sacrifice to make. Yes, Japan was still in the midst of an extraordinary equity bull market, but the competition was intense for the foreign companies operating there and HG just couldn't hack it. I was kept on in London but my responsibilities were less clear. Once again I had to be content with being a jack of all trades, master of none. I was frustrated and heartbroken. And in the meantime the firm continued to struggle.

I have two final memories of this time. The first is of a young SPHG gilt trader, once so arrogant and proud, being led off the trading floor in floods of tears by two colleagues after losing a vast sum of money. He never returned. The second is of a senior manager in the fixed-income division progressively succumbing to what soon became clear was a nervous breakdown. He too was never to return.

CHAPTER 5

A DEAD END

One day in the spring of 1989, Paul took me to one side and told me that he had been approached by the American investment bank, Drexel Burnham Lambert (DBL), with a view to overhauling its international economics group in London. He asked how I would feel about going with him. Paul had had enough of SPHG's petty politicking and rightly sensed that the firm was not going to be one of the winners, or even indeed one of the survivors, in the post-Big Bang world. After the traumas of the 1987 Crash, it was desperately trying to focus on its residual profitable areas, but both the intense competition in global financial markets and the macroeconomic environment were making this harder and harder. By this time, the wheels were coming off Mrs Thatcher's 'economic miracle' and the tougher economic times to come were unlikely to be kind to SPHG.

Given that my prospects at the firm were looking rather uncertain, and that DBL was looking at diversifying its business and expanding its footprint in Japan and more broadly within Asia, I was attracted by the idea – especially as there would be a generous pay rise in it for me. It proved to be a disaster, and looking back on my all too brief sojourn at the firm I cannot but ask myself: 'What in God's name were you thinking?'

Drexel was, of course, the firm that will forever be associated with three things: the 'junk' or 'high-yield' bond market, leveraged buyouts, and Michael Milken, the firm's dominant personality and generator of cash, who was subsequently sentenced to ten years in jail for insider dealing. Although at its peak it was the fifth largest investment bank in the US, it was distrusted by much of the rest of the industry. Few would deny that it employed some excellent individuals, not least in research, where Abby Joseph Cohen, Dick Hoey and Maria Ramirez commanded enormous respect for their economic and strategic insights. But what troubled people was the idiosyncratic business model it adopted and the especially mercenary way in which it was run. Just as I joined, DBL was beginning to reap the unfortunate reward for its hubris and past misdemeanours.

In early 1989 Drexel was at risk of indictment under America's Racketeer Influenced and Corrupt Organizations Act, a law designed to suppress the Mafia![18] In the end, a deal was done that resulted in Milken leaving the firm en route to prison (it was as if he had landed on the 'Go to Jail' square while way ahead in a game of Monopoly) and the firm settling with the US Securities and Exchange Commission for $650m. As if that wasn't enough to raise question marks over the firm's future, in the same way that SPHG was confronted by an increasingly difficult macro environment, DBL's keynote businesses were entering some very choppy waters.

The appetite for leveraged buyouts was on the wane and criticism of junk bond finance was rising along with the default rates on low-quality debt. In the meantime, a number of senior executives had agreed to stay on only in return for the promise of obscene bonus cheques at the end of the year. The fact was that the firm was in deep trouble and required major reconstructive surgery if it was to have any chance of survival. Although much of this had yet to come fully out into the open at the time I was considering joining, I was warned by a number of people to steer clear. As a friend put it: 'It just didn't pass the smell test.' But, attracted by the generous pay cheque, taken in by the propaganda I was fed when being interviewed (which included the flagrant dismissal of the potential effects of the lawsuits the company was facing and the rosiest assessments of the outlook for junk bonds) and reluctant to sever the umbilical cord to Paul, I ignored the advice.

I can honestly say that almost everything to do with my time at Drexel was a farce. What followed next bordered on the absurd.

Paul resigned from SPHG slightly ahead of me. Without shedding too many tears, and probably with more attitude on my part than was warranted, I followed about a week later and then took a few days off. Forty-eight hours later, Paul called me and dropped a bombshell. Because of the ructions associated with the SEC settlement, the man who had brokered our hires at Drexel had been forced out, the firm's headcount was being reduced, a number of its businesses were being wound up, and Asian expansion was off the agenda. Hence, although Paul thought he would be kept on, there would probably be no job for me. Drexel would give me a lump sum payment for my trouble but that was all. I was, in short, to be made redundant and receive a pay-off without actually having worked there! Paul also suggested that I should get on to the phone to Richard at SPHG and ask for my old job back. I was dumbstruck.

Now let me put all this into some kind of personal context. I had been married for less than two years. My wife was six months pregnant with our first child and was about to give up her much-loved job as a conference organiser. We had recently moved in to an apartment in Maida Vale in northwest London, close to the top of what increasingly looked like a grossly inflated property market, UK interest rates were still moving rapidly higher as the government desperately tried to bring an overheating economy to heel, the City job market was only likely to become more difficult, and we had precious little cash to fall back on. This was a personal crisis, and one that I struggled to explain either to my wife or to anyone else. My father, for one, brought up in a different era and with different values about loyalty, job security and thrift, was completely incredulous about my situation.

Notwithstanding the personal humiliation involved, I had little choice but to go back to Richard for help. After briefing him about my situation over the phone, I travelled up to Broadgate to have lunch with him. He was sympathetic on a personal level, and staggered by what had occurred, but his sense was that the powers that be at SPHG would be less forgiving than he was. They were unlikely to take me back, especially if I hung on to the pay-off from Drexel. The feeling was that Paul and I had left them in the lurch at a difficult time for the firm and that I should not be seen to have benefited from it financially. We had made our beds and we now had to lie in them. The next few days were grim. The only note of consolation was my journey up to the Drexel offices at Aldgate to collect my 'redundancy cheque'.

Before long, however, the situation took another extraordinary twist. As I moped about at home and tried to motivate myself to start looking for another role, Paul phoned me again. This time he informed me that he had managed to convince the management at Drexel to take me on after all, but it meant that I had to return the pay-off. You honestly couldn't have made this up. Once again, I had to explain to my disbelieving wife, family and friends the latest iteration of this bizarre tale. Given what we had already been through, I considered turning DBL down but, eventually, my wife and I decided that I should accept, concluding that if it didn't work out, it would be easier to look for something else while in employment than not.

So, after a ridiculous false start, and carrying a personal cheque to the company for the precise amount that they had paid me just a week earlier, I began work at Drexel. I shouldn't have bothered. Notwithstanding the reputation of the High Yield team around the world, it was a smaller and less influential operation than SPHG's London office. Indeed, it was something of a distant outpost rather than the firm's operational hub. Moreover, the roles that Paul and I were to fulfil were to have precious little to do with the High Yield part of Drexel's business. That was walled off from the remainder of the operation on its own separate floor of the building. No, we were to be there to service the rest of the firm's operations, and in particular its plain vanilla bond and foreign exchange divisions, which were having to play a much bigger role in revenue generation than in the past.

By the time I arrived, Paul had already let a couple of economists from the previous regime go and this had not gone well. Accordingly, there was considerable resentment towards us both from the rump of the old group (at least until they too decided to leave). But there was particular antipathy towards me. Their attitude, understandable under the circumstances, was to ask what I was doing there apart from being Paul's 'boy'. What particular skills did I bring that they did not already possess? Well, certainly not much by way of technical understanding of the major sovereign bond markets. Japan? The company's Asian ambitions were largely dead in the water and it didn't trade in Japanese government bonds. Even its foreign exchange positions in the yen were insignificant.

Nor were the salespeople or traders much more sympathetic. Their focus was on whether the firm was going to survive and, if so, whether they would retain their jobs. Paul and I were seen as costly outsiders and I was viewed as little more than his gofer, much as I was when I first started at ITM, three and a half years previously. To say that the atmosphere was challenging would be an understatement. Poisonous would be more apt.

And frankly, a gofer is what I was. I was there to backstop Paul. I undertook a single marketing trip (to Denmark), barely presented to any clients and did precious little media work the entire time I was there. Meanwhile, the generally hostile internal audience encouraged me to keep my head down, look busy, ignore the barbs from my colleagues and just hope that things would begin to change, or indeed that something else might come along to allow me to escape.

Much of my time at Drexel was spent observing the ignominious end of Mrs Thatcher's premiership and the collapse of what had been widely touted by the right-wing press and much of the City economics fraternity as Britain's economic renaissance. Given my political leanings, this caused me to shed few tears on her, or her government's, account, although I thought it tragic for much of the rest of the population. This is not to deny that the Conservative administrations of the eighties did some good. By the late seventies – after a period of stagflation, excessive and destructive government interference, poor management and persistent industrial unrest – Britain could not go on as it was: a sclerotic and pessimistic country that was falling behind its peers in terms of wealth and prosperity. It was ripe for a period of much-needed reform that would temper its rigidities, enhance the flow of resources from the less productive to the more productive, and in the process boost growth potential and the ability of the economy to absorb shocks. What was also clear to me, even as a confirmed Labour voter, was that the Labour Party was at the time singularly ill-equipped to deliver this change. After the Falklands War it was in no position to do much to stop it.

The initiatives of the Thatcher era in the areas of trade union reform, tax reform, privatisation, financial sector liberalisation and the enhancement of domestic product market competition certainly helped to arrest Britain's malaise, with the positive results most conspicuous in the reversal of the economy's long-standing relative productivity decline.[19]

However, I thought that the Thatcher governments went about their business in a crass and unsubtle manner and that enormous mistakes were made, many of which originated from the simplistic, at times fundamentalist, manner in which complex issues were confronted. It was the arrogance and enamelled certainty of Thatcherism – its separation of issues into black and white, good and bad, free-market and socialist, and us and them – that I found so distasteful and which I was sure would mean that it would end in tears. Life, and especially the worlds of economics and politics, was so much more complicated than that. And some of their reforms, whatever their longer-term benefits, involved gut-wrenching short-term human costs that were given inadequate weight.

What is more, if you actually look back at what happened in that decade relative to what was supposed to happen, and indeed what was presented at the time as happening, the ultimate degree of transformation was altogether more modest and less enduring than claimed. Four particular considerations spring to mind.

First, naive monetarism proved to be just that: naive. Despite the retention of published monetary targets for some years, the commitment to hitting them come what may rapidly dissipated. Second, at the end of her period in office, inflation was still the overriding problem it had been at the outset. Third, the average growth rate achieved in the eighties was very close to what it had been in the much-maligned seventies. Fourth, too much emphasis was placed on 'instant gratification'. The idea of creating a British sovereign wealth fund to invest North Sea oil revenues for longer-term gain was eschewed, consumption was encouraged at the expense of investment, and personal indebtedness ballooned. In the meantime, the nation's human and social overhead capital were compromised, the enduring tendency towards mass unemployment meant that inequality and poverty increased alarmingly, and a dependency culture was encouraged. And financial liberalisation was pushed too far – storing up enormous problems for the future.

I have to add that my particular academic grounding had led me to be sceptical about fundamental transformations in economic performance. History is replete with policymakers and commentators confusing unsustainable cyclical boom with (supposed) structural renaissance, an error that I was to encounter repeatedly throughout my career. It was certainly made in Britain during the eighties and many City economists were particularly culpable.

In this context I am a firm believer that all countries are, to a significant extent, prisoners of their own history, and that this probably applies more to the UK than most. Britain was the first country to industrialise and as a result it became the world's dominant economic, political and financial power for much of the nineteenth and early twentieth centuries. But by the standards of later periods, it grew at a pretty sedate pace, and the general population and the nation's institutions became accustomed to this pace of change. They also became conditioned to this position of power and the grandeur and independence that went with it. What is more, the rather hollow victories that Britain enjoyed in both the World Wars and the 'soft export markets' available first via the Empire and then via the Commonwealth only deepened this sense of the country being unique and able to continue to plough the same familiar furrow. For Britain, there were just not the same searing experiences that, for example, befell Germany and Japan and necessitated such attitudinal and institutional changes.

What this meant in practical terms was that, for the British economy to transform itself, the shock delivered to it via Mrs Thatcher's reform policies would need to be both sizeable and, more importantly still, sustained over an open-ended period. After all, reflecting technological advances, rising per capita incomes and changing consumption and production patterns, the processes of structural adjustment are themselves continual. Furthermore, the by-products of these reform initiatives on macroeconomic stabilisation policy were likely to prove very challenging. The risk was, therefore, that if her government didn't get demand management right by controlling the subsequent boom, reform would run out of steam and many of the conservative forces and damaging traits that had constrained UK economic performance over the decades would reassert themselves and drag the country back down. Worse still, Britain was not the only country embracing this kind of reform agenda. It was a global phenomenon, and we needed to do it better and more enduringly than others.

If there is one thing that I have learned over the years, it is that bad macroeconomic policy always results in a bad outcome. British economic policy failed in the eighties in large part because the government failed to come to terms with the broader macro implications of its supply-side radicalism. This criticism holds true throughout the decade but is particularly apposite for the years during which Nigel Lawson was chancellor.

It will come as no surprise that Lawson was not one of my favourite politicians. Rarely have I seen someone who saw the world quite so starkly in black and white terms, who was so convinced of the veracity of his own views and so witheringly dismissive of those who disagreed with him. But for all his arrogance, bombast and condescension, and all his dreams of hallowed status among economic policymakers, Lawson proved in practice to be a rather narrow technocrat who failed to grasp the wider consequences of his radicalism both within the domestic economy and abroad. He got it terribly wrong.

CHAPTER 5

By 1985, although no one could doubt the UK economy's impressive and disinflationary recovery since 1981, the government's Medium Term Financial Strategy, which Lawson had done so much to design and which sought to sketch out how the objectives for key monetary and fiscal variables would dovetail to deliver macro stability, had become something of a joke. This was particularly the case where monetary targets were concerned. Institutional changes in the financial sector and elsewhere, many of which reflected the government's own reform policies, had generated huge volatility in money demand. Monetary growth had proved extravagant, mercurial and difficult to interpret. Lawson therefore sought out alternative nominal anchors for policy, eventually fixating on nominal GDP growth and especially the exchange rate. To his mind, the ERM was the obvious option to embrace, in that it would allow the UK to 'import' German low-inflation credibility via a fixed or quasi-fixed exchange rate. However, what he failed to recognise were the extensive political implications of the UK's membership of this club – implications that the ever-Eurosceptic prime minister was far from ready to embrace. Lawson's initial proposal was therefore vetoed.[20]

As it happened, UK membership of the ERM in 1985 and 1986 would probably have ended in disaster, as this period saw a collapse in oil prices that put the pound (which still enjoyed 'petrocurrency' status) under sustained downward pressure. It is quite possible that there would have been a repeat of Britain's humiliating experience with the European 'snake' in 1972, when sterling was forced out of a managed, Europe-based, exchange rate system after only six weeks.

Undaunted, Lawson subsequently adopted a strategy of shadowing the Deutschmark. But again his timing left much to be desired. As the second half of the decade progressed, unemployment finally began to fall and Britain's recovery matured into an out and out boom as the effects of the government's various reforms bolstered confidence. There was a palpable sense of euphoria among householders and entrepreneurs that was only further encouraged by Lawson's pro-cyclical tax cuts, the demand-side effects of which he tended to dismiss as insignificant and largely in the minds of old-fashioned Keynesian thinkers. Rather than seeking to take some of the steam out of the expansion via tighter monetary policy, Lawson's fixation on sterling's stability against the Deutschmark led him to cut policy rates, and not just around the time of the 1987 stock market crash. He continued to do so into 1988, even though it was becoming obvious that the economy was seriously overheated and central bankers elsewhere were looking to unwind the monetary easing of the previous year.

Eventually, Lawson desperately tried to bring the economy to heel by finally allowing sterling to appreciate, and by reversing course on interest rates, but it was too late. What is more, having abandoned his exchange rate anchor, he was now effectively operating without any serious policy framework beyond his appeal that we should trust him as the great architect of Britain's eighties renaissance. Such unconstrained discretion in the hands of someone whose sense of self-importance was on an entirely different level from most human beings, and whose previous errors had just been exposed, was hardly a credible approach. And the rest, as they say, is history. By the time he resigned in October 1990 (ironically just before Britain actually did join the ERM), inflation was back in high single digits and running far above that of our competitors, UK policy rates had more than doubled to 15%, and recession was a foregone conclusion. The Thatcherite economic miracle, insofar as it ever existed, was over.

One of the few encouraging moments during my spell at Drexel was when I was asked to provide some informal advice to the UK Labour Party, which, under the modernising leadership of Neil Kinnock and with Mrs Thatcher on the defensive over the economy's performance, was seen as having a reasonable chance of success at the next general election. Alastair Campbell, subsequently Tony Blair's director of communications, but then political editor of the *Daily Mirror*, was an old friend and he put me in touch with Mo Mowlem, who was then number two in the Labour Treasury team. At her request I drafted a paper on the case for UK membership of the ERM, on the assumption that Labour was indeed soon to be returned to power.

Looking back, the judgement on my advice is mixed. I was sceptical that the end of a major boom, if not a recession, was really the best time to make such a move, but I also accepted that a Labour government, after its painful experiences with economic policy in the seventies, would need some mechanism to lend it credibility in the markets. I concluded, therefore, that should the decision be made to enter, it should be at a competitive rate that would prove sustainable but with narrow bands either side of the central parity.

Frankly, this was a fudge. The low entry rate (if it could have been negotiated) could well have offset much of the credibility that would have been gained from the narrow bands. However, I suspect it would have been a more enduring strategy than the one that was ultimately adopted, which embodied a central parity with the Deutschmark that was a huge hostage to fortune. As to the paper's impact on Labour policy, I seem to remember a nice hand-written thank you note from Mo, but no more. And, of course, despite Mrs Thatcher's demise and the travails of the economy, Labour went on to lose a fourth successive election.

Overall, this was a miserable time for me, and Drexel was a miserable place. It became increasingly obvious to Paul and to me that the company was a dangerously asymmetrical and poorly managed enterprise and that, despite every effort being made to preserve the myth, the 'high yield' business could no longer generate enough revenue to sustain the whole venture. The vexed departure of Milken's alchemical talents and the circumstances surrounding his demise, together with the increasingly hostile global macro-economic environment, meant that as the second half of 1989 progressed the company looked doomed.

DBL was always more dependent than other investment banks on external funding, and it was struggling to roll over its commercial paper. It saw its lines of credit progressively withdrawn. Only financial sleight of hand was keeping it afloat. Meanwhile, morale among the staff was collapsing, the headcount on the trading floor was being whittled down and, whatever the bigwigs secured for themselves (an astonishing $260m in bonuses were paid out in total at this time), junior and middle-ranking staff were incensed by the paucity of their year-end awards.[18] Some expressed their anger very publicly. One, returning from drowning his sorrows in the local pub, suggested that my 'pointless' employment had 'effectively stolen his paycheque'. To this day, I regret not punching him.

As Christmas approached, many employees didn't even bother going through the motions any more and I noted that Paul, ever the savvy political operator, was spending more and more time tête-à-tête in the office of the formidable Ros Wilton, who ran Drexel's London operation. I requested a heart-to-heart with him at which I said I was deeply unhappy and had begun to try to find something else while there might actually be something else to find. He admitted that he was doing the same himself. My main game plan was to look to Japan as an escape route, and the option I pursued most avidly was to join the large UK stockbroker Phillips & Drew, or UBS Phillips & Drew (UBS P&D) as they then called themselves after their merger with the large Swiss bank.

UBS P&D had been showing some interest in me for a while, as their chief economist in Japan, the respected David Pike, was being moved upstairs to head up the entire Tokyo research operation and they needed a replacement. This was a tremendously attractive opportunity. David had built a great product: UBS P&D was a firm that so far had done well in the free-for-all that followed Big Bang. Moreover, it had long enjoyed a top reputation for research, and especially macroeconomics, not least because the firm invested heavily in it. And UBS was a giant among European banks, seemingly with some of the deepest pockets. This looked like the perfect antidote to DBL and the perfect opportunity for me if I could only secure the job. Oh yes, and on the assumption that I could convince my wife, who was now the mother of a six-month-old baby girl, to up sticks and relocate half way around the world to a country about which she knew virtually nothing.

Christmas and New Year of 1989/90 was an unsettling time, but a series of interviews with UBS P&D in London went well and I was granted dispensation by Paul to fly out to Japan for a few days for a further set of interviews in Tokyo. These were also a success, although I had yet to convince my wife that such a drastic move was the right step for us. This was particularly the case after the pantomime that had occurred when I left SPHG. There were one or two other opportunities in London and in Edinburgh at the time, but they were less attractive, both financially and professionally, and my half-Greek spouse certainly had little desire to experience the bracing climate of eastern Scotland.

My career at Drexel ended as it began, in something akin to farce. At the start of 1990, the High Yield team in Los Angeles decided to head over to Europe on a marketing trip, although whether this was a serious attempt to drum up business or just one last jolly for those involved is unclear. Paul was asked to accompany them to add some credibility and provide some macro insights. The movers and shakers duly jetted into town via Concorde or first-class flights and were subsequently ferried around London and the continent in limousines and private jets, in between staying at a selection of five-star luxury hotels. No expense was spared and the misinformation spread about the prospects both for high-yield bonds and for Drexel knew no boundaries.

The afternoon before the trip ended, Paul phoned me to tell me to grab whatever was on the table from UBS P&D as he had been reliably informed that Drexel was about to fold. There were no interested buyers because of the threat of further lawsuits, and the US government would have nothing to do with a bailout because Treasury Secretary Nicholas Brady had suffered personally as a result of one of the more hostile deals that DBL had sponsored. Having managed to convince my reluctant spouse that moving to Japan was the best option for us, I actually resigned from the firm on the morning it went belly up. I was now faced with the logistical complexities of transcontinental relocation and the professional challenges of coming to terms with both the loss of my mentor and a Japanese economy that had just hit the wall.

But before going on to discuss all this, there is one final footnote about Drexel. After its demise, some of the company's traders went on to work at AIG and there, some twenty years later, one or two of these individuals were to be involved in another dramatic collapse of a major financial entity – a collapse that was to provoke a rather different response from the authorities.

CHAPTER 6

THE RISING SUN

The first instalment of my Japanese adventure began in April 1990. My arrival in effect coincided with the onset of the country's secular stagnation – not that anyone I encountered at the time believed that to be the case. Yes, there were people who had long been sceptical about the 'Japanese economic miracle', and yes, there were those who expected the economy would have to navigate a testing period of adjustment in the years ahead, but no one was predicting the twenty-odd years of purgatory that were to follow. I certainly wasn't. My experience of Japan, such as it had been at that stage, and my knowledge of the broad contours of the country's post-war economic history suggested sanguinity and that it would cope well with the situation it now faced. Indeed, it took me until 1995 and my second spell in the country to fully grasp the extent of its underlying problems.

After the trials of my time at Drexel, it is difficult to describe quite how relieved I was to secure my new job. My elevation to chief economist for UBS P&D in Tokyo was a big jump professionally, representing both an enormous challenge and a stunning opportunity. I remember feeling that I had really 'arrived', even if I was amazed as to how it had happened, given my limited experience and what I saw as the enduring shortcomings in my skillset. It was also a colossal change for my family. We had a nine-month-old baby, we had moved to the other side of the world to an alien culture, we spoke barely a word of the language, and we knew virtually no one.

I well recall the feeling of trepidation my wife and I felt when we stepped off the plane at Tokyo's Narita Airport after our initial fourteen-hour journey. Bleary eyed, we sped into the city on an airport bus, surveying the vast and less than aesthetically pleasing sprawl of suburban Tokyo, before being deposited at the famous Imperial Hotel, which was to be our home until we found an apartment. And no matter how luxurious this might sound, having to confine a jet-lagged nine-month-old to a hotel bedroom for much of the day was anything but fun, especially when you yourself are eight hours out of kilter.

I also remember that I had forgotten to pack my work shoes, so we spent much of our first day in Japan searching high and low for a pair of size tens that would accommodate my gigantic Western feet. In the end we struck lucky just off the Ginza, in the appropriately named Big Shoe. Until that moment I had visions of starting my first day at UBS P&D in a pair of running shoes.

The office could not have been more conveniently located. It was in the Yamato Seimei building in the tongue-twisting area of Uchisaiwaicho (you knew you were grounded in Japan when you could comfortably articulate words like this), next-door-but-one to the Imperial and overlooking the small, but fussily maintained, Hibiya Park, which abuts the Imperial Palace. At least I could get back to see my wife Mick and my daughter Ellen easily enough, and they could come and meet me for lunch.

Thankfully, within a couple of weeks we had found an apartment in Sangubashi, a quiet well-to-do residential neighbourhood close to one of the city's nicest open spaces: Yoyogi Park. Although modest by UK standards, by Japanese criteria our new home was extremely spacious. Indeed, the exceptional status of our living conditions is amply illustrated by what happened the first time we invited some of my work colleagues over to dinner. Halfway through the evening my wife found two of the young women investigating the cupboards in our kitchen. When politely asked what they were doing, they replied embarrassingly that they couldn't believe that we had storage space with nothing in it! Every centimetre of room in their own tiny apartments was occupied. But the fact is that few, if any, foreign professionals would come to live in Japan if they had to live in the cramped conditions suffered by the vast majority of the locals.

The first days in a new job are always a trial and that was especially the case with this role, as I had to make the right impression on the local employees as well as my fellow Westerners. And I had a tough act to follow. My predecessor and immediate boss, David

Pike, was both a lovely man and a proven expert on Japan. He was also universally respected across the firm and beyond, and I was told in no uncertain terms by the Swiss who ran the entire operation in Japan that I would have my hands full if I was to match David's achievements. Formerly of the Bank of England, where his focus was also Japan, he had been in Tokyo since 1986 and had built a reputation as one of the foremost foreign, or Gaijin, economists, not least because of his phenomenal work ethic. David was regularly in the office by 5 a.m. and rarely left much before 8 p.m.!

I immediately concluded that I wouldn't, indeed physically couldn't, replicate his hours, although neither would I be able to restrict myself to the working day I had had in London. Thankfully, my commute was much shorter: around thirty-five minutes rather than an hour each way. In the end, my average day in Tokyo was roughly 7 a.m. to 7 p.m. The locals, many of whom faced hour-and-a-half to two-hour commutes, would struggle in between 7.45 and 8.30 a.m. but rarely left before David. In Japan it is considered bad form to leave before your boss, and my relatively early departure was initially frowned upon – I was determined, though, to spend at least a few hours of each evening with my family.

It is also worth noting that the Tokyo stock exchange closed for an hour at lunchtime and that everyone tended to take that time out, often to sleep. One of my abiding memories of Tokyo trading floors is discovering someone curled up, unconscious, under their desk in the middle of the day. Indeed, the Japanese generally display a remarkable ability to nod off whenever and wherever they can. A French friend of mine would swear that he was once on a Tokyo commuter train and the entire carriage was asleep apart from him – and I can quite believe it. I frequently remember seeing commuters fast asleep while standing up and clinging on to the leather straps that hung from subway-car roofs. Furthermore, for traders and salespeople, the entertaining of clients was an almost nightly occurrence and would begin as early as 5.30 p.m. All in all, therefore, my working hours were as extended as anyone else's; they were just organised differently. And besides, in true Japanese style, once you had established a regular pattern, and it was seen that you worked hard, it was accepted as the norm. Indeed, the first time that I worked late, one of the women in the office rather concernedly informed me that it was time that I was going home as my family would be wondering where I was! Such were the joys of living and working in Japan.

Something else that initially caused amazement among my Japanese colleagues was my habit of running home after work. This was a means to decompress and achieve my regular fix of exercise. I would change into my running kit at the end of the day, leaving my suit and shoes in the office, and head out into the city's packed thoroughfares, dodging the swirling mass of commuters. The next morning I would come into work on the subway in my (clean) running kit, with a freshly laundered shirt packaged up and ready to wear.

Living and working in Tokyo was both exhilarating and fascinating. The city dominates the nation's economic, political and cultural life in a way that few other capitals do, and, as I hinted in chapter 3, this was a city that was alive in every sense. It is a vast sprawling megalopolis, especially when you considered that Tokyo essentially morphs into the port of Yokohama, taking the total population to some 16 million. Tokyo was a thousand contradictions. As my wife and I used to say about living in the city, there would usually be something that would make you laugh and something that would make you cry every day. The fact that it was never boring was certainly one of its primary attractions.

For example, the oppressive and unrelenting heat and the humidity of the summer, when your clothing and hair were often sodden with perspiration and you craved the haven of air conditioning, contrasted sharply with the crisp, clear and dry winters, when there was so little moisture in the atmosphere that it felt as if your skin was about to crack open.

Tokyo is a vast port and yet unless you visited its vast fish market, you would hardly notice.

There was the extraordinary modernity of the technology on show, yet many local shopkeepers would still use an abacus to work out your change and the bureaucracy was archaic: pedantic in the extreme and dependent on an ocean of forms.

The city's main thoroughfares, often clogged with traffic, contrasted dramatically with the labyrinth of tiny residential streets that dominated all neighbourhoods.

With its numerous Michelin-starred restaurants, ubiquitous Americana, visits from international pop stars, exhibitions and theatrical offerings, the city could appear as cosmopolitan as any, yet this was a thin sheen. You only had to scratch the surface to reveal Tokyo's inherent Japaneseness.

The ugliness and noise of the city's endless suburban sprawl was juxtaposed both with the beauty and tranquillity of the Imperial Palace and with numerous ancient shrines.

Most homes were either wooden in construction or part of ugly utilitarian ferroconcrete apartment blocks. When I arrived to live in Tokyo only about a third of Japanese households were directly connected to the sewer system. For all the wealth that had been generated, standards of comfort were low.

Yet, at the same time, despite the chronic overcrowding, the highest standards of public order were maintained. There were remarkably few robberies or assaults. Teenage girls could walk home unmolested late at night, old ladies could sleep with their front doors open, and cars could be left unlocked. Huge sums of cash could be carried safely in one's wallet and lost handbags would be returned in person to the owner with their contents completely intact.

Japanese women were invariably beautifully turned out in the latest designer fashions, and they were probably the best-dressed females outside of central Paris. Yet witnessing a large group of Japanese men is like a scene from *Attack of the Clones*: each is decked out in a dark suit, a white shirt and a conservative tie, and they invariably sport a '70–30' short back and sides haircut.

The public transport system was fast, spotlessly clean and dependable, yet travelling by road could be a nightmare. If you timed things badly, you went nowhere.

Tokyo is also in one of the world's most notorious earthquake zones. The Japanese archipelago rests on a veritable spaghetti junction of geological fault lines and Tokyo was, and still is, considered overdue for another 'Big One'. The last major quake hit the capital in 1923 and devastated both it and neighbouring Yokohama, killing almost 150,000 people. Moreover, as a rather troubling epilogue, the chaotic aftermath saw the mass murder and detention of thousands of foreigners (mainly Koreans rather than Westerners), who were accused of everything from looting to insurrection!

Earth tremors are a fact of everyday life for Tokyoites, and as a resident you will now and then experience a serious one. You are also advised to prepare an easily accessible earthquake kit containing, *inter alia*, canned food, bottled water, sleeping bags, a tent, a torch and a considerable sum of Japanese yen in cash.[21] I felt my first tremor when I visited Japan in 1988 and, woken up by the violent shaking of my hotel room, it scared me out of my wits. And you never get used to them. When they begin, the intensity rapidly builds and you just don't know how they will end. I experienced them in the street, on the subway, at work and at home. My response was to just stop still and hope that the escalating crescendo of movement would soon begin to die down. But I also worked with a fellow Brit whose party piece when a tremor struck was to jump up onto his desk and pretend to surf. I never quite had his sangfroid.

Thankfully, Japanese anti-earthquake technology is absolutely state of the art: some of the larger skyscrapers are built on giant rubber balls to absorb the effects while others are designed so that the higher stories respond to the quake in a contrary fashion to the lower stories, thus neutralising the consequences. Or at least that is the theory. Working as I did in a couple of these tall buildings during my time in Japan, I got to experience first hand how much they would sway when a tremor hit and it was truly extraordinary. That is if you could draw your attention away from the screams of the office girls as they dived for cover!

Talking of disasters waiting to happen, there was also the economy. A supposedly great capitalist success story, it was anything but a classic free-market entity. While it was characterised by low taxes, low interest rates, high levels of saving and high capital formation, and little overt intervention, market forces were rather distrusted. Indeed, markets were in fact managed by a battery of bureaucratically administered licences, subsidies, tax breaks and cheap government-sponsored loans. And with all this went an element of mercantilism, or adversarial trade practices, which in the eighties were embodied in the pejorative phrases such as 'Japan Inc' and 'the Japan problem' that were adopted by Westerners, leading in turn to much Japan bashing. The failure of Japan to fit comfortably into Western characterisations of how economies and societies should behave generated considerable external antipathy and suspicion.

Any description of the inhabitants of a particular country is bound to be subjective and to fall prey to oversimplification, stereotyping and value judgements, for which I apologise.

The Japanese are a proud, nationalistic – some would say xenophobic – people. As is the case in many island nations (the UK being another example) and especially those that have escaped foreign invasion for much of their history, they consider themselves to be different, superior and unique. Japaneseness means a lot to them, and great efforts are made to preserve the concept.

Japanese people are drawn to regimentation, not least in their education system, where learning by rote continues to have a central role. The scope for free expression is limited, not least in the way that their institutions and businesses are organised. There are echoes here of the military rule of the thirties and the war years. An enduring attachment to frugality and a dislike of ostentation can similarly be traced back to previous less affluent periods in the nation's development.

To Western eyes, the Japanese are less free than they should be. Loyalty and sacrifice for the greater good are treasured. Individualism is frowned upon, although there are occasional controlled outlets for individualism to express itself, as long as they do not upset the overall harmony of things. A famous Japanese saying is 'the nail that sticks up will be hammered down'. Collectivity, cohesion, fastidiousness, hierarchy and respect for order are deeply implanted into the national psyche, such that the 'truth' often appears to be almost socially constructed and reality managed. Japanese culture places great stress on distinguishing between *honne*, one's genuine feelings, and *tatemae*, or what one must say publicly. Alone, the Japanese can appear awkward, diffident, naive, juvenile and hopeless prevaricators. Confidence, fulfilment and conviction are derived from the group and from certain cherished institutions, overlapping layers of which form a curiously opaque national pyramid of authority. There is no overall leader. Certainly no prime minister fits this bill and nor does the emperor, who plays a largely symbolic role.

It is difficult to do things in a hurry in Japan. Due process must be followed; short cuts are a recipe for disaster. One should never expect a decision of any consequence to emanate from an individual, and especially not from one who is short of middle age. Japan is a gerontocracy. Age is more highly revered for its own sake than in the West and it is therefore harder for a Japanese to achieve fast-track status and to be promoted beyond his years in a Japanese company. Indeed, one of the biggest problems that I encountered when I first arrived in Japan was my relative youth (thirty-one) and the fact that I have always looked younger than my years. It is only over the last decade on subsequent return visits to Japan that I have felt that the respect I believed my seniority and experience as an economist warranted seemed to come easily.

Along with their unhesitating respect for the aged, the Japanese often demonstrate an almost religious fervour in their loyalty to a firm or a government ministry, with the implicit assumption that they will in return be protected and looked after.

The Japanese are for the most part studiously polite to foreigners and are often fascinated by the freedoms of thought and expression that Western life offers, but they are also distrustful of them. Indeed, this distrust extends to Japanese who have lived outside Japan and have been exposed to Western society for any length of time. Taking any friendship beyond the superficial therefore takes time and effort. At the same time, though, foreigners can provide a convenient mechanism to deliver change in Japan. External political pressure can provide the excuse to 'reluctantly' acquiesce in a reform that is recognised to be for the general good but that would hurt certain domestic interest groups. The term applied is *Gaitsu*.

'Face' is extraordinarily important to the Japanese. In Japanese society the dominant motivational force is shame rather than sin, and while you can be instantaneously forgiven for your sins by those you have sinned against or by your priest or vicar, shame is more enduring. Indeed, in some Japanese eyes it lasts forever. It is therefore an immensely powerful and often debilitating consideration in people's lives and, indeed, in the country's general development.

To function comfortably in Tokyo you must try to take these considerations on board. Unsurprisingly, therefore, some expats never got past first base. Equally, the archetypal 'shoot from the hip' American businessman who expected to do things his way and triumph by force of personality or naked financial clout could get into terrible trouble and be left immensely frustrated. I know this because on occasion I fell into that very trap. But the saying was that if you did not press the eject button within six months, you would probably find yourself a Japanophile for life. I did not, and therefore I did. But this is not to understate the initial difficulties of assimilation, nor the enduring irritations and pitfalls.

Part of the problem was the language, and here I did myself few favours. To say that I never progressed very far with Japanese is an understatement. I can offer any number of excuses: I was always a poor linguist (although I have also acted as a more than capable translator when taking the family back to see my extended family in Liverpool), it's an extraordinarily difficult language to learn, my job was to be a commentator on Japan to the outside world rather than to the Japanese themselves, and I was always short of time to spend on it (or rather, I never made the time).

In hindsight, these reasons all seem rather lame, and it will no doubt come across as remarkable that someone could claim to be an expert on the Japanese economy without being able to write or speak the language. But the fact is that the vast majority of statistics were available in English, the people to whom one needed to speak in high places spoke English, and, amazingly, not speaking Japanese could actually enable one to avoid falling into the trap of Japanese 'groupthink'. This consensual state of mind consumed a great deal of domestic political and economic commentary and, given time, that of many foreigners too.

I would also stress that I was not alone as a non-Japanese-speaking economist in Tokyo. Most Gaijin who could write and speak the language with any degree of fluency had been there for many years or had been in a long-term relationship with a Japanese person. As the old adage went, the best way to learn Japanese was lying down! But there was one problem for Gaijin male heterosexuals: they had to guard against their speech becoming infected by 'female Japanese', with its ultra-polite and self-effacing tone. Failure to make the necessary adjustments when speaking, and especially when speaking in a business environment, could result in much hilarity among the local males. Interestingly, two of the most fluent and widely respected foreign Japanese speakers that I knew were gay men who had been in relationships with their respective partners stretching back to their student days.

With no opportunities to network through work, the initial problems of assimilation were even greater for my wife, although her linguistic skills, which were much more developed than mine (she already spoke Greek fluently, reasonable Italian and French and some Russian, in addition to English) meant that she was less intimidated by Japanese than I was. Having a young child and the need to find playmates acted as something of a saving grace, but the fact is that we suffered several months during which we would accept almost any invitation in the hope of finding kindred spirits. This threw up more dead ends than successes, but eventually we accumulated a number of friends, many of whom remain close to us today.

The expat community in Tokyo in the early nineties was large and varied, ranging far beyond those involved in the financial markets. There was also a surprisingly expansive contingent of young students and people teaching English. Overall, however, it was overwhelmingly dominated by Americans, who had a definite tendency to ghettoise themselves in areas that had been favoured since the post-war occupation. The Brits made up the second largest contingent and tended to be rather more adventurous in their geographical locations. Tokyo had few of the cosy British colonial familiarities of Hong Kong or Singapore, but for most that was seen as a plus rather than a minus. Japan was something different and that was to be savoured.

In keeping with the spirit of adventure that brought much of the British expat community to Japan's shores, Tokyo certainly had more than its fair share of characters, many of whom were renowned for their hedonistic excess. Thursday, Friday and Saturday nights would see the bars and restaurants of Roppongi, Tokyo's most cosmopolitan entertainment district, packed to the gunnels with Gaijin out for a good time, with the seemingly suicidal money-broking community more often than not leading from the front. If you looked hard enough, you could find whatever degenerate pleasure you desired in Roppongi.

As far as work at UBS P&D was concerned, I was lucky to inherit a comprehensive infrastructure of professional support, tried-and-trusted publications, excellent policymaker contacts and a truly global client base. My only problems were that, initially at least, some clients still hankered after my predecessor and the personnel I was now in charge of found my arrival and the change of style that it brought distinctly discomforting. The fact that rather than having to analyse a rambunctious boom we were now having to come to terms with its increasingly painful aftermath no doubt added to their sense that things had moved beyond their comfort zone. I seemed to be much more attuned to the new analytical requirements than were my cohorts.

My two key lieutenants were a young Japanese woman, who although not formally trained as an economist had acted as David's research assistant, and an American bond analyst. They were both immensely hard working and dedicated but I won't pretend that our relationships were always smooth. Part of this reflected my own management inexperience, together with my impatience to make a name for myself and step out of David's shadow. On the other hand, there comes a point when as 'the boss' you have to call an end to discussions, take a view and trust that the rest of the team will follow.

Looking back on that time I am pleased to say that I managed to sustain the reputation that the firm had around the world for thorough analysis of the Japanese economy, although this was helped by the fact that in his new role David remained an influential contributor to our written output. We also worked closely on a number of pieces of research that were well received, not least a detailed survey of the condition of the Japanese economy that we put together for a conference of central bankers that the company held in Bali in 1991. Indeed, I can honestly say that David was both one of the most objective and calm observers of the macro scene and one of the best people to work with that I have encountered over the course of my career. We both loved economics and were both fascinated by the economics of Japan, to the extent that even when we went out socially we would regularly bore the pants off our wives discussing it.

My travel commitments generally proved more onerous than my quasi-jolly to address central bankers in a tropical paradise. I would visit the US for a coast-to-coast road trip twice a year and was similarly scheduled to tour the UK and Europe every six months. I also had to fit regular jaunts to the rest of Asia into my plans, and this included Australia and New Zealand, which I had never been to before. This was all very exciting but also challenging, both physically and intellectually. There were a lot of smart people at the monetary authorities, and among the institutional client base in Hong Kong and Singapore, while the Reserve Banks in Sydney and Wellington always provided tough tests of my still-developing knowledge of Japan and its rapidly evolving circumstances. Then there was Bankers Trust Australia, which was universally recognised as one of the toughest institutional clients in the world to impress: it had been known to reduce seasoned analysts to gibbering wrecks.

These trips were usually exhausting. The initial journey from Japan would often cross numerous time zones: London was thirteen hours away and New York was fourteen. Even when there was little time difference to cope with, the journeys would be long. Hong Kong, for example, was a four-hour flight. Singapore was close to seven hours. Trips to Sydney and Wellington involved journeys of twelve hours or more. Then, on arrival, in addition to a frenetic schedule there would be more flights, and the tedious burden of having to drag your bags from meeting to meeting, packing and unpacking in a different hotel every night.

Road trips in North America were particularly punishing because the client base was so geographically disparate. You had to spend a good few days in New York, but Boston, Chicago, San Francisco, Los Angeles, Toronto and Montreal were major financial centres as well, and there were important money managers in cities as diverse as Milwaukee, Philadelphia, Denver, Nashville, Kansas City and Dallas. I could undertake twenty or more internal flights in a two-week period. Sometimes I forgot where I was, which could have painful consequences. On one of these trips I woke in the early hours with my bladder bursting. I stumbled out of bed in what I thought was the direction of the bathroom only to walk slap bang into the bedroom wall. I thought in my nighttime stupor that I was in the previous night's hotel. I woke with a shocking headache and had to complete the next day's presentations with a large red lump over my right eye.

These trips had their positive aspects, of course. In my UBS days I was accompanied by two of the most maverick and entertaining salesmen I encountered over the course of my career. Steve Main was a hard-drinking, chain-smoking Iowan who seemed to thrive on late nights, hangovers and double espressos. He was also a suicidal driver whose inability to concentrate on the road used to leave me frightened out of my wits, especially when we had to navigate our way around the Los Angeles freeways. Then there was Tom Norton, a former college football star with hands that could crush concrete. He would choose the most fantastic restaurants for us to entertain in and also make sure that we found time in the schedule for a workout or a run, often around New York's Central Park. Both were wonderful with their clients and would make sure that every trip, for all their exhausting qualities, was entertaining. It was with them that I was lucky enough to see Steve Winwood perform in Nashville and Buddy Guy at his Blues Legends Club in South Chicago. As a long-standing fan of the blues these were moments to savour.

While ultimately Steve retired to his mother's ranch in Iowa, tragically Tom died suddenly of a heart attack in his mid-thirties. Given their respective lifestyles, this was not how I would have predicted things would turn out.

Marketing around the world was bound to result in the odd personal disaster. The one moment that haunts me most came in Singapore. The Monetary Authority there held a conference at which I was invited to speak on Japan's prospects. After the various presentations there was a lunch and I found myself sitting next to the director of the MAS's Reserve Management division, a formidable woman by the name of Ms Yeo, who was wearing a gossamer-thin white linen dress. I never normally drink at lunchtime but my wine glass was nevertheless filled (with red wine) by the waiter. While making some point to my hostess with excessive enthusiasm, I knocked this wine glass across the table and into her lap. To this day I can see in my mind's eye the glass spiralling through the air as if in slow motion and the wine plastering the dress to her tiny body. The entire table went silent. It was as if time had stopped. Then, from everywhere, waiters and flunkies appeared with any number of napkins and cloths. Mumbling apology after apology, I wished that the floor of the hotel ballroom would open up and swallow me. The poor woman. Through gritted teeth she told me not to worry and that these things happen. But the fact was that she had no choice but to get up and leave there and then from an event that she was effectively overseeing. Thankfully, she appeared to forgive me: she continued to attend my presentations when I came through Singapore and even made a joke out of it with me once. But just writing this down still makes me squirm.

It was at this time that travel began to really impinge on my private life and become a bone of contention with my family. I remember coming back from one overseas trip to find that Ellen, rather than race to see me, clung to her mother when I walked through the door. Later, when my father-in-law became terminally ill, my wife took both Ellen and the newly born Madeleine all the way back to England while I finished a business trip in Asia and followed on later. In my keenness to make a positive impression at UBS P&D, I hardly took a day off in the first eighteen months. This was ridiculous and, quite rightly, my wife was insistent that I pursue a better work–life balance. And so began one of the most pleasurable aspects of living in Japan – using it as a jumping off point to explore the rest of Asia.

We enjoyed some wonderful breaks in the region over the years and a trip to Vietnam in 1992, when it had only just begun to open up to the world, is especially memorable. The Vietnam War was indelibly stamped onto the psyches of many of my generation, perhaps because it was so controversial as well as being the first global conflict the progress of which one could follow daily on the evening TV news. Having the chance to explore the place for myself was therefore an exciting prospect. Hanoi, in particular, was an extraordinary place: a mad juxtaposition of a communist political system, the first chaotic stirrings of market liberalisation, and the enduring influence of long-departed French colonialism. It also offered up some of the best food I have ever eaten, often from some of the least hygienic places. As an economist I was fascinated to experience hyperinflation first hand. On arrival, and after filling out any number of flimsy filthy forms, I changed a hundred dollars and was flabbergasted to find that I had to carry away the local currency – the wonderfully named new dong – in a rucksack! Purchases would be made by pulling out bricks of the small rotting notes, and these would be weighed on old-fashioned scales rather than individually counted. My wife and I would joke that a particular meal was cheap in that it only cost 'three wodges'. British comedian Harry Enfield's 'Loads of Money' character would have been in his element.

As I hinted at the start of this chapter, at this time neither I nor my contemporaries quite grasped the extent of Japan's fall from grace or the extended economic malaise that was to descend on it in the years ahead. In 1989 Japan looked unassailable. Its development since 1945 had been miraculous – the wealth that its population had accumulated, or appeared to have accumulated, beyond their wildest dreams. Of course, growth had slowed significantly since the reconstruction and 'catch-up' boom of the fifties and sixties, but it had still averaged 4.3% in the eighties and closer to 5% in the second half of the decade, and this was far superior to growth rates in any of its developed competitors. There was virtually no unemployment, no obvious signs of poverty and the Japanese lived longer than anyone else too. Furthermore, the economy enjoyed massive trade and current account surpluses and was backstopped by a vast accumulation of overseas assets, on which it would earn income for generations to come.

The Japanese corporate sector boasted many of the world's most prestigious companies and they were increasing their presence via direct investment and burgeoning export penetration of almost every major overseas market. Iconic pieces of global real estate such as the Rockefeller Centre in New York were being bought up almost daily; Japanese tourists seemed to be snapping their state-of-the-art SLRs in every major capital city that I visited; Japanese buyers were dominating the fine art markets; and Japanese increasingly populated the *Forbes* list of the world's richest people.

Underpinning this extraordinary prosperity were soaring land and stock prices. Unfortunately, though, this asset price inflation was becoming more and more unsustainable, and went hand in hand with a similarly dramatic increase in indebtedness, especially within the corporate sector. Should the trend in asset prices reverse, therefore, the potential for a rapid build-up of non-performing loans at the banks that overwhelmingly dominated financial intermediation within the economy was enormous.

From the mid eighties Japanese real estate prices became increasingly disconnected from the trajectory of GDP, and, from 1988, this developed into a veritable speculative frenzy. Prices in Tokyo jumped 60% in 1987 alone, and those of the country's six largest cities tripled in the second half of the decade. At their peak Tokyo real estate values were thirty times those in London, which was itself experiencing a property boom. Commercial real estate development plans became more and more outlandish, and similar excesses were evident in equity market valuations. In the second half of the decade Japanese stock prices rose three times as fast as profits and, by the end of 1989, the Nikkei index had appreciated by some 237% in five years, with market capitalisation up more than 300%. Over a similar period, paper wealth equivalent to more than twice the country's annual GDP had been created.

These extraordinary gains in asset values and debt, rather than leading to caution, only sparked more outlandishly optimistic and unrealistic assumptions about the future. I remember on one trip to Japan in 1988 being told in all seriousness by a portfolio manager at Nomura Investment Trust that the Nikkei would breach the 100,000 level within five years! Nor was this particular optimist alone in his blue-sky thinking.

By the end of the decade, however, the burgeoning costs of this feverish boom were increasingly manifest. Japanese incursions into overseas markets were sparking political resentment among its trading partners. Domestically, increasing divisions were becoming evident in what had always prided itself on being a relatively homogeneous society. A cavernous gap was opening up between the asset-rich haves and the asset-poor have nots. Two-generation mortgages became increasingly common, but still many ordinary urban Japanese were unable to even contemplate getting on to the housing ownership ladder. What is more, the slack regulation and oversight of Japanese markets meant that stocks and real estate were increasingly the focus of manipulation and criminal activity, with everyone from the Yakuza (Japanese mafiosi) to bureaucrats and senior politicians anxious to take a cut.

When the Nikkei closed at 38,916 on the final trading day of 1989, hopes for another stellar year for Japan, its economy and its markets were high, despite the fact that the global business cycle had clearly begun to turn downwards and some economies, such as the UK's, were already in dire straits. Moreover, the Bank of Japan had become increasingly troubled by the asset boom over the course of the previous twelve months, both because of the damaging distributional impact on society and because officials believed it represented a harbinger of broader inflationary pressures. Reflecting this, it had shifted the focus of policy from exchange rate stability and reducing the nation's politically sensitive current account surplus towards the excesses in the domestic economy. With broad monetary growth running into double digits and the yen weakening, three official interest rate hikes, the last on Christmas Day, were sanctioned, amounting to 175bps in total, while 'window guidance' over bank lending was tightened.[22]

More importantly still, the final month of 1989 saw Yasushi Mieno become the twenty-sixth governor of the BOJ and, as soon became clear, Mieno, a BOJ lifer who had joined the institution in 1947 and a character long groomed for the role, had clearly been given the job of bringing asset prices back down to earth. A conservative central banker down to his boots – and someone who by all accounts had been a stern, if less than public, critic of the BOJ's policies in the late eighties – he went about his remit with considerable enthusiasm.

I never met Mieno but from my discussions with other BOJ officials I could not but be impressed by the high regard in which he was held within the bank. Indeed, he was seen internally as someone who was reclaiming its independence from a Ministry of Finance that had long dominated Japanese bureaucracy. For a time, at least, it would not be an exaggeration to say that Mieno was viewed by many of his colleagues as a Japanese Paul Volcker: a man who would rebuild the central bank's credibility after a period when it had largely ebbed away. Sadly, it never quite worked out that way.

I did, however, meet one of Mieno's deputies, Toshihiko Fukui, who was also a formidable character. He was another BOJ lifer and was cut from a very similar cloth. Indeed, there were those who suggested to me that Fukui, who later became the BOJ's twenty-ninth governor, was just as important in setting policy. If Mieno ever wavered in his commitment to drive the excesses out of the Japanese economy, Fukui would put him straight!

The new year saw long-term interest rates heading higher and the stock market struggling. This was viewed by most observers as merely a temporary pause, but by February the Nikkei was under severe stress. Nevertheless, the BOJ and its new governor kept up the pressure. The discount rate was raised by a further percentage point in early March and, as I arrived to take up my new role in early April, the stock market was trading back under 28,000. Views at UBS P&D about the outlook were mixed, with David now seeing the market close to a realistic value but the locals convinced that this level represented a fantastic buying opportunity.

As it happened, my appearance in Japan coincided with a rebound in the market and, by the end of May, the Nikkei was back above 33,000 and there were audible sighs of relief. These were not to last long, however, as Governor Mieno had not finished applying his sobering deflationary medicine, and nor did I expect him to do so anytime soon. After all, the yen had continued to fall against the dollar, ten-year bond yields had moved up towards 8%, broad monetary growth was still running well into double digits, companies appeared sanguine about financial conditions, and there was little sign yet that land prices, or lending to real estate companies and non-banks, were coming to heel. The economy as a whole appeared to retain considerable positive momentum.

The situation became yet more complicated in August, when Iraq invaded Kuwait, pushing up oil prices and elevating Japan's headline consumer price index (CPI) inflation to more than 3.5%, a rate not seen for a decade. Over objections from the Ministry of Finance, which took a cautious line because of the uncertainties of the international situation, the BOJ hiked the discount rate to 6%, but by this time, following the example set by the Fed, it was increasingly using the overnight call money rate as its primary policy tool and this was pushed up to more than 8% in the period to early 1991. At the same time, increasingly severe restraints were imposed on bank lending, especially for real estate purposes.

The net result of all this was to prove catastrophic. In October the Nikkei fell back to close to 22,000. It had almost halved in value since the turn of the year. More pertinently, by the end of the year the land prices that underpinned the entire edifice of the Japanese financial system, and therefore the macroeconomy, had finally started to decline, albeit from stratospheric levels. And in early 1991 broad monetary growth began to collapse, falling at a rate not seen since the war.

I first became concerned about monetary overkill in the final quarter of 1990 on a marketing trip to the US. By the spring of 1991 I was convinced that the BOJ should reverse course. This was not a view shared in the company's London office at the time, where, to my amazement, some very heavy, complex and ultimately expensive bets were made by one particularly headstrong trader that Japanese interest rates would remain high. Neither were many of my domestic colleagues so easily persuaded. In true Japanese fashion they tended to sympathise with the BOJ's judgement that most of the casualties of the central bank's monetary squeeze had to date been 'bubble companies' that should never have existed in the first place. I was more influenced by the potentially devastating impact of asset price deflation on private sector wealth and confidence, and in the end I had to override the team to put in place a forecast that included 200bps of rate cuts over the course of 1991. To support the forecast I wrote two pieces: one called 'BOJ Monetary Policy: Overkill or Prudence', the other 'How Far for the ODR?' Initially, my interest rate projections looked way off the mark, but, as it turned out, my target was met early in 1992.

Although both personal and business sector spending turned sharply lower in the first half of 1991 and bond yields fell sharply, the BOJ continued to take a hard line, focusing on the enduring tightness of the labour market and the fact that consumer price inflation was still above 3%. It was not until July of that year that the discount rate was cut, and even then by only 0.5%. But insolvencies were surging, evidence of bank distress was accumulating, and there were signs of a slump in wholesale prices. The BOJ was the latest in a long line of central banks to keep fighting the last battle well after it had been won: and it was to haunt them for many years to come. It was only in the final quarter of 1991, when it twice cut rates by half a percentage point, that it began to grasp the extent of the trouble the real economy and financial sector were in, and at this point I had to revise down my own target for official rates. At this juncture, though, the notion that the call rate would get down to zero and then stay there for the better part of fifteen years was inconceivable.

The downturn intensified in 1992. Broad monetary growth continued to slump, turning negative in the second half of the year.

Industrial production was also falling rapidly in annual terms as inventories accumulated and, to compensate for the weakness of domestic demand, Japanese companies increasingly looked overseas for sales. This export drive would only build further international resentment. Property prices continued to fall from their previously sky-high levels, but the most immediate evidence of Japan's malady continued to come in the form of the stock market's woes. In March the Nikkei dropped through the 20,000 level for the first time since February 1987, and by August it had collapsed to a six-and-a-half-year low of 14,309, which represented a decline of nearly two-thirds from its highs. The bull market of the late eighties had evaporated.

The BOJ cut rates again in April and July, but by this stage interest rate reductions had little effect. Few households or companies wanted to borrow unless they were in distress, and even fewer banks wanted to lend. Japan was dropping into a Keynesian 'liquidity trap', whereby the strength of balance sheet adjustments in the private sector greatly diluted the impact of orthodox monetary policy. Nevertheless, the failure of the BOJ to ease policy further in the latter part of 1992 was difficult to understand. Additional rate cuts might not do much, but they were better than doing nothing, not least because, with disinflationary pressures building, they would prevent real interest rates from rising.

If the BOJ was still intent on playing hardball, the government and the Ministry of Finance were becoming less sanguine. March saw public investment spending front-loaded to give the economy a temporary fillip and then, at the end of August, a ¥10.7tr fiscal package was announced. Looking back at the work that we published around that time, I am proud to say that, six months earlier, we had put the case for a shift to a more expansionary fiscal stance. Furthermore, the Ministry of Finance also introduced measures designed to dissuade banks from unwinding their cross-holdings of shares and to temper their burden of ever-increasing bad loans. Finally, not only were the government's privatisation plans for NTT, Japan Railways and Japan Tobacco postponed, but a scheme was announced to help with the disposal of bad loans. Banks would be encouraged to sell the collateral (essentially repossessed properties) on these failed advances to a new agency called the Cooperative Credit Purchasing Company, which would then try to liquidate these assets. This announcement stabilised stock prices temporarily, but the problem was that the scheme would only accelerate property sales and thereby create even more sour loans, especially at a time when the collapse in real estate values was accelerating and now spreading beyond the major urban areas.

Such were the concerns about Japan in the broader financial community at this juncture that I and UBS P&D's top financial-sector analyst were invited to Zurich to brief the UBS board on the situation. Although we were both withering about the new mechanism to help the banks, with hindsight, my presentation was too sanguine. I pointed out that real GDP had not yet begun to decline (that happened in 1993), I suggested that a few years of adjustment after the massive boom of the eighties were only to be expected, I made much of Japan's ability to shrug off previous traumas, such as the oil shocks in the seventies, and I suggested that a combination of more aggressive monetary and fiscal reflation would see it through the crisis before too long. Backing up the latter point, I made much of Japan's then relatively low level of net general government debt and the scope thereby afforded for budgetary largesse. My conclusion was that Japan would remain a world beater: its issues were temporary rather than secular.

Insofar as it went, what I said about Japan's historical resilience and macro policy was true. It was what I left out of my analysis that was the issue. I failed to comprehend the destructive virulence of the interaction between chronic asset price deflation, private sector balance sheet adjustment, especially among financial entities, and confidence. I failed to realise quite how far monetary and fiscal policy might have to go to turn things around. And I largely ignored the other structural issues that Japan was facing, not least its collapsing total factor productivity (it declined shortly after the bubble burst), its rapidly ageing population (the working-age population was set to decline from the middle of the decade), and the constraints, both political and cultural, on the sort of sweeping reforms that were required to encourage a new and more sustainable development model.

If I had any excuse, it lay in the fact that this kind of crisis was unfamiliar in a contemporary context, but really, given my historical knowledge, I should have had a better understanding of what was going on. I could also point to the astounding lack of transparency (if not outright subterfuge) about the true extent of the damage done to balance sheets and the criminal activities that had gone on during and in the aftermath of the bubble. But there were enough rumours circulating about all this and enough exposés in the press that I should have taken it all to heart more and made it central to my analysis. Sadly, the opportunity to put all this right was not to come for several more years.

By the start of 1992 my family and I were happily embedded in Tokyo life. Besides the fact that I loved my job, our second daughter, Madeleine, had been born there in the summer of 1991, we had made some good friends, and we were still captivated by the city's vibrancy and uniqueness – neither of which the bursting of the bubble had done anything to undermine. Moreover, I had become a well-known name in the market in my own right. At a time when the world still cared deeply about Japan, I was a regular performer on CNN and the BBC, and my name was widely quoted in both the domestic and international financial press. I also found myself invited to various embassies to provide informal advice about what was happening in the country. Life was good.

The problem was that, just as I was feeling comfortable, UBS, which had by this time completely subsumed Phillips & Drew into its global investment bank, decided to 'Japanify' its Tokyo operation. This meant a reduction in the number of expatriate staff and the hiring of a local management team. The latter was recruited from the domestic securities giant Nomura, and these individuals sought to bring in people loyal to them. Again they came in the main from Nomura, and often from rather obscure parts of its huge domestic network. Not to put too fine a point on it, some of these people had more in common with Yakuza members than your average Western equity or bond salesman. Fundamental analysis and macroeconomics were not their preferred means of communication. One senior manager was a particularly brutish individual who must have smoked five packs of cigarettes a day (I remember seeing him at a client function continuing to chain smoke while he ate, drank and conversed) and whose every guttural utterance seemed to put the fear of God into his underlings.

The net result was a huge culture clash. I have it on good authority that Zurich realised the mistake it had made almost immediately but felt unable to do anything about it for fear of the reaction of the Japanese authorities. The new management was used to doing things their way, which seemed on occasion to extend to a combination of latent arm-twisting and stock ramping. But what certainly was clear was that they had little interest in a non-Japanese-speaking, independently minded, Gaijin economist whose primary focus was the offshore client base.

My position was tenuous, while David was also looking to further his career elsewhere. Over the previous couple of years, mindful of where jumping precipitously to Drexel had got me, I had turned down approaches from Barings and Salomon Brothers, which at that time were two of the best foreign brokerage houses in Japan. The Barings opportunity was particularly attractive and they invested a lot of effort in cultivating my interest, not least by setting up a 'diner à deux' with CEO Christopher Heath. I was sorely tempted but ultimately rejected their advances. I regretted this enormously at the time, in that it would have given me a fantastic platform and would have meant our stay in Japan could have been extended. But, as matters turned out, this proved to be the right decision. At the end of 1992 the only reasonable option available was a return to London with UBS as Senior International Economist, a job the remit for which I would have to invent myself. So, at the start of 1993, rather than finding myself analysing the next episode in Japan's crisis, I was again focused on a much broader canvas.

CHAPTER 7

THE LOWEST COMMON DENOMINATOR

Arriving back in London under sufferance in mid-winter was tough. And I was immediately confronted with two huge challenges. At work I had to begin to forge a role for myself and start to build a series of important relationships both within the London office and with clients. Away from work I was confronted with the urgent necessity of finding a home for our newly expanded family. In the end, after a fraught period of juggling the new job, pretty shoddy rented accommodation and house hunting, we had an offer accepted on a house in Barnes in west London. We were lucky in that this marked more or less the bottom of the housing market correction that followed the eighties boom. We got a bargain. What is more, Barnes is a lovely place to live. Close to the river, with a village-like atmosphere, an excellent kindergarten for the girls and any number of pubs and restaurants to enjoy. The only downsides were being under the Heathrow flightpath and being a twenty-minute walk from the nearest station, which extended my commute into Broadgate to an hour at either end of the day. This was fine on a beautiful English summer's evening, but in pitch darkness on a wet mid-winter's morning it could be foul. Still, it was worth it for the relative tranquillity the area offered from the hustle and bustle of central London.

The UBS office at 100 Liverpool Street was huge, acting as it did as the global headquarters of the firm's investment banking operations. As at SPHG, there were two enormous football-pitch-sized dealing rooms, one for equities, where my responsibilities were initially focussed, and one for bonds and foreign exchange. And the emphasis on top-quality research endured from the old P&D days. Indeed, I joined one of the largest and most talented teams of economists and strategists in the City – a team that now included my old mentor Paul Chertkow, who, at least in part on my recommendation, UBS had recruited from Citibank to run currency analysis the previous year. The problem was that this group was incredibly top heavy, and my return only made it more so.

Besides Paul and myself, UBS London boasted Bill Martin as Chief UK Economist, Malcolm Roberts as Head of Bond Strategy, Rick Reid as Head of European Economics, Mark Brown as Head of UK Equity Strategy, Andy Smith as Head of Commodities Research, Guy Rigden as Head of European Equity Strategy and Alun Jones as Head of Quantitative Strategy. Each had people reporting into them, a number of whom were themselves talented and ambitious, and who subsequently made names for themselves in the markets: people such as Klaus Baader, Paul Lambert, Paul Donovan and Robert Lind. Then, of course, there were the various economics teams in other major financial centres (including Paul McCulley, subsequently the larger-than-life PIMCO executive). And finally there was another entirely separate large global economics group based in Zurich with the remit of servicing the retail clients of UBS.

Sadly, this impressive ensemble amounted to considerably less than the sum of its parts. There was no one single figure who could consistently harness the team's output into a coherent whole. This reflected the competitive tension not just between the individuals but also between the various business units at UBS. Equities were run by Hector Sants, who would subsequently go on to head the UK Financial Services Authority, while fixed income and foreign exchange were managed by the urbane Conservative Party grandee Richard Briance. But relations between the various groups and the individuals that led them were, at best, strained. Meanwhile, the powers that be in Zurich were constantly trying to take back control from the investment bank, which they saw as dangerously out of control (and, as subsequent events were to reveal, they had a point). And if there was one thing that the Swiss loved, it was bureaucracy. Most of the senior executives at the bank had served in the Swiss army, and it showed. There was a huge emphasis on due process, and one was frequently surprised at how rapidly some relatively unknown Swiss employee rose through the ranks. That is, until one discovered his background in the military.

Numerous times we were encouraged to work together more closely, and bow to the administrative will of our Swiss overlords – not least at a couple of bibulous, but ultimately fruitless, offsites at UBS's spartan conference centre in the Swiss Alps – but any positive results were short lived. My tenure at UBS London therefore proved to be a political, and often emotional, quagmire. Looking back, I recall an endless round of posturing, partial solutions and back stabbing.

As it turned out, with Paul Chertkow's support, and because I was seen as one of the office's few team players, I ended up running the London international economics group. However, acrimonious arguments over the group's reporting lines, responsibilities and funding rumbled on amongst the senior management and were never satisfactorily settled during my time at the bank.

As the grandly titled Chief International Economist I was charged both with liaising with our numerous colleagues in Switzerland (having been told in no uncertain terms by the rest of the London team that my role was to sound sympathetic but to give nothing away) and with trying to inject an element of coordination and coherence into our global views. However, I had no formal authority over Bill Martin's UK economics team, nor over fixed-income strategy, equity strategy, currency strategy, quantitative strategy or those economists operating out of the various satellite offices. Despite the grand title I fell somewhere between the only available honest broker and a lowest common denominator. It was a thankless position. I was in office but not in power, and I was often merely a mouthpiece for other people's often-inconsistent views. Furthermore, I was constantly privy to this group or that person sniping at another. It was stressful and, in an effort to move things forward, it often required me to play one individual off against another. There was no other way to get things done.

It was also the case that by the time I took this job on, some of the best talent at the bank had either moved on or were for one reason or another *hors de combat*. Mark Brown, a Barnes neighbour and a good friend, had left to join ABN. For internal political reasons I was pressured into letting Klaus Baader, another close friend, go – a decision that I thought was bananas. He subsequently proved at Lehman Brothers and beyond to be one of the best Bundesbank/ECB watchers around. Rick Reid was taken seriously ill and was unable to work for the better part of a year. Furthermore, my replacement in Tokyo, who was recruited by the new regime, proved to be a huge disappointment. The net result was that I was desperately in need of a second in command who had the necessary gravitas and on whom I could depend for political as well as intellectual support.

To help me make the right choice, UBS engaged a top firm of headhunters at vast expense. After soliciting my views and those of my fractious colleagues, they came up with a list of candidates drawn from the markets and beyond. The City headhunters that operate at this elevated level are an extraordinary breed. Invariably well-to-do, perfectly turned out and with the most fluent of patters, they are like elite estate agents. I felt that they would sell their own mothers for a deal and I rarely trusted them, especially when I was looking for a job myself. Close management of information was their stock-in-trade, and such loyalty as they retained was almost always reserved for those paying the bill, not for the individuals being sought. Their major plus point was that they could take some of the logistical sweat out of the search process and the administration of candidates. But I would also say that on many occasions during my career I concluded that they added little to what could have been achieved by pooling the market knowledge and connections that I and my colleagues already possessed. Nevertheless, every financial institution I ever worked for spent a lot of money on them, often on a retainer basis.

Anyway, my preferred candidate was one David McWilliams. I have always taken the view that when you are recruiting for your team you should go for somebody smarter than you. They will raise the entire level of the group and, as long as you manage them well, make you look good too. David certainly fell into this category. He was the best and brightest at the Central Bank of Ireland, and he was being courted by numerous other City institutions. In an effort to get ahead of the competition, I flew to Dublin to meet him. Over dinner and a lot of Guinness we got on famously. Intellectually, David was sharp as tack, even though in those days his views on how economies worked, and what governments and central banks should do to manage them, were about as far away from mine as it was possible to be. But he was more than an economist: he was widely read, he spoke Gaelic, he had well-developed views on everything from football to politics, he was confident in his own abilities, and he was a great communicator. He was a showman. I figured we would be a good combination, especially if I could chisel off his rougher edges and keep his feet on the ground. I convinced him to come to London for a day of interviews and managed to persuade the various warring management heads of his worth and potential, although sadly I always felt that some were just waiting for him to fall flat on his face.

David and I remain great friends. He has gone on to become one of Ireland's foremost economic commentators and media personalities and has written a series of superb books about that country's dramatic boom and bust and the recent global financial crisis more generally. But, despite his enormous talents, his time at UBS was difficult for both of us: he is much better cut out for what he does now than what he did then.

In an environment where my group was forever walking on eggshells and there was always someone spoiling for a fight, David's strong and loudly vocalised views managed to wind a lot of people up, often adding greatly to my stress levels. He found the notion of cabinet responsibility on the team's views difficult to adhere to. He often seemed to have opinions that were at variance with his senior colleagues, not least myself, and one Monday morning he managed to enrage every Englishman on UBS's equity trading floor by delivering an extended, unsubtle, public gloat about an Irish rugby victory at Twickenham. I lost count of the times that I returned from a business trip to clear up some mess that he had created. 'Oh Christ David, what have you said/done now?' became a familiar refrain. But I could never stay angry with him for long. He was too nice a guy and always so apologetic. And his thinking was always stimulating.

As if trying to navigate myself and my enormously talented, yet mercurial and verbose, deputy through the political minefield that was UBS was not enough of an introduction to the nitty-gritty of management in London, this period also saw me take on full editorial responsibilities for a whole suite of the firm's written output, in the process integrating numerous contributions from around the world. The production of written research had moved on since my formative days at ITM. Desktop publishing was now a reality, but everything did still have to be funnelled through a central production unit. These were people who you had to cultivate if you wanted your life to run smoothly: their instructions needed to be followed, their rules obeyed, pleases and thank yous needed to be proffered, birthdays remembered and Christmas presents delivered. Those analysts who fell foul of the production team could regret it for the rest of their careers.

But there was another more pressing difficulty with this aspect of the job. I couldn't believe how poorly most people expressed themselves in print, and the younger that people were, the lower the quality of their output seemed to be. I admit that given the uncompromising way that I had been tutored in the importance of good English at both school and university, and the fact that I had written two books by my mid-twenties, I could be precious about this kind of thing. But I found having to spend endless hours correcting and redrafting the lazy, incoherent, sparsely punctuated input I was presented with by a selection of highly educated people immensely frustrating. When I raised the issue with certain individuals, however, I was greeted with indignation, if not explosive anger. As my subsequent boss at Lehman Brothers, John Llewellyn, so wonderfully put it: 'There are two things about which people are reluctant to accept criticism: how they make love and how they write.'

This time at UBS was not without its positive aspects. For all the political infighting I learned a lot. How could I not, given my proximity to all that talent? I also continued to travel the world at a time when UBS's expenses policy was one of the more generous in the City. I stayed at some of the best hotels on the planet and would subsequently regale my hotelier father with details of their opulence. On the other hand, some of the trips I undertook were insane. I once flew to Ottawa for a single dinner with the Canadian Finance Ministry and another time I flew to Tokyo for a day and a half, but most ridiculous of all was a trip to present to the executive board of the New Zealand Post Office for one hour. This involved leaving London on Monday morning, arriving in Sydney on Tuesday night, flying to Wellington on Wednesday afternoon, doing the presentation on Thursday morning, racing back to the airport to fly back to Sydney that same afternoon and then boarding a flight for London that evening so that I could return to the UK on the Friday morning in time to take the family off on holiday for two weeks. As my wife delicately put it at the time, 'Didn't they have a telephone? After all, it was the fucking Post Office.'

There were also a few hilarious moments. Top of the list was one of my senior colleague's unfortunate live appearance on BBC Radio 4's *Today Programme* – a tale that sums up the media pitfalls for a financial markets economist. The person in question would always prepare assiduously for every public event and was one of the best talking heads around. But he was an economics purist and could be hesitant in talking about the markets per se. On this particular morning he had done his customary excellent job in describing the whys and wherefores of the latest Bank of England interest rate move. But when the interviewer, James Naughty, asked him how the stock market would respond, he confused two commonly used market terms: 'bottom fishing' and 'stock picking'. Hence, Naughty's closing remark: 'Thank you very much. I'll let you get back to your bottom picking now.'

But this colleague was not alone in making such an error. A male American economist, who at the time had responsibility for some of the lesser European economies, once stood up in front of the morning meeting on UBS's vast equity trading floor and pronounced: 'Good morning. Today, I am wearing my Dutch cap.'

There was also the infamous mid-summer boat trip around Stockholm harbour that our Swedish sales team would organise for the Nordic client base. Five of us from UBS accompanied thirty regional money managers on a six-hour cruise around the beautiful waterways surrounding the Swedish capital, ostensibly to enjoy some local crayfish and to socialise. The evening ended up like something out of Hunter S. Thompson's *Fear and Loathing in Las Vegas*. It began with bottle after bottle of beer, progressed to vast quantities of wine, and ended with the singing of Viking songs, numerous shots of vodka and, as I recall, trays of gin and tonics. Several attendees were sick, even though, thankfully, the water was flat calm, and on the return to shore around midnight (when, disturbingly, it was still light) one CIO of a Swedish pension fund fell off the gangplank and had to be fished out of the harbour, another collapsed into the gutter and one of my UBS colleagues, confused by the fact that there was more than one Raddison hotel in Stockholm, returned to the wrong one and couldn't find his room. It was, he insisted to staff, on a floor that appeared to have vanished since he checked in.

I also had my own special moment. Returning late the previous night from a business trip, I was ill prepared to chair the next day's morning meeting and, confusing my dates, duly described what I thought was going to be in the Dutch budget only to be greeted with sniggers and traders making throat-slitting gestures. The Dutch budget had actually been delivered the previous day. Nor had my credibility been helped by my references to the Dutch finance minister of the time, who went by the unfortunate name of Wim Kok. I vowed never to talk about Holland again. It was jinxed.

In hindsight, my elevation, such as it was at UBS, probably coincided with the gradual erosion of UBS's reputation for macro research. How much of this was my fault is for others to judge. The competition was growing more intense and others got it more right than we did. They clearly weren't spending as much of their time squabbling as we were.

Given all the politicking, editing and managing that I was involved in, it is a wonder that there was any time left to do economic analysis. Some things passed me by. For example, neither the initial emergence of China as a global economic superpower, the end of the Cold War nor the emerging advances in information technology touched me to any significant extent at this time. Of course I was aware of them, and I remember reading commentary about them by various colleagues, but they were not central to what I did and I failed to fully grasp their importance. These were major oversights, but the fact is that it was often very difficult to see the wood for the trees.

Of the many issues that did dominate my time, the ones I recall most clearly were the broader ERM crisis, the early days of Britain's inflation-targeting regime, and the bond market sell-off of 1994.

The ERM crisis was something that I was consumed by even before I left Japan. As I made clear in the previous chapter, part of my job description while in Tokyo was to act as a conduit to the Japanese investor base for UBS's global views, and interest in the sterling crisis of 1992 had been intense. Indeed, while speaking off the cuff to a senior Japanese asset manager, I enjoyed something of a triumph. When asked a few days before Black Wednesday (16 September) whether the UK authorities would raise interest rates or devalue the pound, I replied 'both' – and that is exactly what happened.

Consistent with the paper I drafted for the Labour Party in 1989, I thought that the UK had gone into the ERM with sterling at a level that was too high and which would leave it vulnerable to the sort of currency crisis that had been a regular feature of post-war British economic history. This was particularly the case should external events keep European interest rates high and constrain the ability of the UK economy to recover. With the unique pressures of German reunification conspiring to keep monetary conditions eye-wateringly tight across the continent and a one-off revaluation of the Deutschmark rejected in Bonn, 1991 and 1992 had been grim. Real GDP fell sharply, unemployment rose to a double-digit percentage, and the budget deficit ballooned. The only bright spot was the precipitous fall in inflation that this deep downturn encouraged. I remember returning to London from Japan at the time and being shocked by the all-pervasive physical evidence of deep recession. It was more palpable than anything I had witnessed in Tokyo.

Under such circumstances – and however astute the authorities might have been in handling the tactics of defending the pound – the devaluation, if not the exit of sterling from the ERM, seemed to be only a matter of time. If I needed any additional proof of this it came in a brilliant paper by Bill Martin and his team that compared Britain's situation in 1992 to the one it faced after the ill-fated return to the Gold Standard in 1925.[23] After reading this, my conclusions were that the only valid questions were how sterling's departure would come about and what would happen subsequently. That it ultimately proved to be such a politically messy and costly exit was hardly a surprise: formal devaluations and expulsions from pegged exchange rate systems invariably are.

I was never one of those who believed that, because of the potential for enhanced risk premia, UK interest rates would necessarily end up being higher outside the ERM than inside it, with the economy in general coming under even more stress. Rather, as long as the unconstrained discretion that characterised the latter days of the Lawson chancellorship was eschewed, the budget deficit was reined in over time and a reasonably credible alternative macro policy anchor was adopted in the ERM's stead, I saw exit as providing the authorities with greater flexibility to calibrate policy rates to the requirements of the domestic economy. Again harking back to the Gold Standard era and its aftermath, this was the lesson of the thirties: a period long associated by economic historians with a successful 'cheap money' policy.[24]

What followed was inflation targeting. In reality, the replacement of ERM membership with a formal inflation target, and greater transparency about official thinking in regard to achieving it, came about largely because it was pretty much the only practical policy option remaining. Everything else, from money supply targets to the monitoring of nominal GDP growth and an exchange rate objective, had been tried and found wanting over the previous thirteen years of Conservative rule.

It is worth remembering that, at the time, among OECD economies only New Zealand and Canada had adopted similar inflation-targeting strategies. Hence, initially at least, it was greeted with some scepticism in the markets. The proof of the pudding would come in the eating, or indeed the targeting. But the systematic failure of policy regime after policy regime in the UK implied that anything other than an initially cautious response would have been foolish. Inflation targeting was certainly not yet the conventional policy wisdom that it was to become over the next twenty years. Nor at that stage was it underpinned by Bank of England independence.

In fact, the depoliticising of interest rate decisions had been discussed by the Tories as early as the late seventies. It also received support from Nigel Lawson in the late eighties but was vetoed at that time by Margaret Thatcher. Norman Lamont, the chancellor during the ERM debacle, resurrected the idea again in 1993, but Prime Minister John Major rejected it unequivocally, not least because of the impact of monetary policy on mortgage rates.[20] Hence, despite an undoubted shift in the balance of power towards the Bank of England and away from the chancellor and prime minister over the interim period, it was only in 1997, with the return to power of a Labour government desperate to establish credibility with questioning financial markets, that the Bank of England was granted full operational autonomy.

Moving on to the broader ERM crisis that followed in 1993, sterling's ignominious ejection did little to ease the tensions within the system. The Bundesbank remained determined not to let the inflationary risks associated with German reunification run out of control, and this imposed an enormous monetary squeeze on the other ERM members. Hence, the speculators continued to attack, believing that other parities would prove unsustainable. In February the Irish punt was devalued, and in May the peseta and the escudo followed. By the middle of the year the market's attention had turned back to the franc. For a period, the French currency benefited from aggressive support from the Bundesbank – considerably greater support than sterling had enjoyed the previous year. However, by the end of July, with French short-term rates at astronomical levels and, despite massive political pressure, the German central bank refusing to offer anything other than a cosmetic cut in the insignificant Lombard rate, it was increasingly clear that the pressure building in the system was irresistible.

On 2 August, after what was an acrimonious weekend of Franco-German discussions that captivated the attention of the global media, and saw me and many of my City colleagues in the office in the dead of a Sunday night, the system was maintained only by means of a decision to 'temporarily' widen the permitted margins of exchange rate fluctuation from 2.25% to 15%. Effectively, this meant that the currencies in the ERM were allowed to float freely. The unspoken assumption was that no member of the system would embark on a policy of domestically focused monetary reflation.

The dominant view, and one shared by me (I personally wrote a withering criticism of French economic policy around this time entitled 'Monetary Masochism') and the vast majority of my (predominantly English) colleagues at UBS in London, was that a single European currency was now off the agenda for the foreseeable future, if not entirely dead in the water. Moreover, we saw virtually no chance that the UK would ever join, even if the project were somehow resurrected.

Not for the first, or the last, time, the Anglo-Saxon consensus was to underestimate the political momentum towards monetary union and the willingness to fudge the economics. But at that juncture we took the view that the events of the previous three or four years seemed to have confirmed that the underlying fault lines in the system were unbridgeable, especially when the Bundesbank remained so consumed with its domestic agenda and so unwilling to give up its dominance of European monetary policy.

As it happened, the widened ERM bands proved much more effective in disarming the speculators than was expected. The greater room for monetary policy manoeuvre was not abused by members, not least because, with the inflationary pressures of reunification easing, the Bundesbank was able to progressively reduce short rates. When the governments in Bonn, Paris and the Benelux countries began to make it clear that, despite the debacle of mid 1993, their ambitions for the single currency remained strong and that they saw 1999 as a realistic starting point for the project, we, like most of the UK commentariat, ignored them. We neglected to take into account that, as recovery became more evident and budget deficits fell, optimism about monetary union, and the economic convergence necessary to achieve it, would return. We failed to understand that the very collapse of the old system was psychologically helpful, as the atmosphere of quasi-permanent conflict and crisis was greatly dissipated.

The only guy at UBS that grasped all this was David, who, of course, had actually worked within the system at the Central Bank of Ireland. And we all, not least myself, took little notice of him. I regret that enormously. But if there is one thing that I have become convinced of over the course of my career, it is that the UK is tone deaf when it comes to the politics of European integration. I have always considered myself to be more open minded about Europe than most of my compatriots, and have in particular made every effort not to embrace the 'Little Englander' mentality that seems to consume the Conservative Party and most of the British press, but I willingly accept that an unduly myopic focus on the immediate macroeconomics to the exclusion of the broader political forces that shape the continent has frequently clouded my judgement and resulted in error.

The second episode from my time at UBS London on which I report is the great bond sell-off of 1994 – a period when market sentiment fell into a trap of complacency, many financial institutions (including UBS) suffered large losses, and an initially good year for equities soured. Furthermore, Orange County in California declared bankruptcy after a huge loss on a derivative trade, and the Mexican debt crisis followed. There is also evidence that the sharp rise in US yields and in the dollar that followed acted as a slow-burning catalyst for the Asian crisis that was to erupt three years later, as it rendered many countries' exchange rate pegs with the US currency increasingly unsustainable.

Government bond markets enjoyed a prolonged rally in 1993, during which yields converged markedly. US ten-year yields dropped by more than 150bps from the end of 1992, reaching a low point in October 1993, while UK gilt yields of similar maturities fell by more than 200bps over a slightly longer period.[25] These trends reflected subdued inflationary pressures, as commodity prices were soft and there was significant excess capacity. Indeed, in many cases resource utilisation rates were declining in the face of soft growth or outright falls in GDP, most notably in Japan and much of continental Europe. But everything changed early in 1994 following a reversal of monetary policy course in the US, and in particular a progressive tightening of Fed policy that began on 4 February. The subsequent reversal in bond yields was dramatic, more than unwinding the previous year's rallies and going far beyond the predictions of most observers – including me and my colleagues at UBS. Indeed, in the first half of that year we were surprised on an almost daily basis by the tendency for bond yields to move upwards, and we continually had to revise our forecasts higher. What is more, the convergence of yields also unwound.[25]

With hindsight, there were tentative signs of a change in the outlook for the fixed-income markets at the end of 1993, not least in a sharp pickup in non-oil commodity prices in response to evidence of stronger US growth. US long-term yields began to edge upwards from this moment, but it was only when the Fed began to push the federal funds rate higher for the first time in five years that yields around the world really started to increase. This trend was then further encouraged by a number of stronger than expected data releases, which revived long-dormant concerns about inflation.[25]

The most obvious reason why we misread this period was that we underestimated the speed with which the Fed would seek to normalise short rates after a protracted period of keeping policy loose to counter the credit crunch that followed the US recession of 1989–90. But this was also a time when the Fed was much less forthcoming about its priorities and future intentions than it is today.

The federal funds rate had been held at 3% since September 1992 and was effectively zero in real terms at the beginning of 1994. But between February and November of that year it was adjusted from 3% to 5.5% and, given reasonably stable CPI inflation, the US real policy rate moved decisively into positive territory. According to Alan Greenspan's autobiography, the reason for the sharp adjustment of policy in 1994 was that the Federal Open Market Committee wanted to be more pre-emptive in its approach. In previous cycles it only tended to tighten when inflation was starting to move upwards, but in the nineties cyclical upswing, the desire was to move sufficiently early to nip inflation in the bud and produce a 'soft landing'. Looking at the way the US economy performed in 1995, that is not a bad description of how things turned out. That year, US real GDP growth averaged 2.7%, while CPI inflation averaged 2.8%.

There was, however, rather more to bond market dynamics in 1994 than US monetary policy developments. Policy rates in Germany and Japan continued to come down over this period and began to go up in the UK only towards the end of the year. By disaggregating nominal yields into their component parts, and in particular the expected real interest rate and the expected inflation rate, it can be seen that the former did indeed move higher. What is more, even though longer-term inflation expectations remained subdued, as they had been in 1993, short-term inflation expectations and the inflation risk premium jumped.

A further technical consideration in the sell-off, at least in the US, appears to have been mortgage-backed security (MBS) hedging strategies. It is common to hedge long MBS positions with short Treasury positions. When interest rates rise, the likelihood of early mortgage repayments is commensurately reduced and the effective maturities of MBSs increase. This 'extension risk' necessitates additional Treasury sales of a maturity appropriate to match the new effective maturity of the MBS.[25] Suddenly, we economists had to become experts on the MBS market – an area that hitherto I had had little to do with.

Two other points of interest in exploring the sell-off are fiscal laxity and monetary policy credibility. Fiscal incontinence seems an unlikely explanation. Both headline and structural budget shortfalls in the major economies were actually lower in 1994 than in the previous year, while government debt levels were little changed. However, the Bank of England has unearthed evidence that the bond sell-offs correlated quite closely with three indicators of inflation credibility: past average inflation rates, past averages of nominal bond yields, and a widely used index of central bank independence. The lower the level of credibility, the greater was the decline in yields in 1993 and the bigger the rise in 1994.[25]

The suggestion, therefore, is that the fall in yields in 1993 was related to economic conditions that were shared by many countries. In particular, the expectation was that inflation in general would remain subdued. This encouraged all bond yields to fall, but especially those in countries with low inflation credibility, as they had the most to gain in yield terms from this perception. In the circumstances, inflation credibility seemed to be less important when it came to achieving price stability. But in 1994 there was a sudden revival of concerns about future inflation, and interpretations of central bank policy credibility were key in relative market performance.[25]

As my time at UBS London wore on, I found that I was coping with the politics and infighting less and less well. The stress was getting to me, and my sleeping habits were suffering. I was waking up when the first intercontinental flight of the day began its descent over our house – and 4.15 a.m. starts prior to a twelve-hour day are not conducive to a happy working or family life. I began to wonder if an alternative career might be a good idea.

It was at this stage, though, that I was sought out by some ex-UBS Tokyo colleagues, who, after the company's ill-suited Japanification, had migrated to Lehman Brothers, where big efforts were being made to expand their Japanese government bond operation. There was therefore a requirement for a new chief economist for Japan. Given my regard for the individuals in question, the sense that my wife and I had of unfinished business in Japan, and my burgeoning misgivings about my role in London I was attracted by this interest, which, after another crazy weekend visit to the other side of the world for a round of interviews, developed into a formal job offer.

This came despite the reservations of the then Lehman Brothers chief economist Allen Sinai, who seemed unable to grasp that any Brit who had not attended either Oxford or Cambridge university could be worth recruiting. But thankfully I received much more encouragement from my old friend Klaus Baader, who was also now at Lehman, and I got on much better with my immediate boss to be, Asian chief economist Miron Mushkat, and with Lehman's chief European economist, ex-head of forecasting and chef de cabinet of the OECD secretary general, John Llewellyn. Finally, my former peers at UBS told Sinai that they wanted me, and as is usually the case in the financial world, what the business wants, the business gets. After all, it pays the bills for research.

True to form, I ummed and ahhed over the move, not least because UBS appeared keen to keep me. I also felt a big sense of responsibility towards my existing team, especially David, who I suspected would be thrown to the wolves after my departure (sadly, I was right, even though he was highly regarded by the firm's clients). Furthermore, at the time Lehman was a second-tier investment bank with a chequered reputation. It was not exactly akin to Drexel in 1989, but there had been precious little stability in its structure or business model for some time and its foothold in Tokyo was not entirely secure. It was my wife who finally convinced me that it was the right move for us all and I subsequently enjoyed the better part of a decade at Lehman, much of which was hugely rewarding. Meanwhile, soon to be subsumed into its Swiss cousin SBC, UBS's light grew progressively dimmer.

Looking back, three considerations sold me on the idea of a return trip to Tokyo: the fact that I was the first choice of a number of former colleagues that I greatly respected, the fact that I was more interested in Japan than in any other economy, and John Llewellyn.

A proud New Zealander by birth, grey haired and balding, forever tired-looking, somewhat full around the middle, a tad dishevelled (one Lehman salesperson used to joke that John needed 'ironing'), he had a kindly smile, no obvious edge and the mental approach and demeanour of a Cambridge don, which was what he was before joining the OECD.

John was therefore anything but the typical financial markets economist. While supremely well versed in theory and a proven macro model builder, he recognised the vital importance for economic policy of history, politics and culture, and he thought deeply about them all. In this sense, we viewed the world through a similar lens. I remember John asked me about my postgrad work when he interviewed me and that we ended up chatting for hours about some of the great and the good of the Keynesian world with whom he himself had worked in the late sixties and early seventies at the Cambridge University Department of Applied Economics. In short, we got on famously. He might not have been my immediate boss, but I couldn't wait to work with him. Moreover, I had a sneaking suspicion that he would end up running the show anyway.

CHAPTER 8

UNFINISHED
BUSINESS

In late February 1995, a little over two years after arriving back
in the UK, and just as the Nick Leeson scandal conspired to
blow Barings Securities to smithereens, I resigned from UBS.[26]
By early April I was ensconced in Lehman's London office (just
across Broadgate Circle from UBS) while the logistics of our return
to Japan were worked out. It was decided that I should head out in
late June and that the family would follow six weeks later.

I spent the interim period in the London office getting to know
my new colleagues and writing two extended reports: one on
'Bank of Japan watching' and the other on Japan's labyrinthine
fiscal policy institutions and the outlook for its public finances
(despite being pretty grim at the time, the outlook was nowhere
near as apocalyptic as it is today). The logic was that I would never
get the necessary peace and quiet that was needed to produce two
such in-depth pieces of research once I was in situ in Tokyo and the
day-to-day grind of the job took over, and that they would demonstrate the seriousness of my approach to the role. To my knowledge, although there were any number of examples of investment
banks' efforts to describe in detail how the Fed operated, no one
had at that stage thought of doing something similar for the BOJ.
The same was true of Japanese fiscal policy, the detail of which
was extraordinarily opaque. Even the locals struggled to get to
grips with it as, since the war, the Ministry of Finance (MOF) had
made little or no effort publicly to consolidate its various expend-
iture and revenue accounts and deliver a coherent estimate of the
direct influence of the various arms of government on the broader
economy.

The explanation that I heard was that under Japan's wartime administration, some MOF officials had been desperate to preserve a few public programmes for peacetime purposes and had deliberately made the accounts difficult to fathom to keep the revenue-hungry militarists at bay. After the war, this complex system remained in place and developed a life of its own. Even today, focusing solely on the published central government accounts and the formal budgetary process in the Japanese parliament will offer up only the most partial view of Japanese fiscal policy. Furthermore, successive governments' noisily announced expansionary fiscal packages have become infamous for their smoke and mirrors and the often brazen exaggeration of their size and impact. The only entities outside the MOF itself that have the manpower, expertise and time to regularly do a fully comprehensive assessment are the IMF and the OECD.

As it transpired, my reports were extremely well received, not least by the Japanese authorities themselves.

I soon found out that the economics research conducted by Lehman Brothers was as lacking in coherence as that of any other major bank that I had experience of. Indeed, it had four centres of gravity. Sinai, who split much of his time between New York and Boston (where, amazingly, he was also allowed to run his own macroeconomic consultancy), was the major public mouthpiece on the US, or at least liked to think he was, but he was largely sponsored by the equity division. He had a large team working directly under him but he merely used them to back up his own views. The US fixed-income division boasted its own senior economist: Steve Slifer. Sinai would sometimes dismiss him as merely a 'Fed watcher', but Steve was very experienced and very good, especially when it came to marketing, of which he did a phenomenal amount, in the US and beyond. His folksy style went down particularly well with Lehman's huge US retail client base.

John Llewellyn had a team of eight economists in London, whose responsibilities were largely European. Under his tutelage they took a decidedly pro-EMU stance – this was rare in the UK. They were also at this time mining a rich seam of structural policy and supply-side research that John had originally begun to explore while at the OECD, and which was path-breaking for the financial markets at that time. As was the case with too much economic analysis, the overwhelming focus was on demand management.

Then there was Miron Mushkat, another extraordinary intellect and, like John, the sort of gentleman who was the exception to the financial markets rule. Based in Hong Kong, he was initially my immediate boss and he also managed a group of five whose focus was the broader Asian region.

Each group was desperately keen to retain its independence and autonomy, and the respective business heads into which they reported championed their respective economists in the turf wars that inevitably followed. Sinai went through the motions of coordinating the overall team, in that he would get us on a conference call every week and encourage us to summarise our latest views, but he often seemed to undermine the entire process by subsequently largely ignoring our input and saying in public whatever he himself believed. I even saw him completely contradict one of the team during a conference attended by hundreds of clients. It was an extraordinary exhibition of selfishness, even in an industry renowned for it. I may have bemoaned what I managed to achieve by way of coordination in the shark tank that was UBS, but when I reached Lehman I realised that I hadn't done such a bad job after all.

The fact was that it was only when John Llewellyn – a proven administrator within the political minefield that was the OECD, and someone who commanded everyone's respect – took over Lehman Global Economics from Sinai in 1996 that the group's output became suitably coherent and coordinated. Indeed, I can honestly say that the period at Lehman during which John was in charge was the one time in my career when there was a team of economists that was well organised and where a sense of cabinet responsibility and team spirit reigned. His door was always open and the members of the group had every opportunity to discuss and debate views among themselves, but once that process was deemed to have run its course we all signed up to one global view and sought to deliver it to clients as our preferred outlook. Sure, we had our personal biases and would on occasion disagree but, by and large, these would be suppressed and presented as risks to the house view rather than as an individually preferred alternative future.

However, any concerns I might have initially had about the structure of the broader team were at this stage secondary to my desire to hit the ground running when I returned to Tokyo. Remarkably, within a week of my arrival I had undertaken my first business trip – a twenty-four-hour jump down to the dreaded

Taipei to see the central bank there – and moved into the house that was to be our home for the following five years. This time we had chosen to live a little further from the centre of the city, in an area that was even less of a focus for expats than where we had lived during my previous posting, but again my commute was pretty user-friendly: forty minutes door to door.

On the other hand, despite the warm welcome I received from the Japanese government bond sales and trading team and from the analysts in Lehman's Japan equity research group, my initial days at Lehman Tokyo were complicated by the decision of my supposed number two to leave the firm as soon as I arrived. Thankfully, however, Miron and I soon arranged for the son of a long-standing Lehman employee in the New York office, who had recently earned an MSc in economics at LSE, to fill in. Matthew Poggi remained at my side for the next five years and ultimately went on to undertake research at the Bank of Japan. Although Matt was never one of the world's more gregarious individuals, he was tremendously diligent and without side, and I couldn't have done the job without him. I also remember that it was Matt who first introduced me to the Internet in March 1996.

Lehman's Tokyo staff were a strange mixture. The head of the operation was Mike Gelband. He was impressive, and destined for great things at Lehman (as well as a certain notoriety during the firm's death throes in 2008). The Japanese government bond sales and trading group – the real reason I was there – was excellent, comprising as it did not just the best that UBS had previously had to offer but also some top talent poached from Morgan Stanley. And it was given the financial muscle by the firm to move the market. It had a global reputation, and any central bank or hedge fund with an interest in Japanese debt had to talk to us. This gave me something of a captive audience, although it also meant that my travel schedule was once again pretty insane.

On the other hand, Lehman's footprint in the domestic equity market was much smaller and less impressive. Notwithstanding one or two excellent research analysts, there was little to challenge the dominant local brokerages or the best of the other overseas operations. From the start, given the Japanese stock market's continued travails, I wondered if it could survive.

My return to Tokyo saw me once again asked to provide informal advice to various diplomatic corps, and in particular those from the US, the UK and (most regularly and perhaps most surprisingly)

Australia. In addition, my media career flourished anew. Bad news sells and rarely a day went by without my talking to a newspaper or appearing on some radio or TV station. I was still in demand from CNN and the BBC, and this period saw the increasing influence of CNBC and Bloomberg TV, with their twenty-four-hour coverage of global markets. I also put in some appearances on local TV stations, including one infamous occasion towards the end of my stay when I shared a stage on NHK (the Japanese equivalent of the BBC or PBS) news with Deputy Bank of Japan Governor Fukui, whom I mentioned in chapter 5.

This was one time when my lack of Japanese language skills left me greatly exposed. My appearance on the programme required instantaneous translations of both questions and answers, which were delivered into earpieces. Despite the complexity of the process, things initially progressed reasonably smoothly, as I strained to show the requisite deference to such an important figure in the Japanese bureaucratic hierarchy and sought to tone down some of my answers. However, the last question I fielded was about the future direction of Japanese policy rates, and I responded that I would not be surprised if they fell to zero. This answer was duly translated into Japanese and Fukui, who had a face like thunder, was asked for his views. He guffawed and gave his response. The only word he said that I understood was 'Gaijin' and there was silence in my earpiece, with the programme then duly coming to an end and Fukui being rapidly ushered out. I thought this was a bit odd at the time but it was already late and I was just glad to get the thing over and head home.

The next morning I asked my Japanese secretary how it had looked. She blushed and was sheepish and non-committal. This was not a good sign. I asked her again and raised the matter of Fukui's final comment specifically. Eventually, she told me that he had said something along the following lines: 'I really don't think that we can expect inexperienced foreigners to fully understand the Japanese economy.' Quite a put-down – and how wonderfully Japanese that, rather than pass the insult on, the translator just fell silent. Anyway, in the end I had the last laugh: I was right.

The family and I all rapidly fell back in love with Tokyo. The girls were soon settled into the relatively new, but increasingly impressive, British School, which gave them an excellent initial education and brought them into contact with children from all over the English-speaking world and beyond. Interestingly, a number of Japanese parents opted to send their children there, rather than force them through the narrow and autocratic local system. I always like to think that living abroad, being part of an ethnic minority and being educated with kids of so many different races, creeds and colours can only have been a good thing for Ellen and Madeleine. To this day they both look back on their time at the British School with fond memories, and they are still in contact with a number of their friends from that time.

Our second sojourn in Tokyo also saw us become rather more adventurous at weekends. At considerable cost, we took on a one-week-a-month 'time share' in a wooden cabin about eighty kilometres outside the city. With stunning views of Mount Fuji and the beautiful Lake Saiko, it gave us access to Japan's beautiful mountainous countryside. Less than two hours' drive away on a Friday night (the Japanese rarely exited Tokyo for recreational reasons until Saturday morning), up there we could swim and sunbathe in the summer, toboggan in the winter, and run, cycle, walk, barbecue and make use of the local *onsen*, or hot spring baths, all year round. It was the perfect antidote to the intensity of Tokyo life.

Our two other escapes were to discover, late in life, the joys of skiing in Japan's wonderful alpine resorts, and to join the extraordinary Yokohama Country and Athletic Club. The latter, which was situated in a nondescript suburban residential area on a bluff above Tokyo's twin city, had been set up by British expats in 1868, the year of the Meiji Restoration. To this day it represents one of the few pieces of privately owned greenery of any significant size for hundreds of miles and the opportunity for the expat both to socialise and to play any number of sports, including football, rugby and cricket. Indeed, I can honestly say that hearing the sound of leather on willow on a sultry Japanese Sunday afternoon is one of the more bizarre and incongruous experiences I had in the country. Rather than playing cricket, though, I decided to risk life and limb and came out of retirement to play football for the club's excellent over 35s team. For five years our side of assorted Brits, Scandinavians, Germans and the odd local were rarely beaten.

While I had been back in the UK, Japan and its economy were rarely out of the news (indeed I was often called on to comment about it on both the BBC and ITV), usually for all the wrong reasons. By early 1993 official interest rates were back at 2.5%, the level that was widely believed to have been the catalyst for the final dramatic phase of the 'Bubble Economy'. But by this stage the country was fully in recession, with unemployment finally breaking above the still extraordinarily low 2.0–2.2% range that had prevailed for the previous three years. Neither was there any sign of an end to the slide in land prices, the escalation in bankruptcies, or the accumulation of bad assets on the balance sheets of the banks that so dominated financing across the economy. The credit crunch therefore intensified even though, in sharp contrast to the three previous years, the MOF was now actively urging the banks to increase lending. What is more, Japan was becoming increasingly embroiled in a trade dispute with the US, the net result of which was a dramatic surge in the yen, which by mid August 1993 was approaching the psychologically important 100 level against the dollar. This meant that there had been a rise of more than a third in its nominal value from its April 1990 low. Clearly, the Bank of Japan had not done enough. The historically low level of nominal short rates was not low enough. Nor were matters being helped by the fact that whatever the MOF wanted lenders to do, the government was also encouraging them to boost their operating margins to help address their bad loan problem. They were therefore failing to pass on lower policy rates fully. This meant that the overall thrust of the monetary policy stance was incoherent, and this boosted the number of defaults.

The economy's extraordinary change in fortune since the late eighties boom was mirrored by a collapse in the popularity of the hitherto untouchable Liberal Democratic Party (LDP). Prior to the deflation of the bubble, Japan had effectively operated like a one-party state, and I was told on more than one occasion by someone 'in the know' that the LDP actually provided funding for the Socialist Party to keep it solvent and encourage the notion that there was a serious opposition in Japan. But at a general election in the summer of 1993 the LDP lost its majority for the first time in more than forty years. The new government, led by Morihiro Hosokawa (a former marquis), was something of a rainbow coalition, with scant experience of running much at all, let alone the world's second-largest economy. It behaved like a rabbit caught in car headlights, and instigated little change in strategy before it fell foul of one of Japan's all-too-familiar bribery scandals. Such initiatives as it did take were largely confined to fiscal policy, which, it was assumed, would also help to buy a few additional votes. In the meantime, despite further cuts in official rates to 1.5%, real borrowing costs remained onerous, and land prices actually fell faster in 1993 than they did in 1992. In the major urban centres the decline from the peak was now approaching 50%. Meanwhile, more than 14,500 companies went bust that year, bringing the total number of bankruptcies since the bubble burst to almost 46,000 and leaving total bad debts at some ¥24.6trn.

February 1994 saw a fourth fiscal package. This one totalled just over 3.1% of GDP and was the largest yet. Moreover, it centred on tax cuts as much as public works spending. Unsurprisingly, given the size of the stimulus, the economy quickly stirred into life, helped by the strength of the global economy. But the reprieve proved short-lived, not least because the Bank of Japan continued to drag its feet on monetary policy and the yen appreciated further, breaking through to a new high against the dollar of ¥96 in November. This period was also noteworthy not just because house prices continued their slide but because it witnessed the first signs of outright goods and services price deflation: the annual rate of change in the GDP deflator turned negative.

The core problem, however, was that the real estate market continued to collapse, with the result that Japan's mortgage lenders, or *Jusen*, found themselves under immense stress, especially as they had increasingly moved into commercial property towards the end of the bubble era. Before the year was up, the Bank of Japan had acted to rescue two credit cooperatives, the first time it had intervened directly to save a financial institution since 1965. Until then, the MOF had always managed to persuade other, stronger, financial institutions to step in. Year-end was also the moment that BOJ Governor Mieno stood down, to be replaced by the moderate and pragmatic lifetime MOF official Yasuo Matsushita.

Mieno had certainly done what was initially asked of him. The problem was that he went on fighting the same anti-inflationary and anti-speculative battle for far too long. Despite a persistently appreciating yen and evidence that Japanese inflation was dropping to dangerously low levels, official interest rates remained on hold throughout his last year in the job. The Nikkei ended the year back below 20,000. Mieno, who began as something of a hero, not least at the BOJ itself, ended up as very much the villain of the peace. Certainly few tears were shed on his departure, either at the MOF or in the prime minister's residence. He was no Japanese Paul Volcker, but rather an eighties version of Clément Moret, the Bank of France governor who almost deflated the French economy to death in the early thirties.[27] An equity trader at Lehman Tokyo used to have a large black and white picture of Mieno taped to his computer. Underneath was a cut-out newspaper headline that said 'Dumber than we thought'. He had a point.

Early 1995 saw Sumitomo Bank write off some ¥800bn in bad debts, and so become the first major Japanese bank to post a deficit since the war. But despite the massive write-off, its outstanding bad debts only fell from ¥1.2trn to just under ¥1.0trn. However, any such concerns one might have felt about this soon faded into irrelevancy after the Great Hanshin Earthquake devastated Kobe on 17 January 1995. I was in London at the time and my sense was that the earthquake offered the Japanese authorities an opportunity to launch a concerted attack on the economy's deflationary problems by instituting a sustained burst of fiscal and monetary reflation. I even wrote something at the time to that effect. What emerged was something altogether more modest. The government introduced a supplementary budget designed to finance reconstruction and relief work in the areas affected by the disaster, and after more than a year of stasis the BOJ cut rates by a further 75bps to 1.0%.

This was also the moment that the *Jusen* crisis went critical. By the time I arrived back in Tokyo in the summer of 1995, it was believed that nearly three-quarters of their outstanding loans were irrecoverable and the government was controversially talking of using taxpayers' money to facilitate a rescue operation. Indeed, it was becoming clear that it would soon have no choice but to act. August 1995 saw runs on a number of small financial institutions and the MOF had to reassure depositors that their savings were still safe. Nor was confidence in the Japanese financial system helped by the revelation a month later that a bond trader working for Daiwa Bank in the US had concealed trading losses in excess of $1bn and that Daiwa had itself deliberately deceived the US authorities about this event! This episode was symptomatic of the slack internal risk controls and highly irregular practices that operated during the rapid overseas expansion of Japan's banks during the bubble years. I remember that this was a regular point of discussion with clients during my first marketing trip to the US after joining Lehman. The general conclusion was that the MOF and the BOJ had little idea what was going on in the Japanese financial sector and that the Daiwa incident was only the tip of the iceberg. It was hard to argue.

The growing difficulties being experienced by smaller financial institutions, the question marks that were being raised over the banking sector's operating procedures, and the stringency of the regulatory environment in Japan began to be reflected in higher borrowing costs in the interbank market: the so-called Japan Premium. This in turn made it harder for the stronger institutions to take over the weak. The 'convoy' system that had long been the default response to periods of financial stress in Japan was breaking down. More important still, the network of trust and consensus that underlay the entire Japanese financial system was failing.

The final quarter of 1995 saw the government respond to the economy's continued difficulties with another fiscal package, this time amounting to ¥14.2trn, and a ¥685bn bailout for the *Jusen*. In September the Bank of Japan had cut the discount rate to a mere 0.5%. For a period there were hopes that this latest round of fiscal and monetary stimulus might be enough to stabilise matters, and I admit that I was one of those temporarily caught up in this more optimistic frame of mind. It wasn't that I believed that the financial sector's travails were in the past, it was just the large amount of macro support being applied, the strength of the global economy and the fact that the mid-1995 surge in the yen had unwound somewhat. In my defence, Japan's real GDP growth actually exceeded the G7 average in 1996, even if that was largely because of the temporary fiscal-policy-induced jump in activity in the first half of the year.

The reality was that few, if any, of Japan's underlying problems had been comprehensively addressed. Nominal GDP actually peaked in 1995 and had begun to drift lower, a trend that has only reversed over the last six months, and tentatively at that. What is more, land prices continued to tumble, driven in part by the banks continuing their strategy of transferring their problem loans to the CCPC. Bankruptcies continued to escalate. Further important harbingers of a full-blown banking crisis were seen in 1996, as Nippon Credit Bank, Hokkaido Takushoku Bank and Long Term Credit Bank, all sizeable institutions, either announced big losses or dramatic restructurings, including the closure of their overseas operations.

Matters really came to a head in 1997. The government began the year in an optimistic frame of mind, not least because it thought that the fall in land prices would soon be over. It was at this stage that it took the poorly timed decision to launch its own financial sector 'Big Bang', based on the experience of London ten years earlier. But most strikingly of all, in an effort to rein in a large budgetary shortfall and soaring public sector indebtedness, Finance Minister Ryutaro Hashimoto opted to go ahead with a hotly debated fiscal tightening in his spring budget. This amounted to some 2% of GDP and extended to a sharp hike in indirect taxes, the curtailment of a temporary income tax rebate and a reduced level of public investment. The official expectation was that this might produce a temporary pause, but that growth should soon resume, not least because the private sector would be encouraged to spend by the prospect of more sustainable public finances. Furthermore, the stock market seemed, initially at least, to take a similar view. I was less sanguine, but nevertheless believed that as long as the BOJ kept monetary policy very loose, the yen remained competitive and the international environment was supportive there was little reason for the economy to drop back into recession or for the financial crisis to intensify unduly.

This stands out as one of the worst forecasting errors of my career, although I would stress that once I recognised my mistake I adjusted my position far more quickly, and to a much greater degree, than most. By mid 1997 I was about as bearish as anyone about Japan's prospects and was publicly characterising the situation as 'the largest financial crisis in a major economy since the early 1930s'.

Around that time I produced a report calling for a change in the then-archaic Bank of Japan Law – legislation that harked back to 1942, when the central bank's activities were necessarily tailored to the requirements of war rather than narrow macroeconomic stability – and for the granting of more formal independence to the Japanese central bank. This research note attracted a lot of attention in the domestic press, went down well with Lehman's international client base, and was applauded by my contacts at the BOJ itself. Moreover, it proved insightful. A new legal structure governing the BOJ came into effect in April 1998 that both increased its autonomy and added to the transparency of its decision-making processes. What it didn't do, however, was make the BOJ a formal targeter of inflation. Rather, its remit remained couched in general terms of the achievement of price stability. As the country's deflationary woes deepened in subsequent years, I increasingly came to feel that this was an error. Indeed, it is a mistake that has only just been rectified.

I first became concerned that my view of the economy's resilience was mistaken during the course of the second quarter, when the short-term data following the consumption tax hike began to come in weaker than I expected, and there was evidence that the saving rate was starting to increase in the face of continued financial sector turmoil. As it turned out, this marked the onset of a five-quarter slide in activity that, peak to trough, exceeded five percentage points of national output.

What really exposed the underlying fragility of Japan's situation and the extent of the errors in both macro policy and my forecasts was the onset of the Asian Financial Crisis in June 1997. In mitigation, I can honestly say that this was hard to see in advance (or at least the precise timing was). In the middle of that month, Thailand was forced to abandon its fixed exchange rate and float the baht in the face of unrelenting pressure on its balance of payments. With a number of other Asian economies suffering similar credit booms, operating similar currency pegs, and similarly dependent on uninterrupted external financing, panic ensued and the crisis rapidly spread across the region.

Japanese banks had lent as recklessly overseas in the nineties as they had domestically in the eighties, and they were heavily exposed to the dramatic turn of events in their immediate geographical vicinity. For example, more than half of the lending that took place in Thailand over this period had been provided by Japanese banks. The result was that the Japanese financial sector was facing another huge increase in bad debts. Needless to say, the stock market came under renewed and dramatic downward pressure.

November saw things take a dramatic turn for the worse, as Sanyo Securities, Hokkaido Takushoku Bank and then Yamaichi Securities, one of Japan's largest and oldest securities houses, went to the wall. Moreover, in each case the extent of the hidden losses on their books and the general lack of transparency around these entities' true financial situations prior to their demise was astonishing, as was the inability of ministers and policymakers in general to come up with a coherent response. Confidence in Japan's financial system had evaporated. Fear dominated sentiment. The markets were beset by rumours about which institution would be the next to collapse. Cash gravitated towards Bank of Tokyo-Mitsubishi, which was regarded as Japan's safest bank. Ten-year JGB yields, which had peaked at around 2.5% in the second quarter, trended persistently lower through 1997 and into 1998, ultimately bottoming out at less than 0.5% (which was, until recently, a record low for a longer-term sovereign interest rate in any economy).

This was an extraordinary and exciting period in which to be a financial markets economist. The pace of events was unrelenting and the interest in what was going on in Japan amongst Lehman's own employees, its client base and the international media was intense. My workload grew exponentially but so did the number and quality of my contacts within the policymaking community and among the great and the good of the Japanese economics profession. Hence, by this time I was, probably for the first time in my career, in full control of my brief and I was getting it consistently right (more or less). It was a very gratifying feeling and it fortified me. Mind you, it needed to. I was producing an endless stream of written commentary. The length of my working day often extended to eighteen or twenty hours, with Tokyo's time zone rather detached from other major financial centres. Indeed, I forget how many times I was woken up by a New York salesperson at 2 a.m. with the refrain: 'Hi Russ, what time is it with you?' Until they work out different time zones, no one will be able to persuade me that Americans understand the rest of the world.

Meaningful action to address the deepening crisis arrived only towards the end of November, when the BOJ injected a record ¥3.1trn of emergency liquidity into the entities most in trouble. Then, in December, the government announced that it would provide ¥10trn of public funds to assist in stabilising the banks and ¥12trn of public assistance to help ease the credit crunch among smaller companies. There was also the promise of an income tax cut. In early January the total sum available to bail out the banks was expanded to ¥30trn (almost 6% of GDP).

The problem was that the authorities had a huge credibility problem. Having persistently understated the size of the banks' bad loan problems in official statements and encouraged any number of accounting tricks to allow them to hide the extent of their compromised assets, any policy initiatives faced enormous scepticism. There was considerable resistance on the part of the banks to the bailout. The funds were to be provided only if a bank explicitly asked for public help, and very few were willing to do so, not least because at that time the domestic papers were full of scandals and the banks were fearful of attracting yet more bad press. But without a broad-based recapitalisation, there was no chance of any stabilisation of the banks.

The upshot of this half-baked bailout was that the government resorted to its default option of more orthodox fiscal stimulus. The biggest package yet was announced on 24 April 1998: initiatives that totalled ¥16.7trn. But before this package could exert much influence on the economy, the government was once again forced to intervene in the financial arena. In late May it announced the so-called Total Plan for the bad-debt problem. Under this scheme, banks that were in trouble were to be subject to public takeover. Once all their bad debts had been removed they would be sold back into the private sector. The new bailout institution would in the meantime dispose of the assets of the failed banks and, it was hoped, help to maintain the flow of credit to borrowers. The problem was that the only problem this addressed was the issue of banks that had already failed. It did nothing to arrest the seemingly inexorable slide towards failure of other banks. Furthermore, by adding to, rather than easing, the downward pressure on real estate prices, it was likely to further accelerate this slide.

In the meantime, a huge corruption scandal enveloped the upper echelons of Japan's bureaucracy as it emerged that MOF officials had taken backhanders in return for favourable inspection reports of banks and tip-offs about the timing of these inspections. Finance Minister Mitsuzuka was forced to resign and the Bank of Japan was also then implicated as the extent of the lavish entertainment heaped on its head of capital markets by various banks and the inside information he had passed on in return became clear. This extended to the advanced leaking of the details of key economic reports, not least the closely followed *Tankan* business survey, the detail of which was pored over by every economist in town and, indeed, by many more around the world.

Ninety-eight BOJ officials were reprimanded for the wonderfully phrased misdemeanour of 'accepting excessive entertainment', and the new governor, Yasuo Matsushita, was forced to follow the finance minister's example and resign. With the media and public understandably unwilling to accept the appointment of a contemporary MOF or BOJ insider in his place, the ageing Masaru Hayami, by then CEO of Nissho Iwai Corporation, was asked to return to run the institution that he had previously served for thirty-four years (starting, as had Yasushi Mieno, in 1947). This was to prove a controversial appointment, but at the time there were few obvious alternatives.

This round of scandal sparked a furious response in the foreign banking community in Tokyo, and not least at Lehman, as there was understandable anger that they had been placed at such a disadvantage relative to the domestic institutions. For what it's worth, my own experiences confirm that senior Japanese bureaucrats relished being entertained in luxury in return for offering up their thoughts on the economic conjuncture. I racked up my largest expense claims in wining and dining my contacts at the MOF and BOJ at some of the top restaurants in Tokyo. Furthermore, on occasion after dinner I was invited to attend an official's favourite club, where it was made clear that almost anything was available for a price. The fact was that neither institution had a formal code of ethics, so it is perhaps understandable – if clearly not commendable – that officials saw themselves as legitimately benefiting from the largesse of the private sector, especially when their pay was often so derisory, particularly in relation to the hours put in.

These scandals did nothing to encourage the public to support the further injection of taxpayers' money into the banks. But it soon became clear that two more of Japan's largest financial institutions – Long Term Credit Bank (LTCB) and Nippon Credit Bank (NCB) – were close to the edge, their share prices plummeting as the continued collapse in land prices devastated their balance sheets. Estimates of the size of their non-performing loans snowballed. Bitter wrangling between the government and the opposition about how to handle the situation added to the sense of crisis, and the LDP's loss of its majority in the Upper House further complicated matters.

Then, to top it all, the Russian sovereign default and the Long-Term Capital Management crisis sent tremors through global financial markets. This caused the 'yen carry trade' (the practice of borrowing in super-low-cost yen to invest in higher-yielding assets elsewhere) to unwind in dramatic fashion, with the result that the Japanese currency surged higher. I well remember coming into the office one morning to survey the distress caused across the trading floor by the fact that the Japanese currency was twenty-odd per cent stronger against the dollar than when I left the previous evening.

In the wake of these events, the Nikkei slumped to new lows and the BOJ found itself under pressure to ease monetary policy again. The target for the overnight rate was cut to another record low of 0.25% in early September 1998 and the central bank subsequently also announced that it would allow a reserve surplus of some ¥500bn to remain in the system while easing collateral requirements for its open market operations and establishing a

new lending facility for refinancing half of the new bank lending in the fourth quarter. Then, finally, with LTCB threatening to
sever its credit lines and default on its obligations to depositors,
on 23 October it was nationalised. The same fate befell NCB in mid
December after an external audit showed it to be carrying bad
debts of ¥3.7trn, far more than it had ever admitted.

The announcement of yet another fiscal package, this time
amounting in headline terms to a colossal ¥23.9trn (4.5% of GDP),
had temporarily boosted stock prices after the LTCB nationalisation, but, following the takeover of NCB, the Nikkei slumped once
again, ending the year at its lowest close for thirteen years. By mid
1999, however, there was a sense that, after two truly horrendous
years, the worst just might be over. The government's efforts to
stabilise the banks culminated in a massive recapitalisation programme, launched in March. The banks had initially been reluctant to accept the funds, which were offered in exchange for convertible preferred shares, subordinated bonds or subordinated
loans, because of the stigma that was attached to them. But once
the Industrial Bank of Japan grasped the nettle, others quickly followed, with fifteen major banks ultimately receiving some ¥7.5trn
in return for detailed restructuring plans overseen by the newly
created Financial Services Authority (FSA), which had taken over
the regulatory and supervisory operations of the MOF. Meanwhile,
the BOJ also did its bit. With the yen strengthening and JGB yields
heading higher, it announced its intention to encourage the call
money rate to trend down towards the zero bound once again in
the context of the provision of ample funds to the money markets.
In April it confirmed that it would sustain the zero interest rate
policy 'until deflationary concerns were over', although at this
time the bank was clear that its primary focus remained the price
of money rather than its quantity.

The FSA conducted an audit of all the major players in Tokyo's
financial markets at this time, including Lehman Brothers. Unsurprisingly, the Japanese authorities went out of their way to demonstrate that Gaijin operations were as much under the microscope
as were domestic institutions, and there was a certain satisfaction
when we foreigners were also proved to be bending rules and pursuing questionable business practices.

Credit Suisse First Boston (CSFB) for one was found to have broken numerous banking laws and was heavily reprimanded and
fined. As for Lehman, I remember looking up from my desk one

morning to see a long line of grey-suited, briefcase-carrying men filing on to the trading floor and our being instructed not to touch anything or try to leave. The locals were ashen faced and rapidly adopted the simpering attitude of supplication always reserved for those in authority in Japan. We foreigners put on a show of either disinterest or irritation at the interruption of our working days.

The audit continued for a number of weeks and appeared to me to be pretty comprehensive. It certainly put the senior management on their toes and left some of the Japanese staff in an unremitting state of terror. In the end, as at CSFB, it was our equity derivatives trading operation, which as it happened was located just behind Matthew and me on the trading floor and was run by an American, that came under the most intense scrutiny. The firm was forced to change a number of business practices and move a few people on, including the head of the group, but by CSFB standards we escaped lightly. But what I recall most clearly is my colleagues telling me about how little the FSA bureaucrats, from top to bottom, understood about what the Lehman traders were doing with their book, especially those who had been brought in from New York and London. This theme of regulatory ignorance was, of course, to prove very familiar a decade later, by which time the complexity of derivative products and the trading strategies built around them had moved on in leaps and bounds.

A full decade before its ultimate demise, this period also saw Lehman Brothers go through some convulsions from which it ultimately would emerge strengthened but which at the time threatened its very existence. The first coincided with the Asian Crisis. Lehman was an advisor to the Thai government and was left high and dry by the latter's decision to devalue and the subsequent financial crisis that rapidly unfolded across the region. The firm's broader Asian operation lost a fortune. Sadly, moreover, my colleagues whose job it was to analyse the economics of non-Japan Asia, and especially my immediate boss Miron Mushkat, saw their credibility fatally damaged, both within the firm and more broadly, by their firmly expressed belief that the baht peg would hold.

I managed to escape back to England for a couple of weeks of holiday in August 1997, but the day before I returned to Tokyo I was warned by John Llewellyn that the firm's entire Asian research operation, including the Hong Kong–based economics group led by Miron, had been pared back to a bare minimum. When I arrived back in the Tokyo office, it was like the *Marie Celeste*! The desks, chairs, computers, files, papers, pens – even the personal belongings of those who had been employed – were still there, but the people, some thirty of them, had gone. They had all been sacked: Japanese and Gaijin, senior and junior, old and young. Indeed, the only analysts who remained in the Tokyo office were Matthew and me. It was a similar picture in Hong Kong.

There were other major changes elsewhere in the firm's research operation. In particular, Allen Sinai had been moved on and John Llewellyn had taken over the job of Chief Economist. I was delighted, as was the rest of the team. John asked me to take over the rump of the Asian economics team and become Chief Economist Asia. Upset though I was to see Miron and most of his cohorts depart, and mindful as I was that I could so easily have gone the same way (especially given the over-optimism with which I initially viewed Japan's prospects in 1997), I was happy to take the additional responsibilities on, although these were to prove pretty challenging.

With Lehman's Hong Kong operation reduced to little more than a rep office, this meant consolidating the Asian team in Tokyo. The net result was that, in addition to Matthew, I had two excellent ex-Reserve Bank of Australia economists, Rob Subbaraman and Graham Parry, to assist me and take on much of the burden of looking at the rest of the region. The Reserve Bank of Australia is a top-notch central bank that offers fantastic training to its regular intake of economists from around Australia. Rob and Graham both benefited from this schooling and proved to be most able and personable supports to me over the course of the following three years. I am glad to say that both have since gone on to enjoy very successful careers.

Two other hires did not go so well though. Management was determined to add more Asian economists to my group to give the firm a little more credibility with the Asian client base. John and I were supportive of the decision (mind you, in truth we had little choice in the matter), but the powers that be were, as usual, incredibly impatient. Hence, we were rather press-ganged into hastily fixing upon a couple of what appeared to be good candidates. They both came through the usual interview process pretty well and offers were rapidly dispatched and accepted.

Unfortunately, both hires soon went seriously wrong. One, while very experienced, seemingly well-qualified for the job and an excellent English speaker proved singularly unsuited to the markets. Clearly resenting having to take direction from a Westerner, especially one who was younger than he was, he proved inflexible, difficult to manage, unwilling to follow any instructions and reluctant to express a team view. We had to ease him out at the end of his six-month trial period in what, given the potential for the Japanese authorities to get involved on the side of one of their own, was a very delicate process. Thankfully, in the end this was made easier by the fact that he had been going to interviews with another firm during normal work time. He also foolishly contrived to insult me in public in the most unsubtle and un-Japanese manner.

The whole episode was extraordinary and just not what one would have expected in Japan. However, the affair surrounding the other economist was more remarkable still. On the basis of his CV and interviews, he also seemed amply qualified for the task. Unfortunately, much of the CV proved to be rather economical with the truth. His first written piece was incomprehensible, and came replete with some econometric analysis that even I could tell was gobbledegook. It was immediately clear that we had made another mistake. He too had to be moved on once the sixth-month trial period was complete.

These two errors cost me considerable angst and the firm a good deal of cash. They also raised legitimate questions about the impulsive tendencies of Lehman's management as well as about both my judgement and the role of the HR department in checking references. In all honesty, though, it's hard to offer much by way of excuses. I subsequently heard 'off the record' that the particular shortcomings of both candidates were well known to their previous employers. But if those employers are reluctant to pass that information on – and throughout my career I have noticed a reluctance to provide honest references because of fear of legal action – there is a limit to what you can do until it's too late. And at that time it would have been considered extraordinary if we had required such an experienced economist as the second hire to undertake an English writing or quantitative analysis test.

This period saw the firm's Asian operations largely confined to Tokyo and, to sustain morale and give the office renewed momentum, a number of high-profile senior managers were drafted in from New York, at huge expense. If Japan was alien to a Brit, it was another universe to most Americans, and they required some major financial incentives to make the jump across the Pacific. Furthermore, the bond and foreign exchange trading platforms were bolstered by some equally expensive local hires. But the good news was that the new additions were deeply focused on macroeconomics. Hence, my team and I found ourselves very much at the heart of the revamped operation.

The Asian Crisis was a powerful event that spread outwards from Thailand across the region. It led to severe recessions in a number of economies and, for a period, left some teetering on the edge of financial meltdown and broad-based default. The crisis dealt a huge blow to confidence and in some cases resulted in a thoroughgoing reassessment of how a particular economy should be run and what the policy priorities should be.

Going into the crisis, these economies were beset by numerous structural shortcomings, not least their narrow dependence on capital accumulation to generate growth, and more generally in their regulatory and institutional architectures. However, as Rob, Graham and I described in a hundred-page report, its proximate cause was an unsustainable credit and asset price boom, reminiscent in some ways of the Japanese bubble. This manifested itself in large external deficits and the build-up of onerous external debt. Moreover, the fixed and quasi-fixed exchange rates that were then common in the region were a source of huge foreign exchange risk for corporate and financial sectors. These pegs were initially defended through a combination of interest rate hikes and the use of foreign exchange reserves, but when they were broken by market pressure the result was a massive increase in foreign currency liabilities in local currency terms that led to a catastrophic surge in corporate and financial sector bankruptcies.

Such was the severity of the crisis that there was no realistic alternative for these economies but to seek external financial assistance, and in particular the intervention of the IMF. There was, after all, no Asia-based international institution with the resources to help out. The network of central banks in the region was neither mature enough, nor wealthy enough, to make much of a difference. Besides, almost every country in the region was to some extent caught up in the events of the day, and therefore focused on its own particular problems.

The IMF's response was to tie financial support to tough 'structural adjustment' programmes, which amounted to draconian fiscal and monetary restraint and the announcement of wide-ranging institutional and supply-side reforms, not least where financial sectors were concerned. The logic was that international investor confidence in the respective currencies had to be re-established, and that the way to do this was to revert to the most conservative of macroeconomic values while at the same time creating systems of governance and incentive structures that would help to not just attract overseas capital but make it stick.[28]

As I was to find out first hand, the medicine prescribed by the IMF attracted some vitriolic criticism. Indeed, it has continued to do so ever since, with some commentators even characterising it as 'neocolonialism'. There is no doubt that, at least initially, the extent of fiscal and monetary adjustment that was imposed exaggerated the downturn and generated considerable misery for many across the region, including those who probably deserved it least. This made me distinctly uneasy, and my sense was that the prescribed austerity was overdone. On the other hand, I am unsure that there was a viable alternative. To have allowed the various depreciations to continue would have been to risk complete financial collapse and hyperinflation. To have resorted to a siege economy behind trade and capital controls might have stabilised things temporarily but would have been distortionary and hard to unwind and would have solved nothing. Indeed, it could have set these economies back decades. As for the structural reforms, even if their timing was less than optimal (such policies usually initially damage growth, even if they enhance it over the longer term), they were overdue and much needed if this part of the world was to successfully integrate itself into the global economy.

Ultimately, I believe that the IMF's medicine worked, in that the incipient threats to social, political and financial stability were overcome: certainly, within a few years the Asian region had recovered sufficiently to resume its position as a dynamic and increasingly important force in the global economy. However, there were unintended consequences of the IMF's bitter medicine. Most pertinently, it encouraged a strong desire on the part of the governments of the crisis-hit economies never to be placed in such an ignominious position again. This encouraged a form of modern-day mercantilism, where export growth and the accumulation of huge stockpiles of foreign exchange reserves occupied an unduly elevated importance in policymaking. This became a primary source of the global macro imbalances that developed ahead of the global financial crisis. Moreover, these war chests came to be seen as an alternative to the persistent-reform agenda suggested by the IMF, and these economies have therefore remained haunted by enduring institutional shortcomings and deficiencies in the area of governance. They are thereby still more vulnerable to a loss of foreign investor confidence than they might otherwise have been.

Although, Japan apart, the direct and immediate impact of the Asian Crisis on the advanced economies was limited, it encouraged a sharp decline in oil prices, which a year later was a major catalyst for Russia's devaluation and sovereign default. This in turn resulted in the collapse of the Long-Term Capital Management hedge fund. These two events had a big effect on Lehman: first, because the firm was caught on the hop by the default (although its emerging-market debt business suffered only minor losses on its holdings of Russian debt); and second, because the subsequent collapse in market liquidity, the tightening of global funding conditions, and the withdrawal of a number of credit lines left the company seriously short of cash. Indeed, for a period, as the rumour mill went into overdrive and even some of Lehman's own long-standing hedge fund clients bet against its survival, the firm seemed to be on the brink.

I was in London talking to clients about what was happening in Asia when Lehman Brothers was under the most intense pressure, but most of the meetings would begin with some sort of inquiry about how things were at the firm. I also recall how fear stalked the dealing room and some of the senior management were themselves to be seen on the phones, exhorting counterparties to cut us some funding slack. Leading from the front was the London chief executive, Bruce Lakefield: a tough-as-old-boots, straight-as-a-dye, former US naval officer. On the morning on which the rumours first hit the screens and a hush settled over the fixed-income trading floor, Bruce took the nearest microphone from a trading desk. 'Ladies and gentlemen', he said, 'this is Bruce Lakefield, your CEO. I understand that there are rumours that Lehman Brothers is going bankrupt. I am a member of the firm's executive committee and I am familiar with all is trading positions. Ladies and gentlemen, let me tell you, this ship is not going to sink.' And it didn't.

In the end, the Fed's decision to ease monetary policy and encourage a private rescue of Long-Term Capital Management saved the day, allowing CEO Dick Fuld, the villain of the piece ten years later, to steer the firm through the crisis. But it was touch and go for a while. Also, Fuld's initial reluctance to contribute to this pooled rescue operation generated considerable resentment on Wall Street, and it would seem that it came back to haunt him when Lehman was again on the edge in 2008. It is worth noting that Bear Stearns was the other investment bank that dragged its feet on this issue. Lehman was eventually hauled kicking and screaming into contributing $100m. Bear Stearns refused to contribute a cent.

With the Asian and Long-Term Capital Management crises overcome, Japanese stock prices began to recover rapidly in 1999. Bureaucrats also began to sound more confident, with some declaring the emergency over. There was much talk in the Japanese press of significant progress in bank mergers, corporate restructuring, the dilution of bank-led stakeholder capitalism, an imminent foreign-led mergers and acquisitions boom, and the rapid assimilation of other Western business practices, not least in the area of accounting and shareholder primacy. This was a remarkable transformation from a decade earlier, when the Japanese economic model encouraged swathes of US businessmen across the Pacific to draw lessons from it. The year 1999 was also the peak of the global dot-com boom, and Japan was not immune to the enthusiasm for high-tech companies and the explosion of the World Wide Web, especially as so many of the globe's top semiconductor manufacturers were Japanese. Exports grew strongly after two desperate years.

I can remember at this time constantly pouring cold water on the suggestions made during internal 'risk' meetings (where I was interrogated over lunch on a weekly basis by traders, salespeople and management about all things macro), and by some of the firm's equity clients, that it was now time to make a solid long-term investment bet on Japan. I was just not convinced. To me, notwithstanding the strength of the global economy, the whole edifice of Japan's economy still looked fragile and vulnerable to shocks and I just couldn't believe that the leopard could change its spots that quickly.

What I was particularly concerned about was the continued decline in land prices, which was only exacerbated by the government's insistence that banks rapidly dispose of bad assets. There was also the continued evidence of broader-based deflationary pressures, the still-elevated level of bankruptcies (which meant that new bad loans were appearing as fast as old ones were written off), and the fact that the US boom was itself looking increasingly bubble-like. This will sound like a cliché, but while waiting for a cab outside the Palace Hotel in New York on a marketing trip around this time, I was given a lecture on what tech stocks to buy by the doorman. That clinched it for me: the dot-com bubble was in its terminal stages. Meanwhile, a number of smaller Japanese regional banks continued to go under and a second life insurer, Toho Mutual Life, went bankrupt as well. These failures seemed to be more than mere aftershocks of the crisis of 1997/98, and the information I was receiving off the record from my contacts at the MOF and the BOJ only added to my sense that this was a false dawn.

The Nikkei finished 1999 at its highest for the year, although given where it had been a decade earlier, an index level of 18,934 was hardly cause for celebration. The rally continued in the early months of 2000, as personal computer and mobile phone sales rocketed and internet usage exploded. This was a period during which some of my colleagues lost the plot. The Tokyo office had cautiously rebuilt its equity research operation in the late nineties, focusing on the banks and technology stocks. Softbank, Japan's leading internet company, became a particular favourite of our tech analysts, and they published a ridiculously optimistic report that suggested that its stock price could reach ¥400,000. This would have meant that it would have accounted for some 16% of Japanese GDP! I wasn't sure whether to laugh or cry about this call, but unsurprisingly it soon proved to be totally preposterous and stands as a reminder of how misguided and irresponsible supposedly well-trained and supposedly objective financial analysts can be.

By mid 2000 and my departure from Japan for England, the tech bubble had well and truly burst and talk of Japan's 'new economy' had largely disappeared from the press. The long-standing bear market had returned and the economy's underlying weaknesses were again exposed. Moreover, by this stage any appetite for reform within the government had largely disappeared.

It was also in 2000 that the BOJ delivered one of the most crass policy errors of modern times. From early in the year Governor Hayami began to hint that the zero-rate policy would not last forever. He also suggested that deflationary pressures were easing, and in any case that the decline in prices in Japan was not the result of a shortage of aggregate demand and therefore not that damaging. This was patently absurd. The evolving balance of aggregate demand and supply will always exert a profound influence on the dynamics of prices, while deflation pushes up the *real* value of debts and exerts an unambiguously negative effect on balance sheets and spending power.

Hayami's real concern was that the zero interest rate policy would encourage companies to become too dependent on cheap credit, and that this would slow restructuring. Here he had a point. Japan's economy was replete with unproductive and unprofitable 'zombie companies', kept afloat by support from the banks and the government. They exerted a persistent drag on productivity, as healthy firms were discouraged from entering markets or prevented from expanding because they had to compete with subsidised firms. But the underlying issue here was the *Keiretsu* system, where banks held large shareholdings in firms and were reluctant to see them deleverage – in the late eighties Japanese banks held around a quarter of all Japanese equities. Addressing this problem by tightening monetary policy in the midst of a bout of debt deflation was madness. The solution lay more with those who oversaw the regulatory environment and the governance of the corporate sector.

By August, and my arrival back in the Lehman office in London, the BOJ had raised its overnight interest rate target back to 0.25%. I certainly didn't expect this to be the beginning of a consistent uptrend in official rates and the normalisation of monetary policy. Indeed, I was convinced it was just a matter of time before it would have to be unwound and the BOJ would have to embrace a quantitative approach to monetary policy.

My return to London was a reluctant one and it reflected four considerations. First, the powers that be at Lehman were increasingly of the view that, if they were to compete with the other major investment banks in Tokyo, their chief economist in Japan should at least be fluent in Japanese if not actually Japanese. Second, after five successive years in Japan as an expat, the Japanese government began to tax you on your global wealth. As Lehman was understandably unwilling to compensate me fully for this, if I stayed in Asia I was faced with little choice but to spend a year in Hong Kong or Singapore. Third, I had learned over the years that one of the hardest things to negotiate as an expat is a bona fide parachute back to the mothership. However valued you may be in your offshore role, you become a problem when you want to repatriate. I knew many people, at Lehman and beyond, who had gone home to non-jobs and soon found themselves either eased out or leaving of their own accord. Yet for me there was a real opportunity. Lehman was in the throes of building up its foreign exchange business and they were keen for me to head up the global foreign exchange strategy group in London. Fourth, our eldest daughter, Ellen, had done wonderfully well at school in Tokyo and had been offered a place at St Paul's Girls' School in London, which was widely regarded as one of the best in the UK. With a heavy heart, we therefore decided to head home.

The late nineties provided some of the most fascinating and overwhelming years of my career. Indeed, they were only really trumped by the remarkable events of 2007 and 2008, when my experiences in Japan stood me in very good stead. Barely a day seemed to go by without some dramatic development, and with Japan and then the rest of Asia barely out of the spotlight for a moment, I was constantly in demand from our global client base and from the media. The hours were often extraordinarily long and my bank of airmiles expanded dramatically. But it was also for the most part a happy time, not just for me but for the whole family. We all loved Japan and we would miss it enormously.

Just before we left Tokyo I was called into the office of the Asian CEO, who asked if I was interested in accompanying him and another senior Lehman executive to see President Bill Clinton give a speech during an official visit to the Japanese capital. I jumped at the chance and later that day, together with my two dyed-in-the-wool Republican Party-supporting colleagues, headed off to the ballroom of one of the city's five-star hotels for the event.

Clinton arrived straight from the airport after the gruelling fourteen-hour flight from Washington and was ushered on to the dais to the slightly absurd musical accompaniment of *Hail to the Chief*. He then launched into a speech on 'The Future of the International Financial Architecture', or, in essence, how the US administration thought bodies like the IMF, the World Bank and so on should evolve in an increasingly globalised world. Now Clinton is no economist and, as I myself knew only too well, he must have been exhausted by the length of the journey and the associated time difference. But, barely glancing at his notes, he gave what I can only describe as a graphic *tour d'horizon* of many of the most important aspects of international economic cooperation and development. He didn't miss a beat. He was totally in control of his brief. It was the most impressive political performance I have ever witnessed. It was absolutely spellbinding.

What was also noteworthy was that at the end of the speech, as I applauded, my two Republican colleagues – who had been heard to dump no end of opprobrium on the president for his sexual mis-adventures and for his policies in general, and neither of whom were exactly youthful or small in stature – immediately catapulted themselves to the front of the auditorium, vaulting chairs, elbow-ing aside old and young, journalists and laypeople, Japanese and Gaijin in a desperate effort to shake the president's hand and be caught on film doing so. I couldn't help but laugh. What a politician!

My final story about Lehman's top brass from my time in Tokyo relates to CEO Dick Fuld himself. Again towards the end of my stay, Fuld was scheduled to come out to Tokyo to rally his troops and meet some policymakers and a chosen few of the firms' clients. We were warned well in advance that we had to tidy up our desks and the trading floor in anticipation of his inspecting the operation (as if he would really care!), and a huge effort was made to choreo-graph every minute of his stay. It was like preparing for a royal visit.

It was well known that Fuld did not travel well and that he was uncomfortable away from New York, especially when it came to dealing with foreigners. And from his perspective, things didn't get much more foreign than Japan. Surrounded by the coterie of lackies that followed him everywhere, he flew over on his private jet. But he apparently felt so discombobulated after the flight that he postponed his set-piece presentation to us poor foot soldiers, preferring instead to recover his strength in his hotel (would that I could have done the same after my trips halfway round the world). The speech was duly rearranged for the next day, but it was poor: macho (he talked about 'ripping the heart out' of competitors that stood in his way), strident, bombastic, replete with psychobabble, and distinctly rose-tinted when it came to the firm. And then, dur-ing the Q&A, he rounded on comments that even hinted at a view about the business that was at variance to his own. I came away thinking about what a narrow paranoid man he must be. And I was not alone.

Later, I was one of a group invited to have dinner with him. But I was sufficiently outside the in-crowd that I was put at the far end of the table, barely got a word in, and when I did it was ignored. Dick didn't do macroeconomics. He didn't do Japan. He didn't do Limeys and he didn't do listening. Dick just did Dick. And then he had to leave early because he was tired. God only knows what the locals thought in their audiences with him. I remember that when, later that night, my wife asked me how it went I replied: 'The man is not stupid but he comes across as narrow and self-centred, and he doesn't know what he doesn't know. I suspect he has become a bit of a megalomaniac.' After the events of subsequent years, I see no reason to adjust my opinion.

Japan's fall from grace after the bubble years was spectacular. Despite average weighted GDP growth in its key export markets of 4.3% over the period, Japan's economy grew at an average real rate of around a mere 1% in the nineties, as against a figure of more than 4% in the eighties, a decade when it was responsible for more than 10% of total global growth. This share subsequently declined consistently: to less than 4% in the nineties, about 2.5% in the pre-global financial crisis period, and about 1.5% in the period after the global financial crisis. Prices and the nominal value of the economy began to decline in the mid nineties and have continued to trend lower to this day. Private sector corporate non-financial debt, which had risen by the equivalent of 35 percentage points of GDP in the decade of the bubble, fell by a broadly similar amount over the following decade. In the process, the non-financial corporate sector swung from a net financial deficit of 8.9% of GDP to a surplus of more than 5% of GDP. Meanwhile, the fall in land and equity prices wiped out wealth equivalent to three years' worth of GDP. Only a dramatic swing into fiscal deficit and an expansion of public sector indebtedness saved the economy from an even worse fate. The economy's total factor productivity (that is, the growth in output due to improvements in the efficiency with which capital and labour are utilised) turned negative in the wake of the initial crisis and, after a brief rebound, again in 1997 and 1998.

On my departure from the country, I wrote an op-ed piece for the *Asian Wall Street Journal* entitled 'A Golden Age Lost'. I reckon it is worth summarising in some detail. Fourteen years on I think it remains pretty apposite as an explanation for Japan's demise as an economic superpower.

In it, I began by warning that the then-emerging cyclical upswing was extremely fragile and that the economy remained acutely vulnerable to shocks, especially as the room for macroeconomic policy manoeuvre was limited. Furthermore, Japan's problems were far from over and huge adjustments still needed to be made across the economy and society as a whole.

The article began with my detailing the hubris which characterised Japan at the time of my initial arrival in the country a decade earlier at the tail end of the 'bubble economy', but also with
the observation that in 1990 few commentators were even hinting
at the demise of the Japanese economic miracle, and I for one was
certainly not among the prescient minority. Indeed, I admitted in
my article that:

> I was firmly convinced that Japan's economic and financial hegem-
> ony would endure, and over the years the sad fact is that the fore-
> casting record of private sector economists has proved only mar-
> ginally less fallible than the Japanese government's own wishful
> thinking. It was only with the benefit of hindsight that we as a
> group learned fully to understand the dynamics of Japan's extra-
> ordinary reversal of fortune.

Following this mea culpa on behalf of myself and my profession,
I went on to outline the sobering deflationary details of Japan's lost
decade, adding that although 'at the micro level many large Japanese companies remain household names ... they are increasingly
multinational in terms of production and outlook'. Furthermore,
I stressed that 'the new tech sector aside, the domestic landscape
[was] notable for a swelling corporate underclass'.

One of my key theses was that 'the frenzy of the "bubble economy" [had] covered up a multitude of deepening structural problems' and that Japan's traditional engines of growth – demographics and capital accumulation – had been increasingly exhausted.
I also pointed out that both the private and public sectors were
weighed down by excessive leverage. In this context, the economy was beset by a chronic misallocation of resources. 'Corporate
Japan', I asserted, had 'too many people, too much plant and equipment and too much debt', and it 'produced too little at too high a
cost'. The country therefore needed to adopt 'a new growth model
based on the more efficient use of labour and capital and built
around consumer rather than producer sovereignty'.

I lamented, however, that the changes necessary to achieve this
transformation had been far too slow in coming. In particular,
'the regulatory environment had failed to adjust adequately to the
needs of society and proved a serious constraint on the development of a modern market economy'. Successive governments had
'merely paid lip service to structural reform and deregulation',
while the public sector's suffocating influence on economic activity

remained too pervasive, both business practices and policymaking were too opaque and 'too many markets remain[ed] distorted, uncompetitive and vulnerable to special interests'. Whole sectors of the economy – construction, agriculture, smaller companies, even telecommunications – remained protected from the chill wind of competition, while the financial sector's rehabilitation was patchy at best.

Another of my points was that Japan's economic difficulties had at least some of their roots in social, cultural and political considerations. My belief at the time, and I would stress that it is a view I still hold, was that the government's failure to recognise and act on the economy's deep-seated structural malaise could be traced in part to the overconfidence bred by previous successes. But equally important in encouraging this inertia were 'the opacity of Japanese accounting and supervisory procedures and the predominance of shame as a motivating force in a consensus-based society'. There was also the fact that

> the intensity of modern, free-market capitalism, with its wide income inequalities, enhanced competition and requirement for rapid decision making, [sat] very uncomfortably in a nation that pride[d] itself on its inclusiveness and homogeneity.

Finally, I asserted that by Western standards Japan's democratic process was immature and lacking in gravitas. Japan was 'effectively a one party gerontocracy where gerrymandering is rife, political debate is all too often shallow and parochial, difficult decisions are fudged and patronage is dispensed with brazen vulgarity'. This system, I concluded, was 'inconsistent with anything but gradual change'.

At the end of my article I drew some tentative conclusions. Asset bubbles, I asserted, were difficult to quantify and just as hard to deflate without inflicting serious damage on the real economy. I noted the difficulties involved in disentangling changes in an economy's structural performance from its cyclical development. I observed that when bubbles do deflate, the shock to the financial sector can be catastrophic, and if not addressed quickly could undermine the natural tendency for an economy to return to equilibrium. I remarked how policymakers, businesses, individuals and private economists can often become prisoners of their own historical experience. I stated that the various levers of economic policy require coordination if they are to work in harmony and the whole is to be at least equal to the sum of its parts. In particular, monetary and fiscal policy must work in tandem, while governments ignore the supply side at their peril. I maintained that while technological change and globalisation could be powerful engines for change, their impact can be diluted by inappropriate structural policies. Finally, I again emphasised the point that culture and social mores could play deceptively large roles in economic development, but these are often the hardest things of all to change.

The fact that this article stands the test of time is all very well, but there remains the question as to why it took me so long to fully grasp the nature of Japan's problems? In answering that question, I would initially fall back on the fact that I was learning on the job and had started from a very low knowledge base. Yes, I knew more than most about debt deflation and depression economics, but at the outset I knew precious little about Japan's history, its culture or its institutional make up. This knowledge deficit, which took time to close, made the difficulties of disentangling the economy's cyclical and structural performance in anything approaching real time even more difficult than it already was. My second explanation is the persistent lack of transparency that surrounded the extent of Japan's asset bubble and the subsequent balance sheet fallout from its collapse. Like everyone else looking at Japan, I knew that the truth was not completely available, but few of us, if any, realised quite the extent of the misinformation and deceit we were being subjected to both by the private sector and by policymakers.

All this also raises another question: if from the outset I had had the full facts about Japan's balance sheet issues and a better understanding of its history and so on, what would my policy prognosis have been? Perhaps my first and most obvious recommendation would have been earlier and more aggressive monetary easing designed to stabilise land prices and prevent deflation more broadly. The second would have been a more persistent strategy of fiscal expansion rather than the episodic bursts of stimulus and the misguided 1997 attempt to tighten budgetary policy. The third would have been a much earlier effort to abandon regulatory forbearance, address the bad-loan problems of the financial sector, and recapitalise and reform the banks. The fourth would have been the instigation of a sequenced programme of root-and-branch structural reforms.

This approach was encapsulated in a paper that I co-authored with John Llewellyn early in 1999 entitled 'Japan: A Radical Proposal'. The report also put the case for the creation of a Japanese Ministry of Domestic Demand, set up along the lines of the old Ministry for International Trade and Industry and with the remit to do for the domestic economy what the Ministry for International Trade and Industry did for Japan's export capacity in the fifties and sixties. More specifically, its job would have been to coordinate the monetary and fiscal expansion in an as unorthodox and as bank-and-land-price-focused a manner as necessary. But in addition, it would seek to sweep away the many structural obstacles to the domestic provision of the goods and, most importantly, services that the Japanese people wanted, while also introducing measures to counterbalance the corrosive impact on growth potential of the country's aging population. Maybe if this had been done, Japan's slide from a lost decade to a lost generation would have been avoided.

CHAPTER 9

A SQUARE PEG
IN A ROUND
HOLE

When I returned to Lehman's London office in the summer of 2000, I was struck by how much more impressive an operation it was than during my brief sojourn there in 1995. John Llewellyn and his team had become central to the firm's operations and had gained considerable credibility from their work on supply-side economics and structural policy – areas that had been largely neglected by most financial market economists at the time (and for that matter by much of the economics profession full stop) – and for being one of the few groups brave enough to conclude that European integration would continue and that monetary union was likely to happen, and on schedule.

Meanwhile, the firm's 1998 Long-Term Capital Management–related wobble had been consigned to history. Not only was the fixed-income division greatly expanded, but it was better coordinated and was populated by a more impressive group of individuals. Foremost among the newer recruits was Jamil Baz, one of the smartest (and nicest) people I ever met: he took bond strategy to a new level. Similarly, the equity division (which had been a rather pathetic operation five years earlier) was, courtesy of a protracted period of investment and the wholesale importation of outside talent, now competing on the same level as the other global investment banks. Then there was foreign exchange. Again, large investments had been made to bring in some big names and there remained a sizeable budget to continue the expansion of a part of the bank that in the past had largely acted as a mini-hedge fund and had never consistently contributed much to total revenues.

Some explanation of the difference between an economist and a strategist is probably warranted here. The answer is, it depends; there is certainly plenty of room for interpretation. Strategists are essentially there to offer investment recommendations rather than economic forecasts and analysis. In short, they tell you what to buy and what to sell and when to buy or sell it. However, some strategists contextualise their recommendations entirely through the lens of macroeconomic developments, focus on broader market developments and are essentially economists by another name. Others barely give economics a thought, preferring instead to focus almost exclusively on the short-term market dynamics dictated by investor activity, market positioning and price and volume trends. Given my skill set and interests, I clearly fell into the former category. Unfortunately, this was going to cause me considerable trouble.

The overall head of the foreign exchange business was Mark Degennaro, an old and respected Lehman hand. He was based in New York and was often a rather distant figure as far as I was concerned. But the head of European foreign exchange and the dominant figure in the London office was Ivan Ritossa. Ivan, very much the Antipodean alpha male, had established his reputation at the foremost name in the Australian financial markets: Bankers Trust, Sydney. He certainly didn't lack energy and he was undoubtedly a big personality that gave the European business considerable credibility, but he was also someone that, from the word go, I suspected I was going to have problems with. And so it proved. We were cut from rather different cloth. What's more, his idea of a good head of foreign exchange research was a strategist who lived and breathed short-term market dynamics rather than an economist with a focus more on the big picture and the longer term.

The group that I inherited was a bit of a cocktail and was in need of beefing up. This in part reflected the fact that my predecessor, ex-Bank of England economist Francis Breedon, had decided to return to academia and confine himself to a part-time advisory role at Lehman Brothers. Francis fell into the same category as Jamil: smart (he is now professor of finance at Queen Mary's College, London) and nice. His work on equilibrium exchange rates, the impact of mergers and acquisitions activity on currency dynamics, and commodity currency indices had been largely responsible for giving the previous Lehman foreign exchange regime the credibility it enjoyed, and I continued to milk it for all it was worth during my tenure. Losing his counsel for all but one day a week was going to hurt, but management had no desire to retain full-time 'another' academic economist who many of the traders couldn't understand. This was misguided as Francis's knowledge of foreign exchange markets was unique in the City. I suspect that part of the management's indifference towards Francis was because they were intellectually intimidated by him. Mind you, we all were – it was just that some of us chose to celebrate the fact rather than bemoan it.

Apart from Francis, the team was predominantly European and female, and what it lacked in macroeconomic competency, it more than made up for with quantitative skills. This compensated for my own shortcomings and it was consistent with state of the art foreign exchange research. Since I began to ply my trade in 1986 under the wing of Paul Chertkow, the manner in which currencies were approached by banks and investment banks had changed dramatically. The primary focus was now short-term, and macroeconomic analysis was typically complemented by a detailed assessment of flows, market momentum, technicals (the forecasting of price movements by looking at purely market-generated data) and investor positioning. Moreover, the more sophisticated clients demanded the investigation of volatility and the provision of detailed trade ideas and structures that made use of complex financial derivatives. However, whether this change of approach improved anyone's ability to forecast exchange rates accurately is another matter.

It rapidly dawned on me that this role was going to take me out of my comfort zone. Indeed, I was consistently reminded by management that I was not just there to regurgitate economics, which they seemed to think barely mattered for foreign exchange markets in anything other than the distant, and to them largely irrelevant, future. I recognised the need to embrace the new approach, if for no other reason than because the competition used it, but I was unconvinced by the veracity of many of the analytical tools and I thought that management had the balance wrong. After all, what did a currency's value reflect if not the broadly defined relative risks and returns on investing in an economy? Moreover, almost every client meeting I attended would begin with a discussion of macro fundamentals, and many of them barely budged from these topics. Quant models were, to my mind, better suited as auxiliary tools to time the entry and exit points of trades rather than the primary means to determine currency direction and strategy.

My initial priority was to develop a weekly research document that could become Lehman's flagship foreign exchange publication and would establish a respected position in the market. This I managed to do within a couple of months, and in a manner that embraced the notion that it had to go beyond economics, even if my own personal essay on the macro environment and how it impacted foreign exchange was positioned up front. However, with most of the team not writing in English as a first language (and some that did doing so in a manner that belied the fact), I once again found that editing was taking up an inordinate amount of my time.

Once the basic product was established, the priority was to find a second-in-command who was a well-regarded foreign exchange specialist, who could operate out of Lehman's New York office, and who was an emerging-market currency analyst. With the world economy in recession, the financial sector was contracting and there was a lot of talent available. Nevertheless, mindful of my previous experiences it took the better part of a year to bring in the people we wanted in the form of Jim McCormick from J.P. Morgan and Steve Ellis from ING. Jim in particular was a big catch. He was a young guy with a natural flair for foreign exchange and he already enjoyed a great market reputation – and I got on well with him to boot. I was especially proud that my diligence was instrumental in persuading him to come on board.

Jim arrived at Lehman Brothers in the late summer of 2001 and I thought that it would be a good idea for him to bed down in the New York office before coming over to London. His first day in the New York office was Monday 10 September 2001, and a number of other Lehman London foreign exchange employees were also in the US that week, including Ivan.

As for all people in the financial markets, and especially those with a close connection to Wall Street, 9/11 was a frightful day, the memory of which will remain vivid for the rest of my life. The World Trade Centre was extremely familiar. Not only was Lehman's headquarters on Vesey Street appended to it and the place of work for 6,000 of my fellow employees, I had been visiting clients there, enjoying its amazing views of the city and navigating my way through its shops, restaurants, cafes and labyrinthine security systems, since I first went to the US on a marketing trip in 1988. Indeed, I had been walking through the complex only a few weeks earlier.

My first inkling that something was amiss that day came when I returned to the London trading floor from a lunchtime gym session. Slumping back into my seat, one of our proprietary traders drew my attention to the screens that adorned the walls and pillars around the huge low-ceilinged room, and which were constantly tuned in to either CNBC or Bloomberg TV. There were the now-infamous pictures of thick black smoke pouring from the middle of one of the twin towers, and within a few minutes it became clear that an aeroplane was responsible. Our US chief economist, Steve Slifer, would subsequently tell me how the first plane had cast a massive dark shadow over his corner office in the Lehman New York office just before it hit. His first thought was that there was an eclipse that no one had told him about! The noise of the impact soon put him right.

Already the newswires were buzzing and soon activity on the trading floor ground to a halt. Everyone was focused on the live TV images of downtown New York. Initially, however, we had little notion that it was a terrorist attack. That became clear only when the second plane hit. Meanwhile, although we in London had received information that the New York office was being evacuated, the full extent of the catastrophe and its potential implications for the firm began to become clear only when the first tower collapsed. It was then that we realised that Lehman's headquarters might well be destroyed. It was then that I grasped the possibility that I might have unwittingly sent Jim to his death and that other people I knew could have met a similar fate.

The rest of the afternoon was madness as I desperately tried to make contact with Jim and his wife, made efforts to find out what was going on in Vesey Street, while all the time keeping one eye on the extraordinary events that were playing out on the TV. The one thing I had no interest in was what the markets were doing. By the time I got home I had received information that Jim had been able to get out, but the prognosis for our headquarters and the firm as a whole looked bleak. I remember sitting out in my back garden late that night with a much-needed Scotch in my hand discussing over the phone with John Llewellyn whether the firm would be able to survive and mulling over the likely response from a wounded and vengeful America. Our tentative conclusions were 'yes, just about' and that there was no doubt that the US military would soon be lashing out in some direction. America would not take this lying down.

Thankfully, the human casualties at Lehman were minimal. Only one employee died as a direct result of the attack, and the firm also had a reasonably robust disaster recovery plan that was put into operation. Even though our headquarters was devastated, with the US financial markets closed, much of the New York office was able to decamp over the next few days to 'alternative accommodation' in New Jersey. When I visited our temporary home a little later, it looked like a refugee camp. It was nowhere near big enough to house the entire staff and some parts of the firm therefore occupied whole floors of hotels and squatted in various vacant office blocks around the city, while desks were shared, shift systems were put into operation and many had to work from home. But at least it allowed the firm's US operation to continue to function, albeit in relatively low gear. Lehman's net income fell 67% in the following quarter. In the meantime, the tragedy encouraged the management to look for a new permanent home. The search ultimately resulted in a move to Midtown and the bank's final resting place on Seventh Avenue, just north of Times Square.

Over the course of the days and weeks following 9/11, any number of stories emerged from the horror, all of them harrowing. In escaping Vesey Street, Jim was witness to people leaping to their deaths from the twin towers, and he recalled the sense of blind panic that gripped people as they desperately fought through the smoke and carnage to get away from the area. My ex-colleagues in the economics department saw similarly horrific things play out as they evacuated the scene. Ivan thankfully also escaped unscathed, although his decision to hire a car and immediately drive to Canada, from where he caught a plane back to the UK, was a reaction to events that was perhaps a trifle over the top. Two years later Lehman employees remained sufficiently disturbed by 9/11 and the 'War on Terror' that a significant number had holdalls under their trading desks containing spare clothes, a sleeping bag, water, antibiotics, iodine tablets and other emergency gear.

Once the immediate furore that surrounded 9/11 had died down, with the firm's future seemingly secure and the weekly publication launched and benefiting from the input of two new high-class analysts, one might imagine that I was left feeling good about things. But nothing could have been further from the truth. Yes, I

liked the young people in my team, and my management responsibilities, even if they occasionally presented a challenge, could
be rewarding. Yes, it was nice to be the figurehead for the team.
Yes, I continued to travel the world and, for the most part, my presentations were well received. Yes, I was still highly sought after for
media work. And yes, we produced some good research, including
a comprehensive matrix that brought together all the factors supposedly pertinent to a currency's performance in one place and
weighted them, and a path-breaking analysis of consensus foreign exchange forecasts that suggested that you could consistently
make money by betting against them! But I was uncomfortable in
the job from the word go, and I never got over that feeling. I missed
committing myself 100% to economics rather than the vagaries of
strategy. I missed 'doing' Japan. I disliked the violent mood swings
of the foreign exchange market, which I believe is the hardest of
all the markets to 'get right'. I found the short-term time horizon
of the traders and sales teams anathema (at one stage I was asked
to explore the construction of a trading model that would generate buy or sell signals on a minute-by-minute basis!). And my
relations with Ivan were fragile at best. We had several incendi-
ary moments, including at one morning meeting where his public
criticisms of my macro approach to foreign exchange markets led
me to walk out of the office and refuse to return until he apolo-
gised. I wasn't happy and I hankered after a return to my spiritual
home.

Looking back at the events of that time, the issues that I remember most clearly are the hubris that accompanied the death throes
of the dot-com boom, the initial weakness of the euro, the debate
over UK membership of the single currency, and what Japan's continued travails meant for the yen.

The global slowdown that ultimately turned into the first recession of the new millennium began around the time that I returned
to the UK in the middle of 2000. With monetary policy generally
having been on a tightening path since early 1999, equity markets
having turned sharply lower earlier in the year, and the dot-com
bubble rapidly deflating, this was anything but a surprise. My
relative pessimism, grounded in my experiences in Japan, was in
stark contrast to the attitude of my US colleagues, who had fully
embraced the new economy story. For the previous two years most
of the rest of Lehman's macro researchers had found their unbridled optimism hard to take and had fought a behind-the-scenes

battle to have it toned down and insert caveats into their astonishing conclusions about US productivity and growth potential. After all, the credibility of the entire group was at stake. But even once the US economy had clearly begun to slow in the second half of 2000 my New York colleagues retained an upbeat outlook.

What this episode underlined is that America is still a relatively young country built on optimism, and the habit of expecting a positive outcome extends to its economics fraternity, and even its policymaking community. One of my clearest memories of those first few months back in the UK is watching Fed chairman Alan Greenspan testify to Congress about how the US public finances, which had latterly moved into surplus for the first time in living memory, were now potentially in such good shape that not only were the $1.3trn of tax cuts proposed by George W. Bush in his presidential election campaign affordable, but all the nation's public debt could soon be repaid. This, he asserted, suggested that the Fed would need to draw up plans for the time when private sector assets, rather than Treasury bills and bonds, would necessarily dominate its open market operations.[30] We shouldn't worry about this, he added, as financial innovation would ensure that there would be a more than adequate supply of AAA-rated credits to utilise.

Talk about hubris. The implicit belief was that US policymakers, and in particular Greenspan and his Fed colleagues, had tamed the business cycle and that efficient markets would provide. I remember thinking to myself that this was wishful thinking, or at the very least a dangerous hostage to fortune. And so it proved. Within a decade the concern was that the US public debt position was unsustainable, efficient markets theory was to many a laughing stock, and there were precious-few AAA-rated assets for anyone to invest in at all.

Once again, the perils for economists of trying to differentiate the cyclical from the structural were there to see, as was the speed with which perceptions and conventional wisdom can change out of all recognition. Nevertheless, Greenspan should be ashamed of himself for the error he made and the false hopes he engendered, not least among politicians.

When I first took up the reins of foreign exchange research, or currency strategy, the euro was on the ropes, having been in a downtrend more or less constantly since its creation on 1 January 1999. The work done by Francis prior to my arrival and by my colleague Francesca Fornasari after I was in situ – to which I wholeheartedly subscribed – suggested that it was bilateral port-folio equity (including mergers and acquisitions) flows in the context of globalisation that had been doing much of the damage. However, we also took the view that the currency was becoming increasingly undervalued relative to fair value and that it would soon therefore rebound. But the rebound seemed to take a long time, or at least that was how my impatient and short-sighted sell-ing and trading colleagues saw it.

The position of senior management, who could say whatever they liked about the market (everyone's an economist) and never have to back it up coherently, was that the euro was only headed one way and that was down. This difference of opinion meant that from the word go I was under considerable pressure, with Ivan a continual critic.

Needless to say, when the euro was finally encouraged to turn by a bout of coordinated central bank intervention that was con-sistent with the relative monetary policy trajectories of the time, management views also underwent a 180-degree turn, and their error and the unpleasant things they had said about the foreign exchange research team were forgotten. Indeed, we came under pressure to produce more aggressive estimates of the single cur-rency's upside potential.

The euro also gave rise to a once-in-a-lifetime event: the practi-cal realisation of an entirely new major currency zone. When the initial set of euro notes and coins was launched on 1 January 2002 I was on my way back from a family break in Portugal, and I was therefore able to witness, and participate in, the process first hand. Indeed, as we trooped through Oporto airport to catch the return flight to Heathrow I remember trying to convince my uninterested children of the historical significance of what was playing out before their eyes as they bought the various items of confection-ery that were indispensable to surviving the journey home. And our painless experience that day was much the same as everyone else's: despite the unprecedented scale of the operation – the cash was simultaneously circulated in twelve countries with more than 300 million inhabitants – the changeover went remarkably well and the macro effects were modest.

There was one other way in which European Monetary Union occupied my attention at this time: the vexed issue of UK entry to the single currency. Lehman had, since the mid nineties, rightly developed a strong reputation for its European economic analysis. More than anything else this reflected the judgement of John Llewellyn, who, as a New Zealander, shouldered none of the narrow-minded Anglo-Saxon baggage that so many other London-based economists carried at this time. Moreover, as a former senior OECD official he had been privy to the discussions on this subject at the highest levels. From his first day at the bank in 1995 he had expressed the strong view that the euro was going to happen, and that it was going to happen more or less on time. And despite the deep-rooted scepticism of the firm's management he had stuck to his guns and been proven right. We were all able to bask in the glow of his prescience.

Recognising the particular politics of the issue in the UK, however, John's position on sterling's entry into the Eurozone was more equivocal and he took the decision to pass the bulk of the analysis and the responsibility for the firm's view on the matter to the firm's chief UK economist, Mike Dicks. We in foreign exchange research would provide input but it was going to be Mike's call. Mike was, and is, a fantastic technical economist. Better than I could ever claim to be. His grasp of modern theory is first rate, and his modelling skills are as good as those of any in the market. As a result, he would produce some of the most methodologically sound pieces of research to emerge from any research department in the City. But Mike could on occasion lack practical judgement.

In 2003 he produced a detailed assessment of the two core economic tests of the five that UK Chancellor Gordon Brown and his advisors had devised to determine when the UK would be ready to join the single currency (by the way, I have it on good advice from UK Treasury officials that there is nothing to the story that these were worked out by Brown's then economic advisor Ed Balls on the back of an envelope in the rear of a taxi).

The five tests were as follows.

- Were the business cycles and economic structures in the UK and the Eurozone compatible?

- Was the UK economy sufficiently flexible to absorb the sort of shocks it would face in future?

- Would Euro membership encourage long-term inward direct investment into the UK?

- How would entry impact the competitiveness of the UK's financial services sector?

- And, in general terms, would UK membership of the Euro-zone promote higher growth, stability and sustainable employment.

The two core tests were the first on this list: those of 'convergence' and 'flexibility'.

Mike's view was that the synchronicity of the two regions' cycles was about as close as it could ever be reasonably expected to get and that, notwithstanding the Eurozone's enduring structural rigidities, it made sense for Britain to make the jump sooner rather than later, not least as he feared that the UK was facing a period of exaggerated currency weakness and higher interest rates. My own view was more sceptical about both convergence and the immediate prospects for the pound and the UK economy. Moreover, UK membership of the euro would be an inherently political decision, and although both Prime Minister Tony Blair and Chancellor Gordon Brown were staunch pro-Europeans (indeed, on many levels Brown was more pro-Europe than Blair), Gordon Brown was by this stage a disaffected and bitter lieutenant and was fighting an undeclared war with the prime minister over who was the rightful leader of the Labour Party and the country. I just wasn't convinced, then, that either the economic or political stars were in alignment. But what I also feared was that this kind of call, ballsy though it was, was going to be as hard for us to sell to our audience in the world of foreign exchange – where I would necessarily be the point person – as it might be for Blair to sell to the disgruntled Brown, and for the British government to sell to the electorate. The danger was that a pro-euro call for the UK would prove to be a nightmare for the group as a whole and for me in particular.

Despite my misgivings I did my utmost to do the story justice on the road, but as I expected, it proved to be a tough task. Opposition to things European was often visceral, and people were not interested in the subtleties of our arguments. This was particularly the case in London and Edinburgh, where the Eurosceptics overwhelmingly dominated the asset management business, and in New York, where the hedge fund community took delight in trying to demolish questionable opinions. The bottom line was that on a couple of marketing trips I got a very rough ride and had to dig as deep as I have ever had to not to get completely overwhelmed by some less-than-open-minded counterparties. I thought I did a reasonable job given the hand I had been dealt, but I had no doubt that senior management would have got the message that I had struggled. The fact was that the vexed issue of sterling and the euro probably marked the beginning of the end of my period as Lehman's head of foreign exchange research.

Soon after this period the Treasury published a 250-page report (plus eighteen supporting studies)[31], on which as many as a hundred officials were at one time engaged, that, as I had feared, concluded that despite the UK having made progress towards passing the five tests, important issues of convergence and structural compatibility remained. Indeed, only one of the hurdles had been decisively cleared and the UK would therefore not be seeking membership within that parliament. Precisely how much this decision was political – and due to Gordon Brown's desire to undermine his boss – and how much was down to economic analysis is still debated, although I find it hard to believe that such an exhaustive examination of the pros and cons of UK entry could have been undertaken by so many officials and then had its conclusions gratuitously manipulated by the chancellor. Whatever the political considerations were, the Treasury concluded that the economics were just not right.

One of the hardest things for me to do when I was running foreign exchange research at Lehman Brothers was to leave Japan alone. But I had any number of other responsibilities, and we had also managed to encourage one of the best possible replacements to fill my shoes in Tokyo. Paul Sheard came to Lehman from Barings Asset Management and took over in late 2000. I had known Paul since the early nineties, when we both used to attend discussion sessions at the US embassy. I got on well with him and had a high opinion of his assiduously thought through views. A very different type of Australian to Ivan, he had lived and worked in Tokyo for almost two decades, including a spell at the Bank of Japan, and he was a fluent Japanese speaker. He was a class act, and he took Lehman's reputation for macro analysis on the Japanese economy to new levels, not least because he could get the message over to the locals.

With Paul providing superb analysis of the economy, and on the same page as me about its prospects, the one avenue left for me to offer an independent view of things Japanese was when it came to the yen. Just as I had feared before my departure from Tokyo, the economy slumped back into another deeply deflationary recession in 2001 in the face of the ill-fated tightening of monetary policy in August of the previous year and the onset of a global downturn. The last thing that Japan needed, then, was a strong exchange rate. Yet in both nominal and real effective terms, the yen had been trading through most of 2000 close to its all-time highs.

In March 2001 the Bank of Japan reversed the tightening of the previous August and announced that it was adopting a new framework for monetary policy based on a quantitative target for outstanding current account balances at the central bank (mainly consisting of central bank reserves), rather than a target for the overnight interbank call rate. This was initially set at ¥5trn and was coupled with stepped-up purchases of long-term government bonds. What is more, the bank announced a commitment to maintain this new policy until its preferred measure of annual core CPI inflation had 'stably' reached zero or above. So began the first modern-day experiment with quantitative easing (QE).

Despite the BOJ's apparent willingness to break new ground, and even though the economy began to pull out of its latest slump in 2002, the yen remained relatively strong and falling prices were a fact of life. My sense, therefore, was that the BOJ needed to do more; much more, in fact, if a sustained recovery was to ensue and deflation was to be defeated. The yen needed to depreciate considerably. The problem was that while my belief that the Japanese currency should fall proved reasonably accurate, it didn't fall by nearly enough. The primary reason was that the BOJ was such a cautious convert to QE. In seeking to fight deflation, the BOJ was its own worst enemy.

As early as the late nineties I recall having discussions with BOJ officials about the pros and cons of QE, and the overwhelming attitude to it was one of scepticism. I also remember a return visit to the same officials in Tokyo around this time when I was told that QE was largely a 'PR exercise'. The refrain was: 'we have to be seen to be doing something about deflation, not least to keep the politicians off our backs, but we doubt QE will do much good beyond keeping the financial sector liquid'.

Expectations are very important in modern monetary theory. If a central bank can convince the public that it is fully committed to, and has the tools to achieve, a certain inflation target, then it helps the public to believe it will happen and such beliefs can become self-fulfilling. But the BOJ never did this. Rather, it continued to suggest that non-monetary considerations were largely responsible for deflation and that monetary policy could do little about it. This is the worst sort of expectations management. It acted to entrench deflation in the economy. Indeed, it created a perverse outcome: the BOJ was able to argue that continuing deflation was evidence that it was right all along.

CHAPTER 10

A WINDOW SEAT

Towards the end of 2003 John informed me that: 'he wanted me back in economics'. This initially came across as music to my ears. But the fact was that management were in the midst of a major recalibration of macro research and the subscript was that the powers that be wanted me out of foreign exchange. John, in his customary gentlemanly fashion, was letting me down gently.

Ivan had left the firm early in the year when, having pocketed his bonus, he succumbed to generous overtures made to him by Barclays. My initial reaction was one of relief, but his exit did nothing to help Lehman's foreign exchange business and little to improve my position within it. The year 2003 was a tough one for Lehman: the foreign exchange business had invested heavily in personnel since 2000 and increasingly the view was that foreign exchange research was top heavy. Moreover, the desire was for a 'real' foreign exchange person, rather than a converted economist, to run the show, and Jim McCormick fitted that bill better than I. He was the natural candidate to fill my shoes and an internal campaign to make this happen gathered momentum through the course of the year.

By December 2003 I had been moved out of foreign exchange and become chief international economist, the same title I held at UBS between 1993 and 1995, only this time I had no team to manage, no product to coordinate, no obvious role as an honest broker to fill. Indeed, neither I nor anyone else had much idea what I was meant to do. I was sent to give a couple of speeches which no one else was interested in doing: one on Japan's economic crisis to a conference at the Anderson Business School at UCLA and another on the future of the European Union at a conference in St Moritz. These events might sound attractive and the trips were devoid of the usual litany of client meetings, but they weren't exactly career enhancing. I had been saved from the sack but my fear was that it was merely a temporary stay of execution. By this stage I could hardly be described as irreplaceable.

My situation reminded me of a wonderful Japanese expression: *Mado-giwa*, which means 'a window seat'. Because of the traditional reluctance to shed staff, employees of Japanese companies who have passed their prime (or proven themselves unreliable) are sometimes given much-decreased workloads and seats by the window to help them while away the hours. *Mado-giwa* employees are typically middle managers who have outwardly impressive titles but no subordinates and little responsibility. Their fate is a kind of in-house semi-retirement. The only difference between the *Mado-giwa* and me was that I didn't even have a seat by the window! I initially occupied the spare desk in the economics department.

It was around this time that I began to keep a diary, and looking back through my initial entries, I was pretty low and uncertain about my future. Nor was my mood helped by the news that, despite the fact that I had been in the business for more than eighteen years and occupied a number of senior positions around the world, Lehman's compliance department insisted that I do the FSA exam to prove that I was qualified to dispense investment advice to customers. I understand why the UK financial authorities had become keener for employees to know what they were doing and to be aware of the legal framework within which they worked – after all, I had seen more than enough incompetence, stupidity and brazen distribution of disinformation over the years – but I don't think that I was necessarily the problem (or maybe, as subsequent events were to indicate, I was).

The process involved the sort of cramming of facts that I thought I had left behind in my teens. It also saw me take the exam with a group who looked like they were still *in* their teens! I resented this episode and saw it as a humiliation and a further indication of my reduced status. After all, in Japan the authorities had waved me through because of my experience, and that was eight years earlier, when, in Japanese terms, I was still a spring chicken. But at least I managed to pass. The stigma and shame of failing would have been appalling. I should add that some people who were forced to take the exam at a similar stage in their professional lives did fail it and had to take it again.

My fear was that my career was now on the slide and that I would soon have to look for another job. I was acutely aware that I was already old for the business. In fact, a year earlier, when he was undertaking one of his intermittent tactless mickey-taking assaults on me, Ivan had worked out that even then, at 43, I was the fourth-oldest employee on the trading floor! I even actively considered asking to be paid off, so that I could start to build an alternative career. The problem was that I couldn't think of anything else that I could do.

In the end, thanks to John's support, it was decided that I should become the equity division's economist, but again no one quite seemed to know how I was to perform the role. There was no available job description. Moreover, although my responsibilities at both UBS and Lehman had at times meant that I worked closely with the equity division, I had always considered myself to be much more of a bond economist in that I was focused on macro issues, and in particular monetary and fiscal policy, rather than sectoral or micro research. But if I wanted to survive and thrive, I was going to have to take the initiative and fashion a role for myself that was separate from the well-regarded Lehman Brothers equity strategy group. At this stage I wrote in my diary that I thought my chances of survival at Lehman were 60:40.

I determined that I would concentrate on my comparative advantages: keeping the trading floor up to speed about anything macro that was relevant, acting as a mouthpiece for the global economics team as a whole, and writing in-depth pieces of research on contemporary global issues that would be of interest to senior equity fund managers and CIOs. Furthermore, I would try to get as much media exposure as possible in the hope that it might encourage another firm to come looking for me.

My views at the time were cautious (too cautious, as it turned out) about the strength of the global recovery and fearful about the accumulation of household debt and the development of regional imbalances. My sense was that the latter represented important underlying sources of fragility for the cyclical upswing. This proved to be accurate, of course, but only five years into the future.

Over the next year I regularly co-authored a publication called *Damocles* with Rob Subbaraman in Asia. *Damocles* looked at the susceptibility of the emerging markets to 'sudden stops' in capital inflows and also included a number of extended essays or 'think pieces'. *Damocles* attracted positive attention from the press and even from the US Treasury (and later the UK Treasury), both of which asked us for the details of the model, and the extended essays included an assessment of whether the US and Europe were likely to go the way of Japan and experience an extended period of deflation and quasi-recession: our answer at that stage was a definitive 'no'. In addition, with policy rates in a number of economies (and not least in the US) close to historical lows, I put together a survey of the options available as nominal interest rates approached the zero bound. Needless to say, this drew heavily on my academic research of the early eighties and on my experiences in Japan and concluded that both central banks and governments had plenty of unorthodox weaponry that they could draw on, should the need arise. I was subsequently to revisit and revise these reports repeatedly during the Global Financial Crisis.

What I also did was travel the world, sometimes on my own and sometimes with Ian Scott, who headed the equity strategy group and with whom I got on well. Indeed, there was hardly a week without a business trip of some sort. This was pretty exhausting, especially given the parental responsibilities that went with having a couple of teenage daughters. As a result I found myself a more regular visitor than I had ever been to Lehman's New York headquarters (the new Midtown building rather than Vesey Street). In March 2002, after a period in which the bank's New York operations had been spread out across no fewer than forty different locations, Lehman had moved into a set of brand new offices.

While I have always loved visiting New York – over the course of my career, marketing trips there proved to be both some of the most challenging and some of the most enlightening – I have found the New York office of every bank I worked for a place I wanted to avoid, and 745 Seventh Avenue was no exception. Although I made some good friends there, I could never understand how they managed to spend their working lives in the place. The atmosphere at Lehman HQ was coloured by posturing, paranoia, stress, fear and greed. Testosterone, insincerity and self-interest were everywhere. Teamwork took second place to the individual. Each salesperson or trader sat at their desk, hunched up and furrow browed, in what seemed to be his or her own private silo, from which they barely budged from 6.00 or 6.30 in the morning until 5.30 in the evening. Their phones were semi-permanently welded to their ears, contacts were jealously guarded, important counterparties were treated with fawning subservience, and underlings were bossed around unashamedly.

Meanwhile, the business heads inhabited their own, largely separate, world on the upper floors of the building, only occasionally deigning to descend to the trading floors, and the investment bankers operated on what amounted to their own pampered and exclusive planet. Despite the outward self-confidence and bravado, people's lives seemed neither balanced nor happy. There was more than an element of the desperate. All that mattered was the next trade, the next sale and, of course, the next bonus.

As far as the attitude of those who worked in the New York office to me was concerned, my reputation from Japan stood me in good stead, while many Americans were a little bamboozled, if not even intimidated, by the well-spoken Brit. Notwithstanding the differences of opinion over the US economy's growth potential in the late nineties, I always got on well with my US economist colleagues. There was a sense that we were in this together: a team of much-maligned and misunderstood economists against the world. With salespeople, traders and management it was more hit and miss. For the most part there was studious politeness. On the other hand, though, you were left under no illusions that you were expected to be able to cope with the clients, however unpleasant they might be, and no prisoners were ever taken in terms of scheduling. Days marketing in New York could be utterly relentless, starting with a 7 a.m. breakfast and going through to an evening dinner, while in the meantime you shuttled up and down Manhattan in taxis or were ferried out in sleek black limos, often cat-napping on the back seat, to the upstate towns that housed various hedge funds. In New York you also always knew that if you were perceived to no longer be of use, they would have absolutely no qualms about ushering you to the door. Thank you and goodnight.

I suppose I would characterise it as the most intense variant of capitalism that you could experience. It intimidated me. It left me cold. It exhausted me and it pained me. It made me glad to be a Brit and glad to be someone who was less gripped by that particular religion. I was relieved to be an outsider looking in.

This period also saw the drums of war beating louder, as the Bush Administration increasingly focused on the removal from power of Saddam Hussein, who, all too conveniently, was suddenly tarred with the same brush as Al Qaida. Then, of course, in March

2003 the US and its 'coalition of the willing', which included the UK, invaded Iraq. This resulted in some deep divisions between the European and US arms of Lehman Brothers.

In the US the sense of outrage that went with 9/11, and the perception that all should pull together behind the Commander-in-Chief, meant that criticism of the Bush Administration was pretty much non-existent, and such criticism as there was was considered almost treasonous. In Europe the standard response was much more questioning of US motives and actions, which had already mutated alarmingly once 9/11 let the Bush Administration's neocons off their leash. Personally, I found US foreign policy almost Orwellian. I was aghast at Washington's jingoism and the seeming belief that US values were the only legitimate ones – that the rest of the world was either with them or against them. This was ridiculously simplistic and dangerous. US foreign policy was sounding more and more like a moral crusade – indeed, it was itself a sort of fundamentalism. Against this background, the limpet-like commitment of the Blair government to the US over this period grated. For all their self-serving obnoxiousness, I was with the French! This was particularly the case when, on one trip to a favourite New York bistro, I was offered 'freedom fries' with my steak. I declined but at great expense ordered the best bottle of Bordeaux on the wine list.

Once the inevitable US invasion of Iraq took place, at John Llewellyn's initiative we began to look at the lessons that history could offer as to the likely outcome. As early as March 2003 we had presented figures that suggested – largely on the basis of UK experience in Northern Ireland – that the US-led coalition in Iraq had insufficient security forces at its disposal to restore, and then maintain, order and stability. A year later, with the Coalition Provisional Authority about to hand over a measure of political control to the Iraqis, we revisited the issue, drawing on all the post-conflict occupations since the end of World War II. I provided a good deal of the input, working with John and John Dew, a clever diplomat who was on secondment to Lehman Brothers from the UK Foreign Office. Two conclusions from our analysis stood out.

First, no post-World War II occupation of a country had been successful at a 'force ratio' of less than twenty troops per thousand head of population. And indeed some occupations – most notably the French in Algeria – failed even with a force ratio of nearly forty. To try to bring order and stability to Iraq with a force ratio of just six, and to Afghanistan with a force ratio of less than one, as was then the intention, was to attempt something that had never been achieved.

Second, while order and stability are necessary precursors of political, administrative and economic reform, the belief that political, administrative and economic reform will be delivered is also essential to achieving order and stability. People who do not believe that they are going to get the political change they desire will resist the occupying forces, often with considerable vigour. The challenge is to enter a virtuous circle rather than a vicious one.

The implication was that, as then configured, US policy in Iraq was highly unlikely to prove successful. Indeed, judging by the force ratio number it was ludicrous. And so it proved. During the course of 2003 Iraq sank deeper and deeper into a Vietnam-like quagmire. Subsequently, the only time that the US force ratio came remotely close to that required was during the 'surge', which was designed not so much to sustainably stabilise Iraq as to facilitate the orderly departure of US troops. Ten years on Iraq is broken: riven by sectarian tensions, violent, corrupt, poverty stricken and addicted to foreign aid (much of it American). It's a tragic indictment of US (and UK) foreign policy about which I feel ashamed. So much for 'freedom'.

Tragically, our full forty-odd-page report never saw the light of day.[32] Despite the fact that we went out of our way to present the findings in a non-partisan manner, New York considered it too inflammatory and likely to hurt the firm in the US, not least in its relations with the Bush Administration in the run-up to a presidential election. John was furious. In fact so were all of us who contributed to what was a superb piece of work. In the meantime, a great opportunity for Lehman to demonstrate the breadth, depth and objectivity of analysis its economics team could offer and its ability to handle controversial subjects with both gravitas and sensitivity was lost.

Putting together the report did throw up one entertaining moment, however. One day, we invited a number of researchers in from the UK Foreign Office for lunch with a view to picking their brains, and I was amazed to find that one of the more senior people was an old acquaintance from my first year at Bristol. We had got on well enough, but in those days he used to dress like a tramp, have greasy hair down to his waist, and was noted for walking around the city in bare feet and cocooned in a fog of marijuana.

His attire and general deportment had changed out of all recognition between 1978 and 2003, and I made no mention of his old habits in front of his colleagues. We did, however, enjoy a great chat about old times afterwards. I won't comment on the similarities with my own appearance, demeanour or social habits thirty-odd years earlier, beyond saying that I always wore shoes.

Towards the end of 2004 Lehman began to move its London headquarters from Broadgate – which, twenty years on, was shoddy, infested with mice and no longer the state-of-the-art complex it had been when I first went there with Hoare Govett – to a new purpose-built office in Canary Wharf. The equity division were the first to make the jump, and I was therefore in the first group to relocate. For a couple of months I was the only economist on site and I was determined to make a positive impression. I therefore chose this juncture to begin writing a weekly comment piece that I loosely tied to global equity market and asset allocation trends.

With its two cavernous purpose-built trading floors, every piece of modern technology imaginable, lecture theatres, TV studios, a gym, cafes, restaurants, copious office space (even I qualified for both a desk on the trading floor and my own room on a separate floor), an underground car park and exquisite views of the London skyline from its upper levels, 25 Bank Street was impressive. Indeed, it was sufficiently impressive that, in due course, it would be formally opened by Gordon Brown.

This gesture from the British government came at a time when its attitude towards the City was altogether more positive than it was to become four years later. Indeed, I remember nothing but gushing praise for the City's innovation, its dynamism, its huge contribution to Britain's balance of payments and its supposed new-found stability in the chancellor's brief accompanying speech. Meanwhile, to put on a show for both Mr Brown and the assembled press, Lehman's PR team had briefed those of us on the trading floor to pick up phones, wave our arms about, bellow market-speak and generally raise the level of noise on what was a pretty quiet day. The next time you see a busy trading floor on the TV news you are probably watching something that has been stage managed.

Notwithstanding the palatial surroundings in which we now found ourselves, for the vast majority of Lehman Brothers employees, the move was an inconvenience. Most, like me, lived in the wealthier suburbs of London's north, south and west. The east of the city was rarely visited except under sufferance. Despite seeing myself as more in touch with the real world than most of my co-workers, prior to working there I couldn't remember the last time I had been beyond Tower Bridge, apart from while competing in the London marathon in 2002 and 2003 and on the odd visit to see West Ham play football.

At a stroke my own personal commute was greatly extended. Every day I would now be travelling right across London and back. That said, while one was at 25 Bank Street it was a wonderful place to work. Canary Wharf had come a long way by 2004. It was undoubtedly an impressive architectural development, and the infrastructure connecting it to the rest of London was first rate. The quality of the cafes, restaurants, bars and shops in the vicinity was high, and there was some excellent housing to be had in the area. The problem was that it still felt so detached from the rest of London. It was like a bubble into which one was injected for twelve hours a day, five days a week.

Despite the excitement of the move to Canary Wharf and the fact that I was in such demand in terms of marketing, my sense was that my career was drifting. Part of the problem was that when I wasn't marketing I had little to do. My diaries for this period suggest I was either rushed off my feet seeing clients or kicking my heels back in the office, often in a state of chronic jet-lag. Having no economy for which I was formally responsible meant that I was excluded from the day-to-day imperatives of data watching and number crunching that most of my colleagues in the economics department were subject to. It also meant that anything I wrote threatened to impinge on others' territory and result in resentment. Indeed, on one or two occasions John told me that I was being seen as undermining his authority as chief economist. This cut deep. He was the last person I wanted to hurt. It was a difficult role to fulfil and one that I was not at all convinced that I wanted to stay in.

At the end of the year, although my bonus was satisfactory, I was passed over for promotion. Not only that, but Jim McCormick, who I had recruited to replace me as head of foreign exchange research, was made managing director. And what is more, my involvement in the annual round of economic conferences that Lehman held across Europe was reduced to a marginal role and I was completely left off the list of presenters for the US and Asian legs. I felt humiliated and considered resigning. After due consultation with my ever-sensible wife, however, I decided that the wiser course was to step up my search for opportunities elsewhere and look to leave on my own terms.

In May I engineered an opportunity to do this. Over the previous six months I had struck up an excellent relationship with Alan Lewis, who ran Sthenos Capital, a hedge fund that specialised in equities. Whenever I visited him we would chew the fat about the global economy at great length, and even if we didn't always agree, we enjoyed the process and learned a lot from each other. Alan had made his reputation, and a considerable amount of money, working under Louis Bacon at Moore Capital, and his fund had done extremely well over the previous couple of years. Although he was American he had been brought up in Europe and spoke fluent French, and he therefore tended to have a broader view of the world than most of his countrymen. One Friday afternoon, at a loose end, I retreated to my office, picked up the phone, called him and asked him straight out if he might need an economist. Although he was clearly taken aback by my direct approach, he asked me in to discuss the idea.

Alan's issue, quite rightly, was how he was going to 'monetise' my skills. After all, he already had access to many of the best brains in the London markets, so why did he need someone like me in house? At his behest I put together a business plan for my integration into Sthenos. To my mind, the overarching rationale for my recruitment essentially boiled down to three things: supply (of high-quality economic analysis) would create its own demand within the firm; my presence would allow him to do more of what he was good at, which was trading stocks; and the fund was about to start diversifying into Japan, where I knew that I could bring a level of expertise that was not readily available elsewhere.

My expectations were low but Alan called up one morning towards the end of July and said that he thought we could do a deal and asked me to come over to work out the details. I was in a cab and on my way towards the West End within a couple of minutes. To say that I was excited by the prospect of working with him and confronting some new challenges in a different sort of environment would be an understatement. All I had to do now was resign.

And resigning was easier said than done. I began by phoning John Llewellyn on the Sunday evening to tell him of my intentions. He had been a close friend, a kindred spirit and a mentor. I was going to miss him enormously. Working with John had been an education and a pleasure. He expressed sadness but was understanding, and he offered to do what he could to smooth my exit and prevent Lehman from attaching too many conditions relating to my departure. The next day I went into the office to attend to the formalities. To my surprise I was greeted by a series of senior Lehman executives who at least went through the motions of persuading me to stay. Suddenly I was a vital member of the team, my elevation to managing director was virtually assured at the end of the year, and I was being asked what it would take to make me change my mind. I found all this a bit rich, a bit late in the day, and to be indicative of the way the firm worked, which was summed up in the phrase 'never give anything up unless you have to'. I rebuffed their efforts to turn me round and later headed over to Sthenos to sign the necessary paperwork.

I had drawn a line under ten years of my life. Much of it had been wonderful, some of it a trial – but precious little of it had been dull. I had had my time in the sun while in Japan, but foreign exchange research had not worked out and now my career had rather lost its way. What was also clear was that the thrill had gone and I needed something new. But first I needed some time off to decompress and gird my loins for the challenges ahead.

Mick and I spent much of the next two months down at the small cottage that we had bought on the south coast on our return from Tokyo. There, I passed the time running, walking along the beach, watching the sunset and local wildlife, drinking pints of beer in the village pub, reading and not getting up at 5.30 a.m. It was blissful. We also headed up to the west coast of Scotland, where we toured around in the car for a week before heading off for a ten-day break in Greece with the girls. By the time I was due to start at Sthenos's office in the St James district of the West End in early September, I was rested, fit and raring to go.

CHAPTER 11

HEDGED OUT

What followed over the next four months was one of the saddest and strangest periods of my professional career. While I had been away recharging my batteries, Alan's marriage ran into trouble and, with two young daughters to worry about, he understandably took his eye off the ball a little at work. What is more, that summer saw global equity markets hit what can best be described as an air pocket. By the time I walked into the Sthenos office, the fund had gone from earning a good return for the year to date to being very much in the hole. Indeed, some investors had already indicated that they could soon pull their money out, and within a week of my arrival Alan had decided to let two of his younger fund managers go.

Notwithstanding the fact that I had by this stage become inured to most things in the financial markets, this was a shock to me. I was assured, though, that it had no real implications for me. The fund was refocusing its efforts a little and the two individuals in question had not quite delivered. Mollified, if still uneasy, I turned my attention to the job in hand, which was rather different to the roles I was used to. There was no longer any need for me to market to endless clients. There was no longer any need for me to have a media presence. There was no longer any need to write anything for external publication. Rather, I became a filter for the macro research provided by our counterparties and by others, I had to write a single 'position paper' every week on my thoughts on the world, and I started to assemble a global asset allocation framework to help guide the firm's investment decisions.

Meanwhile, I suddenly found myself a focus of attention for a vast array of economists and strategists from around the world, and I was in a position to pick the brains of the best in the business. Instead of travelling the globe in an effort to impress people like

Alan, people like my former self were travelling the world in an effort to impress me. What is more, I became a target for any number of simpering faux-enthusiastic salespeople, not least those from Lehman, who were desperate to please. The best tickets to concerts and sports fixtures were made available. Lunch and dinner invitations at the best restaurants in the West End and the City were numerous. Difficult-to-source macroeconomic and market data were delivered in double quick time. Tough questions were answered in minute detail. Meetings with key policymakers were organised. I was, as it were, now seeing how the other half lived. However, I should also add that I turned most of the invitations down and, given my own sometimes-painful experiences on the sell side of the business, I went out of my way to be as polite as possible. In the meantime, I learned a huge amount.

The overall working environment at Sthenos was so much more congenial and pleasant than had been the case at the banks and investment banks that I had worked for previously. The firm's location in the West End meant that when I left the office, rather than being surrounded by other City types, I was now in the midst of people who, for the most part, had nothing to do with finance. My commute was significantly reduced and despite still being in the office at 7 a.m. each morning I was not having to get up quite so early. I no longer had to wear a suit and tie every day, although as my entire wardrobe consisted of either suits or old jeans, T-shirts and shorts, I tended to wear one anyway. Breakfast and lunch were provided from a selection of St James's finest takeaways. The attitude to expenses was to treat you like a responsible grown up rather than someone whose sole intention was to rip the company off. And if I didn't want to spend my lunch hour running around central London's Royal Parks, we had a gym and a disconcertingly young and attractive female personal trainer on site, and she was only too happy to invent new ways to torture you.

In October 2004, just a month after my arrival, Alan sent me off on a fact-finding tour across northern Asia. The idea was to get some insights into the increasingly important Chinese economy and the economies of its satellites and, ahead of our planned venture into Japanese equities, to see how my old stomping ground was getting on. For the Japan leg I was able to make use of the numerous contacts I had developed there during my residency, but for the rest of the trip I prevailed upon the unstinting generosity of the fund's counterparties to set up a series of meetings with policy-makers and their own analysts.

I had an absolute ball on this ten-day trip, hoovering up the mass of information proffered and rediscovering some of the Asian cities with which I had once been so familiar. The Chinese part of the tour was particularly fascinating, and I came back much better informed about the sustainability of its development than I had previously been. Whatever the horrors of the city's pollution and traffic, the policymakers I met during my few days in Beijing were impressive, as was the overwhelming sense of burgeoning wealth. I have no doubt that at some stage the various tensions and imbalances in the Chinese economy and across the nation as a whole will generate some sort of serious trauma or traumas. That, after all, is what happens in emerging economies, and especially in those where the dominant development model and the political system are so at odds with one another. But my sense after the trip was that China might be rather better equipped to get through such periods of crisis than I had previously believed.

Japan, on the other hand, I found depressing. Yes, the economy had recovered from the recession of 2002. Yes, the banks had finally been comprehensively recapitalised and restructured. Yes, the Bank of Japan had embraced quantitative easing. And yes, there had even been the odd bout of supply-side reform. But the flip side was that deflation, not least of land prices, had continued apace, and deflationary expectations were ever more deeply embedded.

When I talked to my old contacts at the BOJ, some of whom were now in much more senior positions than they had been in the nineties, they had little confidence in quantitative easing beyond its role in ensuring that the financial sector had more than adequate sources of liquidity. They adopted it because they had to be seen to be doing something. If the central bank itself was unconvinced of its potency, no wonder, I concluded, that the effects were so disappointing. In the modern era, so much about what central banks do relates to expectations management. If the BOJ was telling people that its policy regime was fundamentally flawed, it was unlikely to encourage the desired result.

Where the supply side of the economy was concerned, the tax system remained remarkably inefficient and skewed towards incentive-destroying direct taxes, little had been done to liberalise agriculture or services, and the vexed issues of female participation and immigration, that were so important to addressing the nation's rapidly ageing population structure, remained largely untouched. Finally, public sector finances had continued to spiral out of control, which was hardly surprising given the absence of nominal growth.

During that trip I also took the opportunity to pay a visit to one of the Cold War's last frontiers. Rather than spend the weekend in Hong Kong or Tokyo, I opted to spend it in Seoul, and on the Saturday morning I headed out on one of the official tours to the border with North Korea, which is just over 50 km outside South Korea's huge modern capital. I had some unfinished business with North Korea. Towards the end of my residency in Tokyo, the head of the Lehman office had suggested that I and an electronics analyst go to the country, which was then in the midst of one of its intermittent 'open' periods, on a fact-finding tour, the hope being that it might soon be 'open for business'. Notwithstanding the horrors of the North Korean regime, I looked upon the idea with enthusiasm: it was a unique opportunity. But sadly, the trip never happened – first, because I opted to go back to London, and second, because this particular period of 'glasnost' proved to be rather short lived.

The border between North and South Korea is one of the strangest and most sinister places that I have ever visited. The highway to the border is peppered with gun emplacements, and the fields to either side are riven with tank traps. Across the road itself are any number of solid concrete 'bridges' that can be blown up in such a way as to collapse on to the carriageway in the event of invasion. Security at the border itself was intense. There were extraordinarily fit-looking South Korean soldiers everywhere. Supposedly because of the threat of snipers, one was allowed to survey the demilitarised zone and North Korea itself only via special periscopic binoculars from an army observation post some way back from the border. The narrow fenced-off demilitarised zone that has separated the two Koreas since 1953 and that runs from one coast of the peninsula to the other was, bizarrely enough, a natural paradise in which flora and fauna have flourished undisturbed, although one could also see the odd wrecked tank or rusty old gun here and there. Beyond the barbed wire, the part of North Korea abutting the demilitarised zone had been denuded of trees, not for military reasons but to heat the population in nearby towns and cities. The most visible evidence that one was actually looking into the world's last bastion of communism was the nearby 160-metre-high flagpole and North Korean flag weighing 270 kg, together with the incessant anti-capitalist propaganda being broadcast through massive loudspeakers.

Panmunjom, the village straddling the border where the 1953 ceasefire treaty was signed, was as scary as I had been led to believe. There was the most extraordinary tension in the air as minutely choreographed, long-standing military rituals were played out. The soldiers from each side patrol in twos, armed to the teeth and wearing mirrored sunglasses to protect their identities (or was it to prevent being hypnotised?) as they face off against each other, sometimes separated by only a few metres. But there was one crack in the facade of mutual distrust and hostility. To the west of Panmunjom, I watched a line of trucks being escorted across the demilitarised zone before snaking its way towards the Kaesong Industrial Zone, where 120-odd South Korean companies employed more than 50,000 North Korean workers, in the process helping to generate much-needed foreign exchange for the pariah state.

Later I also paid my respects at the British war memorial, visited the bridge where over the years hundreds of prisoners of war have been exchanged, and had a look at the brand new railway station that the South Korean government had optimistically built in anticipation of the day when trains would run from Seoul to Pyongyang. On a whim I then decided that I would venture down one of the four tunnels that the North Koreans had dug under the border over the years with a view to launching a surprise attack on the South. As it happens they were caught in the act, and today one can enter these extraordinary feats of engineering from the South Korean side: they run seventy-five metres below the surface, the bedrock is solid granite, they were dug out by hand, and all in all they stretch nearly a kilometre under the demilitarised zone. They are just about large enough for a man to stand up in and for light equipment, including small armoured cars or even tanks, to be transported through. At the end there is a concrete wall that marks the border. Never have I been so pleased to escape a confined space, and never have I been so pleased to return to the sanctuary of my five-star hotel, where I had just one question on my lips: 'How does the 10.5 million population of Seoul live with this threat every day of their lives?'

I returned from my Asian trip in a state of elevated enthusiasm and wrote an extended report on my findings for my colleagues. I loved the job. My wife said that she couldn't believe the transformation in me since my departure from Lehman. Unfortunately, however, my mood was soon to be deflated in dramatic style. While I was in Asia, Sthenos had continued to haemorrhage money. In early December I noted that a stressed-looking Alan was increasingly spending his days locked in his office. Soon I found myself called into a meeting of the entire firm at which he dropped the bombshell that he was going to wind up the entire operation. Although we were down only 5% for the year, we were facing redemptions that could total $500mn out of a $750mn fund. As of the end of December we would all be unemployed.

I was stunned but, however painful, Alan's logic was sound. With the firm's investors obviously increasingly impatient, he felt that the fund had two choices: either we could 'swing the bat', take some exaggerated risks, and see if we could make back the money we had lost, or we could wind things up, return the money invested in the fund and move on, our reputations intact. This would also allow him to put his private affairs in order. He thought the second option best, and it was hard to disagree. In taking this course of action, Alan set himself apart from so many others in the financial industry, and especially those who populate the world of hedge funds. I have no doubt that many in his situation would have taken a different tack, relegating the potential to hurt investors to a less important role and in the process taking much more reputational risk.

Over the course of the next couple of months, the firm's positions were run down and money was distributed to those who had placed it with us, the irony being that global markets were subsequently sufficiently buoyant that by mid 2005, had we stood pat, Sthenos would have once again been comfortably in the black. Alan announced the firm's closure at the end-of-year wine tasting that he held for our counterparties, which needless to say included senior Lehman Brothers representatives. It would be an understatement to say that jaws dropped. I drowned my sorrows with copious quantities of the best Burgundy that money could buy and then walked home in the small hours from the West End to Barnes. Courtesy of Alan's generosity the staff had one last hurrah at a French restaurant in Pimlico where many more glasses were emptied and tears were shed, and that was it. There was nothing that I could do to help in the winding-up process, although I continued to use the office until 21 December to start my job search. It was time to roll the dice again.

My hedge fund career therefore proved to be an all too brief affair. The new beginning I had hoped to enjoy never happened. Indeed, my basic salary at Sthenos was the same as it had been at Lehman, and that in turn had not changed since 2000. But at least I hadn't lost anything, apart from some pride. I am also glad that I had the opportunity to spend those few months there as I enjoyed it and I learned a lot. And when people question the morals of those who work in the financial markets and in particular of those in the hedge fund community, I am only too happy to tell them about how Alan Lewis behaved. He was a man of honour and integrity.

CHAPTER 12

BANISHED TO
THE DESERT

I spent the 2004/5 holiday season licking my wounds. Foremost
in my mind was the feeling that I should never have left Lehman Brothers. But there was no going back. That bridge had
been well and truly burned. Alan had promised to bear me in
mind when he began his next project, but it was unclear what that
would be or when it would come to fruition. As it happened, our
career paths were from that moment on to diverge inexorably, and
our partnership was never to be rekindled. I regret that to this day.

Meanwhile, the offers of help from both former Lehman colleagues and others that were made in good faith prior to Christmas tended to be forgotten in the New Year. People had moved on.
By the end of January the only statement of interest in my services
had come courtesy of an old UBS Tokyo colleague now working
for the Abu Dhabi Investment Authority (ADIA). ADIA's Treasury
Department was looking for a chief economist and had asked me
to go over for an interview.

ADIA was the world's largest sovereign wealth fund and an
investor that I had been talking to in my various professional
incarnations for more than a decade. They knew me and I knew
them. Despite the mystery surrounding what it did and how it did
it, it was also an institution that was so large, and its market influence so pervasive, that every sell-side entity in the world was desperate to have a relationship with it. This was attractive, as was the
fact that the money, although not in the same league as my Lehman salary, was lightly taxed. On the other hand, it would mean
moving to Abu Dhabi: hardly the world's most glamorous or cosmopolitan city and with a horrific climate to boot. I had been there

on business trips when the daytime temperature was nudging 50 degrees centigrade and it was impossible to venture outside for more than a few minutes. The family issues were also huge. Both our girls were in good schools in west London and doing well. Both sets of grandparents were getting on. Nevertheless, we decided that I should at least go out to Abu Dhabi for the interview and that my wife should come with me for a 'look see'.

Our two-and-a-half-day visit to the Gulf had mixed results. ADIA's interest was keen and the interview process, which included a day of rather unnerving psychometric tests, went well. But Abu Dhabi, although it had come a long way since I first visited it in the early eighties, was a dry and arid place, and not just climatically. Moreover, the overriding concern for us both was that the schooling on offer for the girls was unimpressive by comparison with London. We returned home hoping that something else would come up so that we wouldn't have to worry about Abu Dhabi.

But nothing did, and when ADIA came back to me in late February to offer me the job, I felt under huge pressure to take it. As one headhunter had put it to me at the time, the 'half-life' of an unemployed senior economist was pretty short, and opportunities like the one with ADIA were few and far between. When I consulted them, Paul Chertkow, John Llewellyn and Alan Lewis all recommended that I take the position, although they were looking at things very much from the professional end of the spectrum. My wife's position was different and I was torn. It was a horrible time and I couldn't help asking myself how we had ended up in this situation.

In the end, with ADIA's help, we hatched a compromise. I would relocate to Abu Dhabi while my family would remain in the UK, but for ten months out of twelve I would work one week a month out of London, where I could see counterparties and get on with any written projects I had. As the holiday allowance at ADIA was extraordinarily generous by investment banking standards, this would not actually involve my taking much unpaid leave. And, of course, Mick and the girls would be able to come out to the Gulf during school holidays. In this way we hoped to minimise the disturbance to the family. The cost of the flights was going to rack up, but so would the air miles, and the arrangement would allow us to continue to give the girls the best education possible and at least a semblance of a normal home life. In the meantime, my wife and I were confident that our marriage could survive. It was a question of needs must. And so my career underwent another extraordinary twist.

In late April 2005, I arrived in Abu Dhabi, checking into the soulless modernity that was the Millennium Hotel on a sultry Sunday evening in preparation for my first day in the office. Saying goodbye to the family that morning was probably the hardest thing I have ever done in my life, and the sense of frustration and emptiness that engulfed me over the course of that weekend is hard to put into words. The only way I could survive was by focusing on my first visit home, throwing myself into the job, and wading through the bureaucratic labyrinth that greeted an expatriate landing in the UAE.

Abu Dhabi was a massive contrast to London or Tokyo. It is the largest and wealthiest of the seven emirates that make up the UAE, and it is the nation's political, industrial and cultural hub. Dubai tends to get most of the publicity in that part of the world, but Abu Dhabi is where the real power and money lie. Although occupying an area only about a third of the size of the UK, the UAE boasts 9% of the world's total oil reserves and 5% of the world's total natural gas reserves. Abu Dhabi is comfortably the largest emirate, occupying some 87% of the UAE's landmass. It also accounts for more than half of the nation's GDP, 30-odd per cent of its population and, most importantly, 96% of the country's oil. The exploitation of these natural resources has fuelled the country's remarkable development since the late sixties, and today it has the seventh highest per capita income in the world. Its extraordinary wealth has also left it with remarkable political and financial leverage across the Middle East and beyond. The UAE has a voice that has to be listened to, be it in Tehran, Tel Aviv or Washington, and it often exerts its influence in a myriad of subtle ways.

The country is essentially a federation of absolute hereditary monarchies in which the Abu Dhabi royal family is the dominant dynasty. The father of the current ruler, Sheikh Khalifa, and effectively of the nation was the remarkable Sheikh Zayed bin Sultan Al Nahyan. He died in 2004 but remains revered as the man whose vision set the tone for the nation's rise and integration into the global economy. Oil had been discovered in the area as long ago as 1958 but little was achieved by way of development prior to the deposing of Zayed's brother in 1966. Thereafter, Zayed increasingly dominated the region's politics and became the first president of the UAE in 1971. As ruler, although he retained certain traditional

Muslim values, he saw the necessity for foreign expertise to develop the nation's oil revenues, and he made sure that the UAE's burgeoning wealth was channelled into building up the nation's social overhead capital and many modern institutions.[33]

It is a relatively moderate and open-minded Islamic state, and it has latterly made at least some progress towards democratisation and addressing a human rights record – especially in relation to the treatment of the vast influx of manual labourers from the Indian subcontinent that work there – that has historically left much to be desired.[34] However, the justice system differs from those of the West and, as an expat, one was strongly advised to stay on the right side of the law.

Outwardly at least it is a modern country, in that it boasts excellent infrastructure, one of the best airlines in the world (Etihad), a number of excellent hotels, and some of the most impressive architecture in the region, including the quite remarkable Sheikh Zayed Mosque. I would also add that the Indian food in Abu Dhabi is out of this world.

Besides getting to know my new colleagues and developing some kind of modus operandi in the office, I was faced with having to register my presence at various ministries, having a blood test to prove that I was not HIV positive, finding myself some permanent accommodation, buying a car, organising a UAE driver's licence and insurance, joining a gym and beach club, and, most importantly of all, registering for a licence to buy alcohol.

Abu Dhabi is not a dry state and this was a great relief: if ever there was a place where an ice-cold beer was welcome, Abu Dhabi fitted the bill. You can drink alcohol in many hotel restaurants and you can drink at home, but to purchase alcohol you needed a licence – a licence that gave you access to several discreetly located, but well-stocked, concrete bunkers around the city where booze was made available for personal consumption and you could access your monthly quota (which was sufficiently generous to kill most people).

If I had thought that the bureaucracy in Japan had often been overbearing, it had nothing on Abu Dhabi. For the first two months there I seemed to spend several hours a day presenting documents in triplicate, filling out forms, getting them translated, queuing up (often in the midst of hordes of immigrant workers from the subcontinent) for an interview or being bounced, in the soporific heat, from ministry to ministry. It did nothing for my blood pressure.

ADIA's headquarters was on the city's attractive Corniche, over-looking the crystalline blue waters of the Arabian Gulf. The building itself was surprisingly modest and old-fashioned, given the extraordinarily large stock of assets that we managed and the way the Authority was venerated by the international financial community. A massive new half-built state-of-the-art headquarters was located half a mile up the road, but when it would be fit for occupation was anyone's guess. The talk was of bitter contractual disputes and political battles between competing government departments and individuals over the project.

My new colleagues were a motley crew of wealthy, foreign-educated but poorly motivated locals who were typically the sons of well-to-do and influential Emirati families; expats drawn from every corner of the world; and support staff from the subcontinent. The atmosphere was friendly but subdued. The dealing room was the quietest place I had ever worked, and there was little contact with other parts of the organisation, something that I found extraordinary and vowed to change, with precious little success.

The Emiratis that I met at ADIA and beyond were invariably generous and welcoming – indeed their generosity could on occasion be suffocating – and they were proud of their country and what it had achieved. I was forever being asked about my family situation and how my wife and children were coping with our separation. On the other hand, not least because of the climate and the wealth and privilege they enjoyed, many of those I worked with were used to being pampered and to life proceeding at a more leisurely and less stressful pace than we are used to in the West. They were, quite simply, programmed to operate in a lower gear.

This was particularly the case during Ramadan, when the city partially shut down between dawn and dusk, and refraining from eating and drinking during the day understandably made people less productive and less focused. It is also worth noting that during this period we Westerners would, out of respect, tailor our eating and drinking habits; some restaurants closed entirely during Ramadan while others would serve alcohol only behind specially erected screens.

If the different attitude that the locals had towards work could be frustrating, other culture clashes were much less to the fore, or at least the local and expatriate populations had worked out ways of circumventing them. For example, as long as one never drank in public and retained at least a modicum of sobriety, the issue of

Westerners' alcohol consumption was scarcely raised. And believe me, with thousands of foreign oil workers commuting through the city en route to the rigs, a lot of alcohol was being consumed in Abu Dhabi.

Similarly, religion was rarely a bone of contention. Sure, all of the local employees were Muslim and would intermittently disappear from the trading room to pray. It was also sometimes clear that colleagues and acquaintances had rather different views about Western policies towards Iraq, Afghanistan, Iran and so on, and I remember that when London was attacked by Islamic terrorists on 7 July 2005 there was a distinctly tense atmosphere in the office, but Emiratis are by their nature easy going and I can honestly say that I got on extremely well with some of the more devout locals. Two of them were regular and keen attendees at the five-a-side football games many of us played on Tuesday nights – nights that would regularly involve matches between Christians and Muslims! And rather than faith, religion or politics, it was the English Premier League, the European Champions League or international cricket that generated the most heated debate.

Office hours at ADIA were bizarre, reflecting as they did both the time zone and the fact that the work ethic was rather less intense than I had been used to. Despite our operating in a Muslim country, which meant that Thursday and Friday were the 'weekend', because global financial markets operated from Monday to Friday so did we. The working day started at a leisurely 9 a.m., which was a joy after all those years of the dawn patrol. Four days a week we broke for three hours at 2 p.m. before returning at 5 p.m. to work through until 8 p.m. On Friday the break began two hours earlier at noon.

The mid-afternoon siesta was something else that took some getting used to, and I struggled to fill the time. In this I was an exception to the rule. As one of my French colleagues enthusiastically told me: 'It's wonderful. I go home, have some lunch, maybe a glass of wine or two, make love to my wife and then have an hour's sleep. What more could you wish for in the middle of the day?' During Ramadan, the hours we put in shrank further to a single 11 a.m.–5 p.m. shift. At that time of year it was almost as if one hardly worked at all.

With little to keep me at home I was almost always the first in the office and I was also often the last one there in the evening. What is more, I regularly dropped in on my days off. In this I was unique. No one else was of a mind to work any longer than they absolutely had to, and nor was there any criticism if you did the minimum required. Indeed, after a few weeks, one of my colleagues pulled me to one side to ask me why I was doing so much 'overtime'. Others feared they were being shown up!

As was the case at Sthenos, there was no template for the job and nobody's shoes to fill. Remarkably, they had never had a chief economist before, and I had to make the role up as I went along. What was immediately clear to me was that the level of macroeconomic understanding across ADIA Treasury was poor and that this was especially the case among the locals. Hence, a good deal of my job was going to involve educating the various portfolio managers. What also became obvious at an early stage was that we were drowning in externally provided information and research. In a desperate attempt to win business from us, sell-side salespeople sent us everything.

I decided that I couldn't possibly digest it all and instead rapidly identified the particular economists and strategists that offered the most interesting output, and for the most part I stuck with this list for my entire tenure. In addition, I brought a certain amount of forward-looking structure to the group's previously chaotic morning meeting, I ran the visits that we received from counterparty analysts, I wrote a monthly assessment of the global economy that I also formally presented to my colleagues, and I began to work with the quants in the team on a number of foreign exchange and bond models. In an effort to raise the bar of knowledge more generally, I began to give a series of regular seminars on particular macro subjects, and I instigated a twice-yearly investment conference, where we would invite certain economists to Abu Dhabi for a whole day's instruction on the hot topics of the day.

With having to bed myself in both at work and in the country more generally, the first few months in Abu Dhabi were a whirlwind. Mick came out briefly to help me with some of the logistics, and I also got home on a regular basis as planned. Nevertheless, it was for the most part a lonely existence and I really missed Mick and the girls.

My mood was given a brief lift in late May, with Liverpool FC's remarkable comeback victory over AC Milan in the Champions League Final. I watched the game in a bar full of Italian expats. While their initial euphoria collapsed into suicidal despair, my journey was in the opposite direction, and for days afterwards I would intermittently laugh out loud at the memory of that extraordinary night. In fact I still do. Generally speaking, though, I found myself perpetually questioning how long this arrangement could work. From the word go I was on the lookout for alternative employment back home.

By the time Abu Dhabi's unbearably hot and humid summer had arrived I had moved into an apartment on the twentieth floor of a modern block just along the Corniche from the office. This was high enough above the ground that the late night and early morning calls to prayer from the local mosque wouldn't disturb my sleep. Although I had insisted to my employers that my particular circumstances meant that I needed only the bachelor's accommodation allowance, I still ended up with a vast three-bedroomed, three-bathroomed apartment with the most stunning view of the Gulf. My commute was now a mere three minutes door to door by car or ten (very sweaty) minutes on foot.

Living in Abu Dhabi was a challenge. As well as the unpleasant climate – basically, nice for three months a year, unspeakable for four or five and just about bearable the rest of the time – life was dull. Abu Dhabi has opened up a lot over the past five years (the last time I was there, in 2012, Madonna was in town) but in 2005 it was pretty closed. The Formula 1 race track had not yet been constructed, the availability of English-language books was limited, the Western films that were shown were cut so dramatically as to be incomprehensible, and the theatre was almost non-existent. Hence, free time tended to orientate around the various beach clubs (although in the height of summer sunbathing was near-suicidal), other people's homes (which were often in soulless gated expat compounds), the city's dozen or so top-class restaurants (most of which were in the main hotels), and one or two bars (which were also situated in the hotels and would show all the major sporting events from around the globe).

I spent a lot of time on my own. I exercised a tremendous amount and did a couple of marathons while I was there (despite starting before dawn and taking place in the winter months, they were the toughest physical challenges I have ever undertaken), I read and I watched a huge amount of sport on TV. But there were weekends when I barely spoke to another human being apart from a restaurant waitress or a shop assistant. This was hardly healthy.

Getting out of town was easy but there were not that many places to go. While Dubai was only an hour and a half away by car, was more cosmopolitan than Abu Dhabi and certainly had a more varied and exciting nightlife, it was not really my scene. It had a shallow, artificial quality and there was too much conspicuous wealth and consumption, much of it derived from questionable sources. Abu Dhabi might have been dull but at least it was relatively genuine and largely free of Russian mafiosi and their bejewelled, excessively made-up and botoxed companions.

Driving out into the desert was wonderfully peaceful and a couple of times I just drove into the middle of nowhere, lay on my back and watched the stars. With very little man-made light, the night sky was spellbinding. Other than that, some close friends owned a boat on which we used to visit various small islands and sandbars out in the Gulf, and the wildlife on both sea and land could be magnificent; I also occasionally used to explore the remote and mountainous northern emirates in the horn of the peninsula. There it would snow in winter and the geography was more redolent of Mars than the planet earth. Fujairah was a particular favourite, not least because it was on the Indian Ocean and the surf was spectacular.

My time in Abu Dhabi coincided with the middle of the last cyclical upswing, and in looking back on the period I am rather struck by the absence of major traumas in the OECD economies. It really was the apotheosis of what Bank of England Governor Mervyn King appropriately characterised as the 'NICE' (non-inflationary, continuous expansion) decade. The recession of the early noughties was over and there was little hint of the extreme trials and tribulations that were to follow from the middle of 2007 onwards. Growth was at or above potential. Excess capacity was being progressively used up with unemployment rates trending persistently downwards, yet wage inflation remained quiescent because of the competitive forces unleashed by globalisation. Labour shares in national income decreased. Hence, although global commodity markets were in a bull phase, advanced-economy core CPI inflation remained historically low at around 2%. Although nominal long-term interest rates were edging up, they too remained quite low in historical terms. This was also the case for credit spreads, which, although beginning to increase, were indicative of a remarkable sanguinity on the part of investors.

By this time the growing influence of China and India was clear for all to see, and the emerging economies in general were a hugely positive influence on global growth. Even Japan seemed to be finally getting over its protracted malaise. Its mid-decade expansion, although very much driven by the buoyancy of external demand, was the longest on record, and it again encouraged the BOJ to suspend quantitative easing and edge policy rates up from the zero bound in 2006.

Central banks generally were in the process of changing tack from the outright monetary accommodation and very low levels of nominal policy rates that accompanied the early stages of recovery, but the pace of adjustment was gradual, with the Greenspan Fed leading the way with its strategy of edging the Fed funds target higher by a quarter of a percentage point at each Federal Open Market Committee meeting. Nevertheless, yield curves bear flattened (a market phrase meaning a rise in the term structure of interest rates led by the shorter maturities), which suggested that the markets thought that the central banks were broadly coming to grips with the developing expansion and had it under control.

As for fiscal policy, headline consolidated budget balances were on a shallow improving trend, but this was as much down to cyclical considerations as to underlying policy adjustment. Hence, although gross and net government debt ratios generally stabilised (Japan was a conspicuous exception to the rule), the progress was limited. As had proved typical over a long period, governments, while happy to relax fiscal policy in cyclical downtrends, were slow to reverse the process in uptrends. This was something they were to regret, especially in the Eurozone periphery.

Beneath the surface, however, the forces that led to the Global Financial Crisis were coalescing. The housing booms in the US, the UK, Spain and Ireland were there for all to see. Household debt ratios were marching upwards to unprecedented levels. Banking sector credit standards (not least for mortgages) were being progressively loosened. Risk premia on corporate and emerging market debt securities were wafer thin, not least because the superlow default rates of 2003–6 were similarly unlikely to last. Global macro imbalances were burgeoning, and the disparities in Eurozone competitiveness between the core and the periphery were increasingly manifest in trade and current account data.

There was an active debate about all these issues at ADIA. This was driven in part by the fact that a couple of my expatriate co-workers were followers of the Austrian School of economics and were of the opinion that a decades-long and unsustainable credit boom was approaching its endgame and that the extended tendency towards monetary accommodation on the part of central banks was to blame. For my part, as might be expected, I tended to look at things more through the lens of Keynes and Minsky than Hayek and Von Mises, and was less absolutist in my analysis. But I certainly recognised the underlying fragilities and vulnerabilities in the business cycle, and I was keen to make sure that my colleagues were aware of the excesses in the US housing market and the structure of finance that upheld it. For example, I remember passing on the detail of important statements on these issues by Janet Yellen of the Federal Reserve and Raghuram Rajan of the IMF,[35] and telling some incredulous portfolio managers about the absurdities of the so-called Ninja (no income, no job, no assets) loans that were being offered to house buyers in the US. I concluded that just because US house prices hadn't suffered a protracted decline since the Great Depression, that didn't mean that it couldn't happen. In fact, that was probably a very good reason to believe that it would.

I was in addition keen to point out the asymmetrical failures in OECD fiscal policy and the trouble that these might cause, if for whatever reason a serious downturn were to ensue. On monetary policy, I was cynical about the way Greenspan had been pretty much canonised. I agreed that central banks might have leaned more against the wind of asset price inflation over the previous two decades, but I was more practically minded than my Austrian School-following colleagues. I emphasised that, given the huge influence of globalisation on factor shares and a tendency towards inflation targeting, there were distinct limits as to what central banks could do to address the underlying issues. A more aggressive approach to monetary restraint could have been extremely destabilising and would have been politically unpopular, even to the extent that it might have led to some central banks having their independence diluted. I was also struck by the fact that it is particularly difficult to say precisely when an accumulation of debt becomes sufficiently unsustainable to spark a period of aggressive deleveraging. Much depends on the behaviour of asset values, the level of interest rates, the availability of credit, the labour market, and the ever-mercurial matter of 'confidence'. Overall, my conclusion was that if there was excess in riskier asset markets and risk premia were on the low side, such problems were as much a job for the regulators as for those who set the level of policy rates.

Where I also disagreed with my Austrian School colleagues was over what could and should be done by policymakers should a credit bust beckon. I unashamedly believed in policy activism, and I thought that even if unconventional options had to be explored, they would be able to exert some positive impact on financial stability, output and prices. In hindsight I will accept that I was perhaps too optimistic in this regard, especially where output and prices were concerned, although I still stand by the basic judgement that it is neither a warranted nor a viable public policy option for governments and central banks to stand idly by and let an economy go to hell. That attitude is what made the Great Depression great and it is a recipe for social and political chaos.

One of the Austrian School's great failings is an inability to say much at all about the timing of readjustments in balance sheets. Another is a failure to live in anything that remotely resembles the real world of politics and social pressures.

Japan, needless to say, also took up a good deal of my time at ADIA. Despite the lengthy upswing of the mid noughties and the sense that the country's financial sector problems had been brought under control, I continued to see it as an economy that was inherently fragile and structurally compromised. Domestic demand remained subdued, deflation continued apace, and nothing much had been done to address its supply-side shortcomings, especially in the area of demographics. Meanwhile, its fiscal policy metrics continued to deteriorate year by year. When the BOJ once again began to tighten monetary policy in 2006, I feared it could be a costly error – and so it proved.

Despite the occasional vibrancy of the internal debate at ADIA and the sense that one was working for an institution that exerted a significant degree of influence on global markets, life there was less than fulfilling. Yes, I had access to the best research around and my own stock of knowledge was growing exponentially; yes, I enjoyed the educational aspects of my job; yes, I enjoyed first-class travel; and yes, when I phoned a government or central bank with a view to arranging a meeting, senior officials were only too happy to make themselves available.[36] But the flip side was that the decision-making processes were glacial, the bureaucracy was suffocating, one could not escape the feeling of geographical detachment from the major markets, the days dragged, and, despite my best efforts to change the agenda and the modus operandi of the Treasury group, I achieved very little by way of success. The absence of pressure on my time is summed up by the fact that during the World Cup of 2006 I would go back to my apartment to watch games and no one noticed my absence.

I could have stayed at ADIA until the end of my career (it was very hard to get the sack), picked up my lightly taxed salary and enjoyed the perks of the job, but Stephane Monier, who initially recruited me, had resigned in March of 2006 and with his departure there was a sense of drift in the place. More than ever I appeared to be operating in an elephants' graveyard, when I felt that I had so much more to give and perhaps not much time left in the industry to give it. In the meantime, despite my regular visits home and my wife and children's occasional visits to the Gulf, I desperately missed my family. I was bored and lonely and I had the sense that life was passing me by.

I was once again looking around for alternative openings. I came close to a return to Japan with RBS (in retrospect a job that I am delighted to have missed out on), and I also furtively travelled to Toronto for a day of interviews for the post of chief economist at the Canadian Public Pension Board. This did not go at all well. They wanted a quant with real expertise in portfolio management, and the entire process saw me at cross-purposes with my interlocutors. Furthermore, as I subsequently found out, this was very much a political appointment, so quite why I ever appeared on the shortlist I will never know.

In the end, in the late summer of 2006, although I had no alternative on the immediate agenda, one day I just walked into my boss's office and tendered my resignation. After just over two years, I had had enough. He was understanding, as indeed were all the locals, and I agreed that I would stay on until I had found a replacement, which, as it transpired, took about four months. In the end I teed up Ryan Shea, an ex-colleague from Lehman Brothers, to take over, and I am happy to say that he did an excellent job.

So, in early December 2006 after having waded my way through another bureaucratic labyrinth to leave Abu Dhabi, and turned down an absurdly timed offer of a job in another part of ADIA on my last day, I returned to London and a period of self-imposed unemployment. The question was whether, given my age, I would be able to find anything consistent with my skill set and the sort of income I was accustomed to.

The first half of 2007 was tough. Besides looking for a new job, I also had to spend another month out of the country in an effort to keep the tax man off my back, although as I subsequently found out some bad advice meant that despite this supplementary sojourn overseas I still ended up owing him rather more than I would have liked. What this tells you about my skills as a financial markets economist I leave you to judge.

Meanwhile, I knew that finding a suitable post for someone as experienced (for which read old) as I was would prove difficult. I was after a role as chief economist or head of research. These jobs are few and far between, turn up rarely, and a good number of them are filled internally. Besides engaging various headhunters and using the contacts that I had built up over the years, I also made direct approaches to just about every major financial institution in town. But by the time that March rolled around and I was forced to again head offshore, I had achieved little.

It was a frustrating time that, when I wasn't pestering potential employers, I filled by transcribing the World War I diaries of my paternal grandfather and trawling through the National Archives for background information about him (ironically, most of his service records had been destroyed by a Luftwaffe bomb in World War II). Decorated and gassed at the Battle of Passchendaele, the experiences he related with such brutal honesty and pathos helped me to keep things in perspective.

I decided to spend my enforced period of 'tax exile' in Ireland. It was close to home, it was a country that I loved, and my old friend David McWilliams had found me some reasonable accommodation close to his home in one of the plusher suburbs of south Dublin, so I would have a kindred spirit close by. Nevertheless, after the enforced separation from my family over the previous couple of years, it was hard to take. Thankfully, however, it was brief. I spent much of my time reading and trying to keep up the interest of the various headhunters I had engaged, although, as I feared, it soon became clear that they were much more beholden to the companies paying them retainers than they were to individuals like myself.

I did have one interview while I was there, however: Depfa Bank, the Dublin-based German entity specialising in mortgage and public sector financing and the leading underwriter of German covered bonds, was looking for a head of research. I got down to the last two candidates for this job, but the head of HR and I did not see eye to eye and I was passed over. At the time this felt like quite a blow but again, in hindsight, it proved to be a blessing in disguise. Depfa got into all sorts of trouble in the Global Financial Crisis and the German government had to bail it out.

My time in Dublin also afforded me a first-hand look at the last hurrah of the 'Celtic Tiger' and in particular at Ireland's housing bubble (Irish house prices essentially peaked during my stay). In early 2007 the evidence of excess was ubiquitous. Indeed, the speculative frenzy of Ireland's all-consuming real estate boom, plus all the hubris, extravagance and evidence of corruption that went with it, reminded me of Tokyo in early 1990. Having risen by more in real terms over the previous decade than in any other major economy, house prices had reached stratospheric levels relative to incomes or rents. You only had to look around you to see the intensity of building activity, whether it was related to new homes, the renovation of old homes or to non-residential property. And you only had to keep your ears open to understand how people were swept along by the whole episode. Irish property prices had quadrupled over the previous decade and, at its peak, total construction accounted for some 9.5% of the country's GDP, housing construction for 7% of GDP, and almost 13% of the workforce was employed building things. These are absurdly high numbers for a developed, or indeed any, economy, and completely unsustainable. The only questions were when, how far and how fast house prices would fall, and what the fallout would be.

David had much earlier than most concluded that Ireland's economic miracle was built on shaky foundations and that boom must ultimately turn to bust.[37] Indeed, I was interviewed by him on his TV show as far back as 2003 about the similarities between the Irish and Japanese housing bubbles. Such opinions had got him into trouble both with the local press and with politicians, who were keen to characterise anyone with a more sceptical viewpoint as a pessimistic killjoy. But when the two of us met up for a Guinness or two, my advice to him was to stick with it. He was going to be proved right before long. However, neither of us predicted quite what was to unfurl over the course of 2008 and 2009.

I eventually returned to the UK in April and resumed my job search, which remained a challenge. Initially, the only expressions of interest came from the Middle East, which I was obviously less than keen on, and Asia, where my mind was more open, but the opportunities didn't really merit following up. I kept myself sane by training for, and running, another marathon and by immersing myself in Liverpool FC's (sadly unsuccessful) assault on another Champions League.

What I also began to do was send out comments on key issues of the day to the contacts that I had in my Rolodex. By doing this I could keep myself up to speed with global events, but I also had it in mind that if interest in my utterances took off, perhaps I could make a living from them. In the end, however, I managed to draw in only one paying customer – I am proud to say, though, that that customer was Goldman Sachs Asset Management.

Mindful of that headhunter's comment about the limited half-life of an economist, by mid 2007 I was beginning to despair of finding the sort of job that I craved. Then, rather like proverbial London buses, two attractive offers came along at once. The one I chose to pursue was at Royal Bank of Canada (RBC), who were looking for someone to run their global fixed income and currency research from London.

RBC was an excellent name: they had a strong credit rating and a dominant position in Canada's financial markets. Moreover, the job was a big one. RBC had teams of strategists in Canada, the US, the UK and Australia, and they were also looking to branch out into Asia and into European emerging markets. What they had never had was someone to act as a figurehead for the whole group. The interview process was arduous but I secured the role, an outcome that at the time felt like a resurrection of Lazarus-like proportions. What was extraordinary, however, was that at no stage was I put in front of any of the people I was to manage. But keen to get the job and reluctant to further complicate an already extended period of evaluation, I kept quiet about it. This proved to be a mistake that I would pay for dearly over the next few years.

CHAPTER 13

TEMPORARY RESURRECTION

My time at RBC's offices, situated on the Thames close to the old Billingsgate fish market, began in early September 2007, more or less as the Global Financial Crisis erupted. Although I had signed the contract to join the firm at the end of July, I insisted that I be allowed to take a long-planned family holiday first. This meant that I landed just as the sub-prime issue went critical and there was the first run on a UK bank (Northern Rock) since 1866. So, my appointment was made at about the moment that the bottom fell out of the job market. Indeed, it could be argued that my arrival at RBC coincided with the beginning of the end of the golden age of the global financial sector that had begun around the time that I started in the City in 1986. If the RBC job had not come along, goodness only knows how much longer I might have been out of work.

My initial period at RBC was frenzied. I remember barely sleeping for the first week and for some time feeling that I was drowning under the weight of the role and all the expectations that came with it. My career had run in a lower gear at both Sthenos and ADIA, and during my last year at Lehman, which amounted to a period of four years. And on top of all the usual worries that accompany a new position and the fact that global markets were descending into an extended period of turmoil, I was confronted with some thorny personnel and territorial issues.

First, as soon as I arrived I was asked to take on the running of emerging-market research, which was not in my original remit. This meant having an additional four Toronto-based strategists under me and having to recruit two more. But most pertinently, the atmosphere within the group I inherited in London was toxic. Although they clearly knew their stuff, they were surly and defensive. There was precious little joie de vivre or evidence of teamwork. Indeed, at the end of my first day I remarked to my wife that my new colleagues were reminiscent of a litter of beaten up puppies. It was clear that macro research was not held in the same regard at RBC as it had been at Lehman or UBS, although judging from their manner and demeanour I suspected that the individuals in question had not done much to help themselves. Their attitude towards the salesforce and traders was particularly questionable. Most tasks seemed to be undertaken grudgingly. And if I had learned one thing over the years, it was that sales, trading and management want their researchers to interact, to be visible and to be easy going. They have enough problems with the client base and the last thing they want to deal with is a grumpy and insular research department.

Meanwhile, as hinted above, no one had ever done my job at RBC before. Previously, there had been a global head of foreign exchange research and a global head of fixed-income research, but it turned out that they disliked each other: they rarely spoke and they cooperated even less. The former had moved on and her deputy – a technically gifted, if rather sullen, character – was promoted in her stead. But he was the least of my worries. On the other hand, the head of bond research had been given no inkling of my appointment until he came back from holiday a day or two prior to my arrival in the office. He had been with RBC for a long time, was hitherto the London office's primary spokesperson on things macro, and had dominated the marketing calendar. He was clearly of the belief that if anyone was to be given the new overarching role, it should be him.

He was bound to be resentful and I would have been the same in his position. Not surprisingly, therefore, our relationship never progressed beyond the tense. Managing him was to prove a challenge, and I was incredulous that the business heads at RBC had put us both in such an invidious position. Here, once again, was evidence that many of the people who ran large financial institutions during my time in the business left a lot to be desired, especially where personnel matters were concerned.

My second problem concerned the structure of RBC's research effort and forecasting responsibilities. Unlike most banks and investment banks, RBC employed few pure economists, and the few they did employ were confined to a group based in Toronto that was responsible for analysing and forecasting the Canadian economy largely for the bank's retail clients. However, this group also forecasted the US economy and 'owned' the Fed view, which is the most important interest rate forecast of all. Moreover, although eminently qualified, they were not financial market economists in the same way that I was. They did not believe it was their role to do anything remotely controversial, and their views and published forecasts reflected this in spades. Meanwhile, although we strategists outside Canada were forever being told by management that we were not economists and that our primary responsibilities were to concentrate on market themes and generate 'actionable trade ideas' for clients, we were also charged with the production of forecasts, including those of interest rates for the rest of the world.

This view of the role of the strategist largely reflected the mistaken belief that economists were invariably unduly academic and therefore a luxury that could largely be dispensed with. But it was hard to imagine the sort of model that RBC favoured working in a large institution when the global economy was going to hell and clients wanted a coherent, well-researched and decisive view on so many macro issues. I rapidly realised that the remit initially handed to me was poorly specified and that I was going to have to take liberties with it. This was especially the case after I had paid my first visit to Toronto.

RBC's Canadian economics team were a friendly and open group. They extended me a warm welcome and expressed a strong desire to cooperate, all of which was music to my ears. The problem was that they had yet to fully grasp the extent of what was going on. Indeed, one of the first pieces of detailed research that I saw from the team claimed that the sub-prime crisis was eminently manageable, that the US housing market would enjoy a soft landing, and that the cyclical upswing was not under serious threat. Consistent with this, the team was less than convinced that any easing of US monetary policy was warranted at that time, although in the end they were willing to countenance a call for a single 25 or 50 basis point rate cut. The phrase they liked to use was 'one and done'.

I was incredulous. To my mind, the US housing market was in the early stages of a major, probably catastrophic, correction: to me, 'sub-prime' had the whiff of Japan and Ireland about it. Things were therefore going to get a lot worse in the US and everywhere else, and probably very quickly too.

What had particularly troubled me on arrival at RBC was what the money market traders were saying. And they were crystal clear: the wholesale funding markets had seized up and counterparty confidence between the major banks had evaporated. A vital part of the financial system had therefore become dysfunctional. In such circumstances, my sense was that US (and, for that matter, global) monetary policy was going to have to be loosened dramatically. Forget 'one and done', policy rates might drop to zero!

But my Canadian colleagues were reluctant to embrace such a view. I sensed that perhaps they were unduly influenced by the apparent lack of excess in Canada's relatively small and parochial financial sector and by the fact that the domestic authorities had been early and successful devotees of the sort of macroprudential intervention that has almost become de rigeur in recent years.[38] Anyway, despite some extended discussions, their firm position remained that a call for a big US monetary policy response was unnecessary, especially as they feared that an aggressive US interest rate forecast would frighten the bank's customers and undermine the bank's credibility. For my part, I feared the same if we *didn't* publish a much more adventurous view.

As I wearily climbed on to my overnight return flight from Toronto to London at the end of that initial four-day visit to Canada, we were not much closer to a resolution of the issue. All I got was agreement that I could continue to talk publicly about the bias of risks in interest rates being to the downside. Clearly, I was going to be pushing this interpretation of future events to the limit.

Thankfully, my pessimistic view of the global outlook struck more of a chord with the London-based sales and proprietary trading teams. The former were less concerned about the veracity of my arguments than they were in having a non-consensus story that they could push to their clients. The latter, and especially the head of the desk, were on side with my analysis, though, and they saw it as providing the necessary ammunition to support some aggressive trades. The fact that I was so clear in my opinions and that these opinions seemed to be accurate meant that I rapidly developed the sort of internal credibility at RBC that had taken considerably longer to build up at Lehman, or for that matter anywhere else.

Besides coming to terms with the breadth of my new role and the vexed issues related to it, the Global Financial Crisis rapidly came to dominate my life. To the human casualties of the crisis this will all no doubt sound thoughtless, but despite it often being exhausting, it was a tremendously exciting time. It was like Japan in 1997 and 1998 all over again. Every day seemed to reveal new evidence about how deeply compromised the major economies and their financial systems were. I was thrust into a maelstrom of client meetings, with my diary of the time revealing that between early September and mid December 2007, I visited Toronto twice, Montreal, Ottawa, New York twice, Boston, Paris, Stockholm, Frankfurt, Milan, Rome, Zurich, Glasgow, Edinburgh, Dubai, Abu Dhabi, Qatar, Hong Kong, Tokyo, Singapore, Sydney, Brisbane and Melbourne.

What is more I was regularly on TV, and this led to one of the nicest moments of my professional career. While sitting in the green room prior to going on set at CNBC's London studios, I heard a voice that I had not heard 'in the flesh' for almost thirty years. On being led on to the set I was amazed to see none other than Willem Buiter. The show's presenter looked up at me and said: 'Oh hi Russell, this is Willem Buiter, who is our guest host today'. I reached over, warmly shook his hand and said: 'Actually, we have met already'. He raised an eyebrow and looked nonplussed. I went on, 'The last time would have been at my last third-year international economics seminar at Bristol University in the early summer of 1981.' At this point a huge smile broke across his face and he said: 'Well, by the look of it, you've recovered!'

Now my memory of Willem from my undergraduate days was that if you weren't in control of your brief, he could, if he chose to, eviscerate you. And I knew of instances in his professional life where his intellectual prowess was harnessed to humiliate much smarter and more important people than me. I was therefore immediately nervous that this could turn out to be a nightmare, and a horribly public one at that. As it happened, though, he proceeded to provide me with a succession of easy questions and then nodded sagely at everything I said. In the aftermath of the interview I wrote him a note expressing my thanks for his treating me so generously and explaining how what he had taught me all those years ago had stood me in good stead.

There was one memory that I was particularly keen to share with him. When he initially started teaching that third-year course, he used some pretty complex maths that was above the heads of myself and some of the other students, and three of us went to see him to explain that although we enjoyed his lectures, we couldn't cope with all the algebra and we'd have to drop the course unless he changed tack. He admitted that he didn't realise that he was dealing with such a range of mathematical abilities and subsequently recalibrated each lecture to reflect our shortcomings in this regard. He didn't have to do this, but the fact that he did meant that when I left Bristol my knowledge of international macroeconomics was state of the art.

After a ten-day break over Christmas and New Year, it was back to the grindstone – and there was no respite. The crisis was deepening, with equity markets now coming under huge stress and, as I had predicted, the Fed slashing interest rates. In January 2008 it cut the federal funds rate by 125 basis points in nine days! So much for 'one and done'. Yet my Canadian colleagues still failed to grasp how grim things were and what the consequences of this grimness were for monetary policy. As I had learned in Japan, in an asset price collapse the central bank has to act quickly and decisively. Half measures and attaching undue weight to other issues make things worse.

In this kind of environment, my marketing schedule remained hectic, as did the calls on my time from media. I found myself appearing on the top story on the BBC evening news and I also remember, one freezing snowy February morning, being quizzed on the prospects for UK interest rates by a CNBC reporter while standing six feet off the ground on the plinth of a statue of the Duke of Wellington directly opposite the Bank of England. The cameraman was periodically wiping snowflakes off the lens and I was desperately trying to stop my teeth chattering. All around me hordes of rugged-up commuters hurried by on the way to work. God only knows what they thought.

The other pressures on my time also mounted. I was in the throes of redesigning our flagship weekly: I started to put out a series of detailed notes on particular subjects of interest ranging from the characteristics of deflation to the policy options at the zero bound and a comparison between the US and Japan (the latter two both rehashes of pieces I had written at Lehman in 2003). Meanwhile, the personnel issues were relentless. At the behest of the gilt desk I put a new sterling bond strategist in place in London: an appointment that ruffled the feathers of the existing members of my team, one of whom was sufficiently piqued to threaten resignation. Moreover, I came under pressure both to run RBC's quant research group based in Chicago, something which I was reluctant to take on because of my own quantitative shortcomings, and to replace our US strategist.

The latter two issues meant that I was again commuting across the Atlantic with some regularity. And as at Lehman, I hated the New York office. It was dark, dingy and cramped, and it overlooked the huge hole in the ground that was Ground Zero. Indeed, the physical damage to the RBC New York office as a result of the collapse of the twin towers was still in evidence in a couple of the meeting rooms, where the walls and doors had been pockmarked by flying debris. The atmosphere there was poisonous, to some extent reflecting the personalities of the New York employees, but in addition this part of RBC's business had been the victim of a failed merger and was losing money. Everyone was therefore looking over their shoulder.

In mid March, the Fed brokered the fire sale of Bear Stearns to JPMorgan Chase, and, regardless of another 75 basis point cut in the Fed funds rate, the stock prices of both Lehman and Merrill Lynch were hit hard. Despite the best efforts of Ben Bernanke and the US central bank it appeared to me that the US authorities were struggling to get to grips with the crisis and that it had several more iterations to come.

It was at this stage that I first began to query the sustainability of my old shop. Ex-colleagues were sanguine enough, but I was not so sure. There were just too many rumours circulating about Lehman's creative accounting and its exposure to the crumbling US real estate market. I, like most others, therefore assumed that Lehman would be forced into a shotgun marriage with another US securities firm. I couldn't believe, given its interconnectedness and, in particular, its importance to the US repo and derivatives markets, that it would be allowed to fail. Surely moral hazard would have to take a back seat to financial and macroeconomic stability?

I also believed that it was only a matter of time before Europe, Japan and the rest of the world followed the US's example and slid into a serious downturn. I became dubious about the ECB's rather precious determination to divide its policy response into the 'standard' and the 'non-standard' and to eschew rate cuts because of the temporary impact of higher commodity prices on inflation.

I saw the latter as an error on a par with Governor Mieno's reluctance to sanction an easing of Japanese monetary policy in 1991. The trend in output growth would soon be decidedly negative and higher commodity prices were unsustainable. All they were doing was adding to the nascent downdraft by squeezing real incomes. The real issue was the potential for falling prices. Additional monetary restraint was the last thing that was required. When the ECB actually raised rates in the middle of 2008 I thought it ridiculous and warned that it could be one of the biggest policy errors since the thirties.

I blew off some steam in April by running the London Marathon, but then it was back to travelling the world trying to calm the nerves of investors, not least those at the various central banks we entertained at a big and ostentatious conference in Dubai. This was the occasion when we managed to lose the representative from the central bank of Mongolia for three days (to this day no one knows where he went between his arrival at the hotel on the first evening and his appearance at the conference on the last morning), when I spotted one of my Muslim former ADIA colleagues with a beer in one hand and a gin and tonic in the other, and when our senior central bank salesman won a six-hour vodka drinking contest with representatives of the Polish central bank! As for the substance of the conference, it was a tale of unmitigated woe, with my own presentation being the most pessimistic of the lot. The attendees were drinking to forget.

At this stage in my RBC career I was on a high, despite the problems I continued to have with my team. Management, sales and trading were happy with me and put me on a special leadership development course with a number of other supposed high-flyers. The problem was that I couldn't see it. I remained insecure and my inability to bring the staff that I had inherited around to my way of thinking, or to convince them that they were their own worst enemies, rankled enormously, colouring my own overall demeanour. Furthermore, the relentless travel – which in the middle of the year extended to some unfamiliar territory: a whistle-stop four-day tour of Latin American central banks – was taking me away from home too much and was pushing me close to exhaustion when I was there. Part of the problem was that I just didn't feel I could delegate much and I was therefore putting myself under too much pressure. I was working weekends and a couple of times I found myself drafting articles on my Blackberry in the back of taxis on the way to airports or in between meetings. It's a wonder that I didn't dislocate my thumbs in the process.

In early September I returned from a desperately needed holiday to be confronted by the effective nationalisation of Fannie Mae and Freddie Mac, the two government-sponsored enterprises that effectively underwrote the secondary mortgage market in the US. A week later, Lehman Brothers – a firm that had existed for 158 years and survived the US Civil War, the financial panics of 1907 and 1929, the Great Depression, two world wars and numerous other crises, and at which I had worked for almost a decade – was declared bankrupt. What followed was to prove the most intense interlude of my career. The period through until Christmas 2008 was, as I remarked to numerous audiences at the time, the biggest financial and economic crisis since the Great Depression. By the end of the year no large independent investment bank (in the old sense) remained, the US financial system had changed beyond all recognition, and devastating macroeconomic aftershocks were rippling around the world.

This time of almost unprecedented turbulence in the markets and beyond coincided with my also having to address yet more personnel issues, which included finally letting our New York strategist go, finding a replacement, culling the Chicago quant group and trying to placate the London sales force, who were increasingly critical of one of my less-than-loved team. My holiday resolutions to achieve a better work–life balance sank without trace immediately. I have never worked as hard as I did during the last four months of 2008: my days would start with an alarm call just after 5 a.m. and I would rarely be asleep before midnight. Weekends ceased to exist in any real sense. If I wasn't travelling, I was working most of the time. Thank God I had an understanding wife and sympathetic children. I even missed my eldest daughter's departure for her first term at Oxford. I was not alone in all this: it seemed that every serious economist or strategist I knew was doing the same.

I did, nevertheless, manage to keep a functioning diary going through this period. In one entry, I likened going back into the office after a brief business trip to 'falling into a washing machine'. Indeed, this metaphor applies pretty well to most of that period. What also comes across is the overwhelming sense of fear and panic that overtook so many of my contemporaries and which, as the crisis deepened, began to overwhelm everyone I met. Even when I was at home, if I wasn't fielding after-hours work calls or desperately sending emails on my Blackberry, I was inundated by calls from journalists, friends and family. In the country of the blind, the one-eyed man is king – and at this juncture I was the one-eyed man.

The willingness of the US authorities to allow Lehman Brothers to collapse is widely considered to be the event that tipped a deepening drama over into a crisis. Certainly, when I heard that no deal to subsume Lehman into another major financial institution was forthcoming I was stunned. I thought it a major error. This was less because I had any special insights into the extent of the bad assets the company was sitting on or the overall complexity of its trading book (although one of RBC's risk managers who had previously worked at Lehman had hinted to me that the situation was likely to be 'ugly') and more because I thought it suggested that the old-style 'liquidationists' in US policymaking circles had won an important battle.

This was potentially catastrophic when the fear factor in markets was so all-consuming and the scope for contagion so high. Contagion could prove to be anything but rational. I just hoped that the Keynesians and policy activists at the Fed and beyond would soon be able to re-assert control, but I also fretted that it might be too late. The failure of Chairman Bernanke and his colleagues to slash the federal funds rate in the days immediately after the Lehman decision did not bode well. My view was that they should have immediately gone to a zero-rate stance. As it happened, it took the Fed until 8 October to do anything with official rates, and until 16 December to effectively set the key policy rate at zero.

In my diary entry of 13 September I noted how the Lehman share price had dropped to $3. I had always sold my Lehman shares as and when they vested, as I thought that having my job and cash salary linked to the firm's fortunes was enough without having much of the rest of my personal wealth linked to its performance too. As such I was incredibly lucky. This is particularly the case as the share 'lock in' for Lehman employees became much tighter after my departure. With such a high percentage of employees' remuneration paid in stock, many of the people I knew who remained at Lehman after my departure saw their net worth seriously reduced.

A day or two after its demise I took John Llewellyn to lunch to try to cheer him up. John was, unsurprisingly, bitter about things, and especially about the way that a small coterie of New York executives had ignored so much sensible advice from elsewhere within the bank and taken so many poor decisions. My own memory of the modus operandi of Lehman's senior executives was of a macho locker room mentality. Egos were huge. Weaknesses were denied. Minds were closed. Self-aggrandisement was desperately pursued, often dressed up as 'doing what was best for the firm' and its shareholders, which, of course, meant doing what was best for their own bank accounts.

But it was not just at Lehman that people I knew were questioning their wealth and were worried about their futures. My old friend Klaus Baader phoned to tell me that Merrill Lynch, where he worked, was on the brink too. My fears of virulent contagion were thus well founded. I also heard on the bush telegraph that ADIA had gone into the pre-Lehman bankruptcy weekend holding a large position in the firm's commercial paper and, as a result, had lost the sort of sum that would have bankrupted a small developing country.

In the beginning of the final week of September – with Lehman's failure having effectively triggered the demise of Merrill Lynch, Washington Mutual and Wachovia, with AIG bailed out (an insurance company was obviously considered more important by the authorities than an investment bank), with money market funds and the commercial paper market under intense stress, and with the equity markets in free fall – I found myself in New York. I was there to give the introductory address at an RBC investment banking conference and also to try to recruit some of my old Lehman colleagues to RBC. But what made this particularly strange was that RBC had just relocated into the old Lehman building on Vesey Street. I therefore ended up interviewing a number of old workmates in offices that neither I, nor they, had seen since just before 11 September 2001. The overarching sense of Armageddon was complete.

Ahead of my speech I was apprehended by a senior RBC banker who asked me what I was going to say. When I gave him a summary, putting special emphasis on the point that the US banking system could well end up like the French banking system, in that it would be largely publicly owned, he begged me to tone it down and to come up with a more positive conclusion, not just about the banks but about the macro outlook. I suggested that he open his eyes and take a look around at what was happening in New York and beyond, but his reaction sums up much about what was wrong with the business, and explains how it had found itself in such a mess. What is more, his refrain proved to be a familiar one from salesmen and senior executives alike over the next few months.

At this stage panic was ubiquitous, and no one quite does financial panics like America. The media was hysterical, with the search for a scapegoat in full cry and commentators at some of the more vocal entities – CNBC and CNN, for example – openly calling for just about every policy, or non-policy, that could make things worse. Meanwhile, the gold price was gyrating by $80 a day, US Treasury Bill yields were negative, and exhausted policymakers appeared to be at the ends of their tethers. A senior Bank of England official subsequently told me that he was at this time working 85-hour weeks and that the governor was more or less living at the bank. The same was broadly true of other senior central bankers and finance ministers.

Towards the end of September, the US authorities, who had quickly come to appreciate the gravity of their error where Lehman Brothers was concerned, frantically sought a circuit breaker for the crisis. Working under incredible stress, the Treasury cobbled together the horribly named, but urgently needed, Troubled Asset Relief Programme, or TARP, which sought to make available $700bn of public money (a number by all accounts largely plucked out of thin air) to clear up the mess in the US financial sector once and for all.

The rescue process required greater democratic legitimacy and the TARP appropriately shifted much of the responsibility for financial sector support back onto the shoulders of the Treasury and away from the Fed, which had hitherto effectively been operating as a 'bad bank', accumulating huge amounts of compromised assets in return for cash. Born out of chaos, fear and exhaustion, the initial draft of the TARP legislation was painfully thin, politically naive, and even unconstitutional. It was a red rag to America's anti-interventionist bulls. A Republican-dominated Congress first dithered over it and then rejected it, thereby sending another massive wave of nausea through the markets.

Thankfully, however, this concentrated tired minds. Redrafted, the bill was signed into law on 3 October, and by 12 October the decision had been made to apply the available funding to a blanket programme of recapitalisation. To paraphrase Winston Churchill, America will invariably end up doing the right thing, but generally only after exploring every other alternative. But what all this also demonstrated was that it was a country suffering from a chronic lack of leadership. By this stage, George W. Bush was a lame-duck president, lacking economic policy gravitas and credibility in the markets. He had, to all intents and purposes, vanished from view, and Henry Paulson was effectively running the government. What a contrast to Bush's grandstanding during the Iraq War and to the calm assurance projected by Franklin Roosevelt in 1933.

Despite the eventual passage of the TARP, the similar bank recapitalisation programme announced in the UK, the slew of globally coordinated official interest rate cuts that followed, and growing talk of quantitative easing, stock markets continued to bleed. It was clear that the world was tumbling into a deep recession, one as bad as anything seen since World War II. The question was whether it would turn into something altogether worse. And I was hearing some scary things from the policymakers I knew. In particular, in the wake of the Lehman collapse, the UK banking system came close to complete collapse. That is to say, no operating ATMs, no cheques cashed, no wages paid. If this had happened, we might well have been faced with social breakdown and martial law. It is also worth considering what such an eventuality would have meant in a US context. As Mark Blyth succinctly put it in his excellent book on the history of austerity, at that time the US had 150 million or so workers, 72% of whom were living from pay cheque to pay cheque, and 70 million of whom possessed hand guns.[39] In my diary, I for my part mulled the possibility of a collapse into protectionism, and for the first time began to question whether the euro would be able to survive.

Meanwhile, I continued to be used as RBC's primary interface with clients of all shapes and sizes and to travel maniacally, with two end-of-year trips to Asia: the first, which lasted a mere twenty-four hours, was to formally sign up a strategist for our Hong Kong office; and the second was a three-city, five-day tour of Australia. One trip to Milan in October 2008 especially sticks in my mind. On a day when global stock markets were down by between 4 and 8 per cent, every meeting we had painstakingly scheduled was cancelled, including one after I had actually been taken up to the office of the client in question by his secretary. The Italian institutional investor base was living up to its hysterical stereotype. With our flight home hours away and the sun blazing down on a beautiful autumn day, my salesman chaperone and I decided to make the best of things – after all, we concluded, there might not be a global financial system in a few days' time. We sat down to a long lunch in the garden of one of the city's many excellent restaurants. From that vantage point, and after a glass or two of Chianti, it all seemed rather surreal.

Things were not helped at this time by the extension of the panic to the emerging markets and to commodities and currencies. One day, as I stepped off a flight in Hong Kong, the local stock market was down 12.8%. The next day it was up 14.5%. Most of the people I worked with were by this time shattered, and I was no exception. It was relentless, and I often felt overwhelmed. Indeed, this period probably marked the closest I ever came during my career to 'karōshi': a wonderful Japanese term, literally translated as 'death from overwork'. In the background, the team continued to make life difficult, although the end-of-year bonus season went off without too many problems. Given the environment all financial market firms were operating in, even my egocentric group thought better of complaining about their awards.

I just about got through to Christmas, but was suffering from a chest infection, the result of too many aeroplanes and too little sleep. By this time the Fed had launched its first programme of quantitative easing, focused on the purchase of mortgage-backed securities, and, as I had predicted its arrival well in advance, my light shone brightly as I departed for a ten-day break, much of which was spent licking my wounds with the family on the south coast. The only sour note was that, over the holiday, I heard that the Russian head of our Chicago quant group had resigned.

After a single day in the office at the beginning of January I was on a plane to Canada to give a series of start-the-year presentations in freezing snow-bound Toronto and Montreal. Thereafter, work soon ratcheted up to fever pitch again. My travel diary rapidly filled up with trips to the four corners of the globe, and I was also in demand to speak at various conferences in the UK. In the meantime it was becoming increasingly clear quite how damaged the OECD economies were by the events of the previous autumn. Unemployment was soaring and the City was suffering disproportionately, with the rising tide of redundancies engulfing numerous friends, not least Klaus Baader, who was released by Merrill after its shotgun marriage with Bank of America.

In late January Barack Obama was inaugurated as US president and was given one of the worst macroeconomic 'hospital passes' of all time. But if I have one abiding recollection of that day, it is of tapping the youngest guy in my team on the shoulder and instructing him to disengage from the spreadsheet he was poring over, turn around and watch what was playing out on the TV screens hung on the walls of the RBC dealing room.

'Chris', I said, 'For Christ's sake, history is being made here. There is about to be an African-American president in the White House. When I was a kid forty-odd years ago they there still lynching black people in America, and one of the major presidential candidates was an unrepentant segregationist. Suck it up.'

That said, I have to say that I was always a sceptic about Obama, suspecting that there was rather less substance to him than met the eye. And besides, the expectations for him were so high, and the challenges he faced so complex, that the world could only ever be disappointed. Although he won a second term, I think that this judgement holds.

In general, 2009 proved to be another insanely busy year. I always seemed to be either on a plane or recovering from a trip. However, there were a number of highlights. I produced more well-received pieces of work, including one on potential exit strategies from quantitative easing (not that those strategies have yet been required), one on public sector debt sustainability, and another on the similarities between Britain in the seventies and Britain at the end of the last decade. The firm also hired former Bank of England MPC member David Blanchflower to undertake some client presentations in the period immediately after his departure from the policymaking community, and I acted as his escort. David, or 'Danny' as he was known, had been the Bank's arch dove as the crisis broke and his views were therefore in high demand. He was an entertaining companion: easy going, amusing, insightful and delightfully indiscreet. He must have driven Mervyn King mad. The four days I spent with him were some of the most interesting and entertaining of my career.

Policymakers were a big focus of the firm's attention that year, and on one US trip I found myself addressing the New York Fed (my presentation there was rather stiff, not because I was nervous, but because I had been press-ganged into an early-morning twenty-mile run around much of Manhattan by our head of proprietary trading), the US Treasury, the IMF and the SEC. I also gave a keynote presentation on quantitative easing at our annual central bank conference, which on that occasion was held in New York.

The latter part of the year saw the usual ridiculous travel schedule. Between mid November and Christmas I visited Scotland, Italy, Scandinavia (twice), Switzerland, Abu Dhabi, Japan, Russia and India. Both India and Russia were new territory for me and, although they were brief, I found both trips absolutely fascinating.

In Mumbai the juxtaposition of newly acquired wealth and abject poverty was stomach churning, and in general the city represented an extraordinary assault on all one's senses and sensibilities. It was total chaos from the moment I arrived at the airport at 2 a.m. to the moment I left the next morning at 3.30! The central bank was a noisy building site, with the ceiling flapping in the air conditioning, stray dogs wandering around the ground floor, white-shirted messengers scurrying hither and thither, and waiters carrying trays of tea around from one shabby office to another. There were security guards everywhere, yet no one seemed to know where to take us and I felt anything but secure.

However, we were overwhelmed by the hospitality (which in part reflected the fact that the previous summer we had employed the daughter of a senior official as an intern) and I will never forget the wonderful dinner we were treated to after our meeting at the Reserve Bank of India. We were also lucky enough to stay at the old colonial Taj Hotel, which had recovered from the terrorist attack it had suffered the previous year, and where for the first and only time in my life I found myself being looked after by a butler: a classically turned out young man in his mid twenties who spoke perfect English greeted me at around 3.30 a.m. and duly prepared a very eagerly awaited Johnny Walker Black Label on the rocks as I registered. Then, five hours later, he woke me up with a perfectly arranged tray of English breakfast tea.

Moscow generated a similar mishmash of emotions. Walking around Red Square on the evening of our arrival (which, bizarrely, was one of the hottest December days on record), I was transported back to my youth when, on the BBC News, I would uneasily watch the serried ranks of soldiers, tanks and intercontinental ballistic missiles parading in front of a line of stone-faced Soviet leaders. But when we were there, the only other people in evidence were a few tourists from New Zealand and a couple of young lovers unable to keep their hands off each other. Things had clearly moved on, although I can honestly say that the meal we ate in a Ukrainian restaurant was one of the worst I have ever tasted. Russian hospitality also proved to be less subtle than that offered so deferentially in

Bombay. The most conspicuous example was delivered by the hotel doorman who, hearing that I was from the UK, rapidly informed me in highly accented English that he could get me whatever I might want to make my stay memorable: cocaine, crystal meth (?!), girls, boys or all of the above. Just ask Sergei! I politely declined.

Nor did the magical mystery tour end in Moscow. In the new year of 2010 I broke further new ground by following a visit to the South African Reserve Bank in Pretoria with day trips to Botswana and Namibia. The central bankers in Gaborone were one of the most charming groups I met in my career, and their country was a joy to behold. A real African success story, of which they had every right to be proud. Windhoek, on the other hand, was just odd. A city in a time warp: tiny, landlocked, surrounded by a barren, but beautiful, landscape, and with the feel of a small German market town in the sixties! Certainly none of the edge that one associates with South Africa's major cities.

CHAPTER 14

THE CRISIS

At this point I will offer some thoughts on the whys and wherefores of the Global Financial Crisis (GFC). These were originally developed back in 2009 in collaboration with my ex-boss and business partner John Llewellyn and others, and the conclusions that we came up with then still hold water, albeit with one or two tweaks.[40]

In essence, the GFC – the aftershocks of which continue to reverberate to this day – demonstrates how the human instincts of fear and greed can coalesce within a particular macroeconomic and regulatory framework to undermine both confidence and trust, creating mayhem. But there was no one single origin. The crisis was systemic in nature and reflected a number of causes that interacted and mutated. Furthermore, there is more than one layer of explanation. These considerations rendered the policy response extremely complex and challenging, and this continues to be the case.

Let us begin by discussing the macroeconomic and policy context prior to the crisis. For some time the major advanced economies had been struggling to maintain final demand at a high level. Or, at least, numerous policymakers, through their willingness to keep official interest rates historically low and soft-pedal on fiscal consolidation, were behaving as if this were the case.

Globalisation and Factor Shares

Consistent with the writings of Keynes, Kalecki and Marx (yes, Marx), globalisation played a central role in this. As China, India and other low-wage developing nations increasingly entered the system of world trade, an excess supply of workers and a significant related shift in factor shares (the shares of output taken by labour and capital incomes) in favour of profits ensued. Investment spending and its share in GDP initially responded positively to this development, first in Asia and later beyond, not least in the US. But excess capacity and a slowdown in capital accumulation then followed. The Asian and other developing economies retained the ability to export their way out of this demand deficiency problem, but this response was less open to the more advanced economies. Hence, in the US, where domestic political considerations also exerted a significant influence, the net result was the stimulus of domestic spending.

Macroeconomic Policy

Under the Bush administration, the US cut taxes in both 2001 and 2003, while also embarking on major overseas military operations. The fiscal stance was more conservative elsewhere in the OECD, yet, in truth, the efforts to reduce government deficits were rather half-hearted. Politicians always seemed to find an excuse for delaying budgetary consolidation or a justification for tax cuts, especially in the run-up to an election.

That said, central banks bore the brunt of the task of supporting domestic demand. In the US, the Federal Reserve's response to the collapse of the nineties tech bubble and to the subsequent recession and deflation scare was to slash policy interest rates to historically low levels and then normalise them only gradually. US monetary policy was extraordinarily loose in the early noughties, especially in the wake of the September 11 terrorist attacks, and it remained expansionary for some time after.

The bias of monetary policy was similarly, if less egregiously, lax across Europe and the rest of the OECD, and it was only in 2007 that official interest rates in the advanced economies had in any sense returned to normal.

The Generation of Imbalances

These policy preferences encouraged enormous macro disequilibria. Despite Alan Greenspan's Panglossian assessment of the budgetary outlook at the beginning of the millennium, the reality was that the US ran consistently large consolidated budgetary shortfalls from the 2001 recession onwards, and Europe and Japan also struggled to bring their deficits to heel over this period.

US property prices surged and the housing market began to account for a historically high and unsustainable proportion of output. In the meantime, household debt, which had been on a rising trend relative to disposable income since World War II, and which had already increased rapidly in the eighties and nineties, really took off, and the personal savings rate collapsed. Rising personal wealth and debt accumulation greatly stimulated domestic final demand, such that the US economy absorbed considerably more resources than it produced. The US had been running a persistent current account deficit since 1981, but the shortfall in the mid noughties reached new records, approaching 6% of GDP. A similar pattern of real estate excess, household sector balance sheet inflation and external deficits developed in the UK and in one or two other peripheral European economies. But in the Eurozone as a whole, the current account was close to balance, not least because of neo-mercantilist pursuit of surpluses in the core economies.

This is not to suggest that this constellation of international macro imbalances was entirely down to developments in the advanced economies, and in particular in the US. The penchant for fixed, or micro-managed, often artificially depressed, dollar exchange rate pegs in China, the Middle East and elsewhere amplified the effect of loose US monetary policy. And the counterpart current account surpluses of much of the non-US world, reinvested in significant part in the US, as the home of the world's most liquid asset markets, helped to keep US interest rates low. Nor was the US action unwelcome. Had the US not sustained domestic demand, expanded credit and run a large external deficit, then final demand everywhere else would necessarily have been less robust. As always, the counterfactual has to be considered.

Potential Consequences

The circumstances outlined above were unprecedented, and I would assert that there was no way of knowing in advance precisely how things were likely to play out, or when things would begin to unravel. However, there were some indicators of relevance.

First, there is the essential point that no entity, be it a person, a household, a company or a country, can indefinitely consume more than it produces. There comes a point, even for the world's largest economy, where lenders begin to become more circumspect about advancing further credit.

Second, as I have already mentioned, while I was at Lehman Brothers I helped to develop a tool called *Damocles* for identifying crisis potential in developing economies. Before I left Lehman, we would intermittently feed US and UK data through the model to see how these economies performed. This process continued after my departure and I was occasionally informed of the outcomes. By 2007 the US had been in the danger zone for some time, ranking down at similar levels to Iceland and Romania, with the main negative signals coming from its mounting external indebtedness, its current account deficit and its burgeoning household debt ratio. The UK also performed poorly, but not as poorly as the US.

Formal models such as *Damocles* have their place, although it can also on occasion make sense to cross-reference them with simpler rules of thumb. One that has always appealed to John and to me for its simplicity and proven veracity was the '4 Per Cent Rule' of Jan Qvigstad, the deputy governor of the Norwegian central bank. He has long believed that an economy risks trauma if the public sector deficit (as a proportion of GDP), the current account shortfall (as a proportion of GDP) or the inflation rate exceeds a value of 4%. On this basis too, the US was in the risky category in the run-up to the GFC.[41]

In the years before the crisis, the US, and to a lesser degree the whole global macroeconomic configuration, was looking unsustainable, and as the American economist Herbert Stein so succinctly put it: 'Things that can't go on for ever, don't.'[42]

Regulation

Let us now turn to regulation and how it interacted with the macroeconomic background both in the run up to the crisis and beyond.

Towards the end of the previous boom, a number of fundamental changes that had gradually emerged in US regulatory architecture were formalised by the abolition of the Glass–Steagall Act. This had both founded the US Federal Deposit Insurance Company and separated commercial and investment banking in an effort to eliminate the conflicts of interest that arise (as they had arisen in the thirties) when the granting of credit (lending) and the use of credit (investing) were undertaken by a single entity. In effect, Glass–Steagall said that if you want to have your deposit base insured, we will impose tough regulatory controls on the riskiness of your lending. You will be a commercial bank regulated by the Fed. If, on the other hand, you want to embrace much greater risk, then your shareholders must carry that risk. You will be an investment bank, regulated by the SEC.

With the abolition of Glass–Steagall, the stage was set for these conflicts to re-emerge. Equally important, however, was the manner in which these conflicts reappeared. There were, in essence, six routes by which this occurred.

First, savers who were seeking higher yields were relaxed about moving into assets that had traditionally been high risk. This was in part because inflation was quiescent. Indeed, as noted earlier, in the early years of the millennium the fear had been of deflation, not inflation. But more generally, macroeconomic stability was ostensibly greater than at any time in living memory.

Second, US investment banks borrowed heavily on the wholesale money markets and lent increasingly generously to households through mortgages and other loans, and this fuelled the property boom.

Third, mortgage mis-selling generated additional distortions and excesses. In the US, salespeople were paid per sale while bearing no responsibility for the resultant consequences.

Fourth, investment banks, responding to the stretch for yield, invented complex and highly geared investment vehicles, many of which they funded on the wholesale money markets and then sold on to other parties, so that they never appeared on their balance sheets. This was the so-called originate and distribute model.

Fifth, the explosion of leverage was further fuelled by the shadow banking system of hedge funds, private equity firms and other unregulated entities, which invested heavily in instruments such as collateralised debt obligations, mortgage-backed securities and credit default swaps.

Sixth, other countries became embroiled. Britain, Spain, Ireland and Australia replicated the housing boom, and investors and financial institutions in general bought substantial quantities of the new products that the investment banks had manufactured in industrial quantities.

Then, when asset values turned, paper wealth disappeared, confidence and trust evaporated, and leverage, which had hitherto been everybody's friend, turned into a savage enemy.

As the queen asked Mervyn King (the governor of the Bank of England at the time), why wasn't all this recognised, and why wasn't it stopped?

The explanations for why things played out as they did are many and various.

As I suggested in the introductory chapter, incentive structures often appeared to be dangerously one-sided, encouraging traders to take unduly risky bets. If the bet paid off, they were rewarded handsomely. If it didn't, it wasn't their money that they lost, and they simply moved on. That said, all traders are subject to individual risk limits and the ultimate responsibility therefore fell on the banks' management, which set and oversaw those limits.

The fact was that corporate risk analysis left a great deal to be desired. Within the financial sector, numerous economists (though fewer in the US than elsewhere) issued repeated warnings about the unsustainability of the global macroeconomic configuration, and in particular the configuration in the US. These warnings were typically ignored. Meanwhile, some mathematical risk models did not adequately take into account macroeconomic risks, while some risk managers were reluctant to admit that they really did not understand their banks' models and others failed to recognise that, for contractual or reputational reasons, sponsors would not be able to avoid responsibility for their supposedly 'off-balance-sheet' products.

There was undue reliance on value at risk analysis, which had two serious limitations. First, while there were many observations around the median of a distribution, there were very few tail observations, and it is at the extremities that catastrophic risk is manifest. This was particularly the case after such an extended period of low macroeconomic volatility. In practice, the probabilities of extreme events were obtained almost wholly by assumption. Second, the framework conditions within which a model operates evolve, and accommodating this requires the sort of structural framework that a statistical distribution alone does not provide. Many models therefore barely described reality at all.

My own direct experience in corporate risk management is telling. Belatedly asked to provide input to RBC's stress testing and financial planning in 2009 (i.e. rather after the horse had bolted), I was surprised to find that both the assumptions that were being used by the risk management department and the conclusions that were being drawn as a result were wildly off the mark. For example, they had blindly assumed that all the monetary policy stimulus then being put in place would prove inflationary in relatively short order, and most of the scenarios they sketched out for macro variables and the bank's balance sheet were, as a result, based on that view. The whole exercise needed to be recalibrated to better reflect the debt deflationary reality of the situation and the rather different threats this represented to the balance sheet of the bank. Why I had not been brought into this process sooner was beyond me, although I would also stress that the risk managers themselves were only too pleased to receive some additional guidance.

The management of financial institutions proved very reluctant to act, even when it became clear that their modi operandi were putting their companies and the entire financial system at risk. Chuck Prince, the chief executive of Citigroup, captured this shortcoming perfectly in July 2007 when he asserted that, 'When the music stops, in terms of liquidity, things will be complicated. But as long as the music is playing, you've got to get up and dance. We're still dancing.'

Boards of directors also proved to be too weak, or too ill-informed, to challenge so-called successful CEOs. Managements increasingly appeared to have run companies for their own benefit, and shareholders proved unwilling or unable to rein them in. This was certainly the case at Lehman Brothers. The Lehman board was predominantly composed of worthy individuals, but they had little knowledge of finance and were often indebted to the CEO for making them wealthy.

Grade inflation by the credit rating agencies didn't help, either, implying as it did that a mortgage vehicle rated as 'triple A' carried the same risk as the US sovereign. This was absurd. And the credit rating agencies also became conflicted, in that they accepted fees for certifying that the new vehicles were high grade. At root, the credit rating agencies' business model contains an unsolvable conundrum: the people who pay for their services are not those who use them.

The regulatory authorities did a poor job. They relied too much on companies doing the right thing, and failed to ensure that they did so.

Capital ratios proved inadequate. When asset values collapsed, not only were shareholders wiped out, but the investment banks were revealed as having huge systemic importance. Remarkably, the total amount that the financial sector wrote off following the crisis was considerably more than a hundred times its collective value at risk assessment before the crisis.

The pro-cyclical impact of 'mark to market' valuation techniques exacerbated the capital inadequacy of banks. When crashing 'fire sale' values were used by auditors to value a bank's assets, fire sales were encouraged to spread, thereby deepening the crisis.

Deficiencies in the understanding of corporate self-interest led regulators from Alan Greenspan down to believe that managements would always have their company's survival as their primary objective and would therefore eschew actions that would undermine that survival. This judgement underestimated managements' short-term objectives, their shortcomings in the area of macroeconomic understanding, and the extent to which competitive pressures encouraged each set of managers to do much the same as the others.

Finally, international organisations such as the IMF, the OECD, the BIS and the G-7 failed to press the point about the burgeoning risks forcefully enough.

The Policy Response

There was never any doubt in my mind, given the extent to which I had been steeped from a young age in the economic and financial dimensions of the Great Depression and its aftermath, that the situation wrought by the considerations outlined above would require a comprehensive and extended policy response at both the macroeconomic and microeconomic levels and that the necessary adjustments might well venture some way into unconventional territory. Such was the virulence of the crisis and the threat of a collapse of confidence and the onset of debt deflation that this was not a time for half measures. There could be no repeat of the errors of the thirties that so deepened and prolonged the Great Depression. If ever there was a case for Keynesian policy activism, this was it. But equally, the regulatory environment and the incentive structure required serious recalibration.

Clearly, the initial priority was macro stimulus to moderate the downdraft to final demand. Policy interest rates needed to be slashed and action taken to flatten the yield curve and bring down corporate and other spreads. Notwithstanding historically high public sector debt (which was clearly unfortunate, or even tragic), where it was not completely inconsistent with any notion of sustainability, discretionary fiscal stimulus was required to supplement the operation of 'automatic stabilisers'. But in addition, policymakers had to respond with bank deposit guarantees, bank recapitalisations, efforts to remove compromised assets from financial institutions' balance sheets, support to ensure that important financial markets continued to function, short-term loans to non-financial corporations, and the easing of repayment terms for mortgagees.

These options were all exercised to some degree or another, and the net result was indeed that the downside to real activity was mitigated and to some extent recovery was encouraged. However, especially in Europe, where close trade linkages magnified the associated multiplier effects, fiscal policy was subsequently thrown into reverse gear far too quickly and far too aggressively, and this greatly extended the difficulties of the Eurozone and UK economies. Even if 2008 and 2009 saw substantial fiscal largesse, this had largely run its course by 2010 and was being dialled back by 2011, at a time when few economies had seen their levels of real GDP return to their pre-crisis peaks. The recessions that follow financial crises are invariably enduring and intractable, and the lessons of premature fiscal tightening in the US during the recovery from the Great Depression had clearly not been fully learned.[43]

It is also true that the initial macro policy response essentially left unaddressed many of the fundamental macroeconomic conditions that gave rise to the initial situation. All it did was buy time for adjustment.

Lessons for Policy

Outlined below are eleven broad policy recommendations that, had they been in place, might have reduced the likelihood, if not the severity, of the crisis. However, whether they will help with the next crisis, which is bound to be different, is another matter.

- Narrow inflation targeting is not enough. Central bank mandates and policymakers in general need to pay greater attention to imbalances, not least in financial sectors.

- It makes sense to direct policy at any major macroeconomic variable that departs significantly from any stable historical relationship.

- Do not place undue emphasis on interest rate policy. It is not a universal panacea.

- Fiscal policy can still be very effective, especially within closely knit trading blocs, when private sector confidence is acutely depressed, and when policy interest rates are at the zero bound. However, there is a need for transparent and accountable fiscal policy rules that emphasise greater symmetry across the business cycle.

- Agree a better method of identifying bubbles. Alan Greenspan was reluctant to classify any period of stock or real estate inflation as a bubble, arguing that asset prices are an important signalling device and that their appropriate values are unknowable. Minsky, however, identified bubbles by the behaviour of people, focussing on any occasion when large numbers of people start trading in markets that they don't understand. He had a point. Macroprudential policy also has an important role to play in encouraging financial stability.

- Require the regulatory authorities to report on the potential financial sector implications of macroeconomic imbalances.

- Establish *ex ante* the conditions whereby it is appropriate to take over a distressed bank. Ideally, a failing bank should be taken over when its net worth is still positive, so that it can continue as a going concern.

- Capital adequacy ratios must be significantly higher for any bank that operates with its deposits guaranteed.

- There should be two types of credit rating agency: one to carry out legislated supervisory responsibilities; the other to conduct ratings for business for profit, with no role in supervision.

- Restrict proprietary trading and discourage off-balance-sheet activities. Put the onus on any entity taking such risk to explain why doing so is in the public interest.

- Undertake detailed planning of the exit conditions from present monetary policy settings that, though necessary, cannot be sustainable in the long run.

CHAPTER 15

FROM HERO
TO VILLAIN

To say that I departed RBC under a cloud would be something of an understatement. It marked the nadir of a career that has been noteworthy for its ups and downs. The way things ended seems odd given my professional performance for the two and a half years after my arrival at the firm in September 2007: for the vast majority of that period I called the global economy and its major markets pretty well; I enjoyed an excellent reputation for my written and verbal output; I more than matched any reasonable expectations where travel and marketing were concerned; my media exposure represented a major PR positive for the firm; and I was highly regarded by the majority of my peers in sales and trading, both in London and further afield. So how did things go so catastrophically wrong?

My fall from grace reflected a number of considerations – some circumstantial, some uniquely personal. It reflected a lack of support from my team. It reflected my own lack of faith in that team. It reflected management that was never satisfied. It reflected the fact that I took too much on. But above all, and this is the really painful piece of the equation, it reflected my own insecurities and a belief that I was never quite good enough – never quite in the same intellectual league as the best in the market.

This cocktail of factors led me to cut corners, and in particular it led me into an area that had more than a whiff of plagiarism to it. Now plagiarism is an emotive phrase and it is a very grey area. The reality is that there is precious little truly original thought in financial market economics, and much of the time economists and strategists, who have for the most part been trained in the same skills and in the same manner, reach similar conclusions by resort to similar analytical processes. It is also the case that information in today's financial markets is almost unlimited, it is rarely protected and it is very cheap to access. Indeed, the marginal cost is close to zero. Furthermore, as events play out, one is being constantly bombarded with comment and opinion. This can be communicated directly, it can be communicated second hand, it can come via the media or it can come via some piece of research that one has seen. The choices one has if one 'borrows' or 'inherits' an idea (and I would stress that everyone does it) are to include the necessary attribution or to cover your tracks, rephrase it, repackage it or tweak it in some way that allows you to present it as your own, or at least as your own interpretation.

I made two mistakes. These foolish errors cost me my job and, without the support and faith of certain individuals, they could have cost me my career.

First, I circulated a draft note among my team for comment that failed to include the necessary attribution to another article on the same topic. And although I firmly intended to revisit the piece in question before publication (why else would I have asked for comments?), and in fact wrote an alternative piece that I subsequently actually preferred to publish, my initial oversight was identified by my second in command and the information was passed on to my boss (as was required under the firm's code of practice).

Second, in a note I wrote over a weekend for internal circulation I made use of a time line of future events relevant to the developing European sovereign risk crisis that was drawn from a competitor's research (which had in turn been transcribed from a central bank website). My weekend email was subsequently forwarded to clients by a salesperson, even though it was not originally meant for such a purpose. Someone noticed the similarity with another piece of research they had read and the next thing I knew I was called into a room and confronted by management and one of RBC's lawyers and asked to explain myself, albeit, I would stress, in a manner that suggested that they believed there must be some reasonable explanation for all this. They couldn't seem to grasp that I could have put myself in such a position.

I, on the other hand, knew that I had. I was mortified and, aware of both the conservatism of the firm and the broader hyper-critical environment in which the banking sector found itself in the wake of the GFC, I resigned on the spot. Indeed, I walked straight out of that meeting, picked up my briefcase and walked out of the door. I didn't say goodbye to my team or to any one. I am not proud of this fact, but I just couldn't face the humiliation or the scorn.

I was devastated. How could I have been so lazy, so foolish, so misguided? How could I have let so many people down? How could I have let myself down in this way? Explaining the situation to my wife, family and close friends was as difficult a task as I have ever faced. And there were broader issues, too. My misdemeanours would tarnish my professional record: that was unavoidable. But would RBC report me to the FSA? I was, after all, a managing director of the bank. And would the FSA fine me or would it prohibit me from working in the financial industry? Also, RBC had just introduced a 'claw-back policy' on bonuses, and I feared that they might ask for their money back. What really concerned me, though, was that I would have to come clean about my behaviour with any future prospective employer, and they would then have every right to drop me like a stone. I sought legal advice, but the prognosis was hardly positive. I was in the wrong and I had admitted it. However, I was advised that it was unlikely that RBC would want this to be made public, especially as I had immediately fallen on my sword. And thankfully, so it proved.

Quite how I managed to pick myself up and dust myself down after this potentially fatal self-inflicted wound I don't know, although the support of my family and close friends, not least John Llewellyn, made an enormous contribution to my maintaining my mental equilibrium. In the end, I took the view that I had to try to rebuild my career – this was not how I wanted it to end.

My strategy was initially to tell the headhunters and others I contacted that I had left RBC because of internal politics. I would only reveal the truth as and when I had attracted some serious interest from a potential employer, at which point I would endeavour to be scrupulously frank about what I had done and how much I regretted it.

Thankfully, I rapidly found myself the subject of attention from various sources, with two roles sounding particularly interesting. Westpac, one of the 'Big Four' Australian banks that had come through the GFC in good shape, was looking to broaden its horizons and saw the recruitment of a head of fixed income strategy with a global purview as a potentially powerful way of achieving this. Within a month of leaving RBC I was on a plane to Sydney for a couple of days of interviews. Initially, the notion of relocating

Down Under was not something that my wife and I were keen on. One of the girls was already happily ensconced at Oxford and the other was about to start her first year at Sussex. But we both recognised that, given the situation I had put us all in, we could not afford to rule anything out.

What I found in Australia was a firm, or at least a global head of the fixed income business, that was crying out for the international expertise I could bring. The notion of putting some distance between London and the next leg of my career therefore rapidly became a more attractive proposition. But first I had to come clean. This I did at the end of the interview process, when I knew that they were seriously interested. What I had also done was ask three highly regarded close confidants of mine to be ready to speak up on my behalf. Westpac were fantastic. They discussed my situation long and hard but took the view that my honesty about the matter suggested that it was a one-off. I came away from Sydney under the firm impression that the job could be mine if I wanted it.

My experience with the second opportunity was altogether less positive. This was with another Canadian bank that was trying to expand its presence in London, and while the initial discussions were encouraging, once I made it clear why I had left RBC everything changed. The Canadian financial sector is an incestuous beast, and it contains few secrets. Soundings were taken from senior RBC figures in Toronto and I was soon informed that 'reputational issues had intervened that made my recruitment impossible'. I was hurt but hardly surprised. How could I be?

After this rejection, Westpac became an even more attractive option, especially after we all discussed what it might mean to us as a family. In particular, the girls were happy enough to remain in the UK for their university careers but to spend a significant portion of their holidays in Australia. However, dotting the i's and crossing the t's of my contract took rather longer than I thought, not least because the man initially responsible for my recruitment decided to move on. Once again, the vagaries of financial sector management had intervened at an unfortunate time. In the end, Westpac decided to honour their commitment to me regardless of the change in personnel, and while I of course wondered quite what this would mean in practice, it was certainly a case at the time of a beggar not being in a position to choose. I still needed to work, and Westpac had offered me a lifeline that was not readily available elsewhere.

CHAPTER 16

RESURRECTION DOWN UNDER

My time at Westpac began in their London office in the summer of 2010. As I walked into the building I remembered that when I first started talking to them I had very nearly not shown up for the interview. After my embarrassing ejection from RBC I was so knocked off kilter, so disappointed in myself and so unprepared to search out another job, especially one on the other side of the world, that when I got up to the City I debated turning around and going home again. But life never fails to surprise. My initial spell with the bank in London gave me time to rebuild my stock of knowledge after the months out of the markets, do some homework about the Australian and New Zealand economies (I had some familiarity with them but was certainly not an expert), and get acquainted with one of the more important outposts of the firm's international operations. I also undertook a few brief business trips, including one to Brazil, where the central bank was keen to start buying Australian government bonds to diversify its reserve holdings.

By early September I had decamped to Sydney and Westpac's modern headquarters on the western edge of the central business district, overlooking Darling Harbour and the disused dockyards at Barangaroo. There was a certain familiarity about upping sticks and moving to the other side of the world, but unlike my move to Abu Dhabi, my wife and I did our house-hunting together, and even if the girls would be with us only intermittently, they were young women now, and it was comforting to know that, from the New Year, the family home would be where I was situated.

I had been coming to Australia on business since 1990 and one of my most cherished memories of the place is of the first time I landed there. Having flown down overnight from Tokyo, I checked into the wonderful Park Hyatt Hotel, situated underneath the Harbour Bridge, as dawn broke. When I reached my room I pulled open the curtains to find the most exquisite view of the Opera House. Although it was only 6 a.m., I opened the minibar, poured myself a beer and sat on the balcony to watch the city come to life. (I should add that my first meeting of the day was not until mid morning.)

In addition to my happy experiences of Australia, my Anglo-Greek wife had spent most of the eighties working for the Australian Tourist Commission in London. Not only did she therefore know more about Australia than most Australians, we also had a network of friends to call on when we arrived. This overseas jaunt was consequently rather less daunting than previous escapades. We both knew Sydney and the delights it offered well, and it was clear from the outset that this was not going to be a hardship posting. In fact I couldn't quite believe how lucky I had been to receive this opportunity to rebuild my career after my ignominious exit from RBC. Unsurprisingly, this was also the view of some of my ex-colleagues and acquaintances in London, who found themselves caught up in the UK's most obdurate recession ever. The City of London was under acute stress because of both the macroeconomic situation and the desire of the public and politicians alike to extract compensation for its many excesses and failures over the previous couple of decades.

I made my debut in front of Westpac's domestic clients at the firm's annual economics and strategy conference the day after my arrival. As I said at the time, I felt privileged to be working alongside some of the best macro research talent in Australia. Chief Economist Bill Evans boasted a wealth of experience (he was even older than me) and I was also a long-standing fan of Robert Rennie, the head of foreign exchange research. He, like me, was a Pommie who had built his reputation in London before moving Down Under, although a major difference between us was that he was a Glaswegian rather than a Liverpudlian. Jokes at our own expense about our respective home towns became commonplace during the presentations we gave together. I was also lucky enough to inherit the best fixed-income strategists in Australia and New Zealand in the shape of Damien McColough and Tim Jung in Sydney and Imre

Speizer in Auckland. One could not have asked for more congenial and supportive colleagues.

I am proud to say that throughout my time at Westpac, the team was ranked number one in industry surveys. This was a first for me. Despite working with some incredibly smart people over the years, a top ranking was something that always eluded the teams I was part of or had led. Some might say that Australia is a small and relatively unimportant market, and in some senses that is true, but the Australian dollar is the world's fifth most traded currency, and in recent years it has become a prime focus of global investors, not least because central banks and sovereign wealth funds have been looking to diversify their asset holdings in a search for yield. At the same time, Australia has one of the most 'over-broked' debt markets in the world. The competition is intense. I think I am therefore entitled to be as proud as I am of what the team achieved during my time there.

My long history of venturing down to Australia also meant that I had some knowledge of both the client base and the policymaking community. The former were invariably easy-going and welcoming, yet smart and thoughtful, and their interest in the global situation was keen. How could it be otherwise in an economy that was so dependent on the international demand for its commodities? Senior Australian economic policymakers were an impressive breed. As I mentioned in chapter 8, I had two ex-RBA economists working with me at Lehman in Tokyo, and when I moved to Australia I found the people I met at the central bank and the Treasury well informed and astute, and not just about their local economy. They offered valuable insights into the global picture, and especially when it came to China. It should also be remembered that Australia has not had a recession since the early nineties, and that not only did policymakers in Sydney and Canberra successfully steer the economy through the GFC, they also had a massive terms-of-trade boom to contend with. This is a remarkable record.

Where Westpac was lacking was in its international analysis. Bill knew his stuff, Rob was an innovative foreign exchange strategist whose knowledge spread far beyond the Antipodes and, in Huw McKay, the company also had one of the most original commentators on China in its ranks, but there was no one to pull a view of the global environment together and assess it thematically. This was where I came in, and I gave the firm something that no other major Australian bank had.

My employment by Westpac worked in that the period from 2010 to 2012 was dominated by international considerations, and in particular by the aftershocks of the GFC. Australian investors and the firm's risk takers could not ignore Europe, they had to be aware of the extraordinary monetary policy initiatives being put in place in the US and the UK, and they had to have a view on Japan, China and the rest of Asia, given that these economies meant so much to Australia. My commentary sought to address these issues and, once I had come up to speed with domestic developments, I tried where possible to put Australia and New Zealand's macroeconomies and their fixed-income markets into this context.

Where my role worked less well was that, aside from highly commoditised foreign exchange, the company sold little product that was not Australian or New Zealand in origin. Nor, therefore, were the salesforces anything like as worldly wise as those I had worked with before, and if I am being frank, both the quality and the quantity of the bank's offshore sales effort were poor. Indeed, with one exception in New York, shockingly poor. Hence, the business struggled to directly monetise my input. I might have made the right call on the Fed or on Greece, but how many times could a salesperson in Sydney turn that into a profitable Aussie swap trade, for example?

This was particularly the case as the global ambitions that had attracted me to the bank in the first place soon withered and died. Ahead of my employment at Westpac I had been asked to put together a business plan on the basis that the firm would be expanding its offshore operations and looking to trade and sell international bond market product in London, New York and across Asia, as well as at home. This, I suggested, would require a fixed-income strategy team of up to twelve, based in the major financial centres as well as in Australia and New Zealand. This proposal was accepted, and indeed I was assured that setting it up would facilitate my ultimate repatriation to the UK in four years' time, from where I would continue to run the group. It was no wonder I was so attracted to the role.

But none of this ever materialised. Instead, as the reverberations of the GFC continued to generate enormous macroeconomic and financial market volatility, Westpac pulled in its horns and reverted to its default option: that of trying to be the best within its home markets. And when the management of the fixed-income division changed in late 2011, and there was no longer anyone in a senior position who had been directly involved in my recruitment, the reversion to type deepened. I knew that my stay in Australia was likely to prove shorter than I originally believed when the new head of the division blurted out to me: 'I can't understand how we hired a Brit international macroeconomist to run fixed income strategy.' From that moment on my sense was that, as a relatively expensive and mature member of the group, with expertise that was anything but the norm, I would be in the firing line as soon as the business suffered a major hiccough. Mentally, I began to prepare for such an eventuality.

This is not to suggest, though, that I did not enjoy my time in Australia. The truth is the opposite, on both a personal and professional level. Sydney is a beautiful city in which to live and work. It can appear a little small after London and Tokyo, it is a long way from anywhere, and it is certainly a young person's town. But on the other hand, my commute into the office was twenty minutes on the bus or a fifty-minute walk, and at lunchtime I could go for an hour's jog around one of the world's most majestic harbours. In the evening, for eight months of the year, I could jump into my car when I got home and be swimming off Bondi Beach in ten minutes. What a contrast to the trials and tribulations of getting to work and back on the tube in London and the misery of its winter climate. What is more, an hour and a half out of Sydney and you can be in the sparsely populated wilds of the Blue Mountains. An hour and a half out of London and you are in Birmingham.

Workwise, I greatly enjoyed doing tag team acts with Bill, Rob and Huw, and the firm's annual macro strategy conference was always an excellent event to be part of. At one of these I was lucky enough to see Paul Keating (a former Australian prime minister) deliver a pugnacious tour d'horizon of global geopolitics that proved one of the more astute and entertaining speeches I have ever witnessed. I'd venture that it was close to being on a par with the speech I saw Bill Clinton make in Tokyo just before my departure from Japan. Keating also happily hung about afterwards to sink a few beers, chat and answer question after question. I was deeply impressed. At another of these events, the guest of honour was another former Australian prime minister, John Howard. While a much more understated and less abrasive animal than Keating, and of a rather different political hue, he too offered some fascinating insights into the world and was incredibly patient and friendly during the drinks reception that followed.

I was also lucky enough to be able to ride the wave of the diversification trade. As a rare positive exception to the OECD rule of deep recession and hesitant and uneven recovery, Australia and its debt found themselves in huge demand from the international investment community, as indeed was New Zealand, albeit to a lesser extent. Australia was a high-yielding economy for most of the right reasons, and it was increasingly seen as a safe haven: a more worthy 'triple A-rated' sovereign credit than many of the others that were desperately struggling to hang on to that moniker. This meant that our research was in huge demand offshore, and I again found myself travelling all over the world to see reserve managers. From China and Japan to Poland and Russia to Mexico and Chile – the interest in Australia and New Zealand was unrelenting.

I also enjoyed the atmosphere, both within the office and with clients. In some ways Australia's financial markets proved to be something of a throwback to my early days in the business. People would have a few drinks on a Friday lunchtime and client entertainment enjoyed a higher and much less stuffy profile than was the case in London, where over the years an attitude seemed to have developed that, to be worthwhile, a client event had to be serious. Pub nights were common. Visits to one of the plethora of sporting events that Australia excels at were both de rigeur and great fun, especially when the opposition was a team of Poms.

Indeed, one of my initial client events was at the First Test between Australia and England in Brisbane in November 2010. To secure their attendance, clients had to listen to me for half an hour, in that during the lunch interval the group left the stadium and took up residence at an excellent restaurant over the road and, as they ate and drank, I provided a few thoughts on the global economy. After lunch we retired to watch the rest of the day's play, which, I am happy to say, England dominated.

Perhaps the only aspect of Aussie business that I didn't wholly embrace was the heroic drinking. I find Australians' sociability an extremely attractive aspect of their national character, but their approach to alcohol consumption could be pretty juvenile. My first insight into this came during my first weekend in the job. On the Friday evening I decamped with the entire fixed-income team to a resort in Port Douglas in Northern Queensland for their annual offsite. What followed over the next thirty-six hours was a monumental piss-up that began at Sydney airport, settled into a steady rhythm on the three-hour flight to Cairns, was sustained by a couple of cases of beer in the minivan to the hotel, and then progressively descended into a series of scenes from *Fear and Loathing in Las Vegas* once we arrived at our destination. Some people were virtually stretchered off our Qantas flight when it landed back in Sydney on Sunday afternoon.

From that moment on I was recognised as someone whose presence at similar occasions was unlikely, although I would stress that I was rarely (at least publicly) the subject of any 'Pommie-poofter' jokes as a result.

One of the positive elements of my job at Westpac was that I was granted the freedom to write about whatever I wanted, provided, of course, it was pertinent to what was going on in global markets and, in particular, in the Australian and New Zealand debt markets. Over my two-and-a-half-year spell in Sydney I produced up to four 1,800-word briefing notes per week on subjects that ranged far and wide. What I also tried to do was put out a weekend commentary, as I had done for RBC in London, that sought to provide at least a partial framework of thought for the next seven days. This was something I borrowed from Jim O'Neill's Global Economics unit at Goldman Sachs, which I looked upon as the best around. I also found that putting my thinking down on paper away from the hurly burly of the trading floor helped to clarify my thoughts. And I knew that, as the Aussies and Kiwis valued their free time so much, none of my domestic competitors would be following my example.

The bulk of my utterances focused on various aspects of the European sovereign risk crisis and its broader implications, the development of unconventional policy responses to the GFC and its aftermath, the sustainability of historically low global bond yields, and, of course, the impact of Australia's mining boom on the economy.

In assessing Europe's trials and tribulations, never having been a fundamentalist Europhile (or, for that matter, a Little Englander), I have largely taken European integration and the evolution of the European Union for what it is. That is, a basically laudable project that began for all the right reasons but in which political ambition has tended to develop in advance of the underlying macroeconomic fundamentals.

From the start, the euro was a half-baked hybrid. There are essentially six textbook conditions for an optimal currency zone.

- The members should enjoy synchronised business cycles and similar economic structures.

- There should be competitiveness convergence and wage and price flexibility to sustain it.

- There should be a high degree of labour and capital mobility.

- There should be a sound and consistent macro-prudential framework and a single lender of last resort.

- There should be a powerful and symmetrical system of fiscal oversight and transfers.

- There should be an efficient system of governance and decision making.

The sad fact is that the Eurozone has never fully met any of these conditions. Some have been met at different times, at least in part, but none in their entirety and none over the whole life of the project. This rendered the entire edifice vulnerable to shocks, and in 2007 it was struck by the largest shock to impact the global economy since the war. Moreover, in the run-up to the crisis, much of its financial sector had been as culpable for excess as any other. Hence, its numerous fault lines were exposed and the net result was near-catastrophic.

Although the situation is now more stable than in 2010 and 2011, and any imminent fragmentation of the single currency looks unlikely, huge uncertainties endure. Moreover, the Eurozone economy remains acutely depressed and the level of joblessness, especially among the young, is a tragedy. The effects of this will reverberate for decades.

The region desperately needs sustained growth: its sovereign debt crisis is impossible to overcome without it. I also remain concerned about France, a country at the very core of the European project but one whose economy is persistently failing to compete with that of Germany and which is overseen by a government that has yet to grasp the extent of the nation's structural shortcomings. Whether the euro survives in its present form over the longer term therefore remains moot. What would happen if it were to disintegrate is even more unclear.

The immediate collateral damage from a break-up would depend on precisely how it played out, and in particular on whether there remained any vestiges of the existing single currency – a hard core euro, for example. But it is difficult to believe that the outcome could be anything other than extremely damaging, both for Europe and for the world. The Eurozone's influence on global trade, capital flows and confidence is quite simply too big for it to fail painlessly. One must also ask what kind of economy would emerge once the initial trauma had passed. Europe might still be criticised for its lingering attachment to old-style social models and excessive government interference, but the fact is that, over the past three decades, it has gradually become more market orientated. Indeed, the crisis has accelerated this process. Can we really be sure that this pro-market momentum would be sustained in the event of a break-up? Or would Europe collapse back into the quagmire of red tape, financial repression and trade and capital controls that marked its previous history and all the political infighting that went with that? Personally, I suspect that we would see more of the latter than the former.

In my presentations for Westpac, for two and a half years I used much the same slide to outline what I thought would provide an enduring solution to the crisis. I saw the following as priorities.

- Slower fiscal austerity in the periphery. The pace of fiscal adjustment had in many cases proved self-defeating. Fiscal austerity really cannot work well when every country in a close-knit trading bloc is embracing it simultaneously, and when the private sector is dead set on deleveraging too.

- Greater fiscal policy symmetry. There should be some budgetary expansion in the core, and particularly in Germany.

- Further sovereign debt restructurings in the periphery, and perhaps even in parts of the core.

- The application of real quantitative easing, rather than the half-hearted variations on the theme represented by Long Term Refinancing Operations or the threat of Outright Monetary Transactions.

- The expansion of the European Stability Mechanism bail-out fund's firepower to some €2trn.

- Latitude for the European Stability Mechanism to recapitalise the Eurozone's banks directly and address legacy asset issues in conjunction with the rapid creation of a banking union, extending to a common deposit guarantee, a common system of regulation and supervision, and a common resolution authority.

- Root-and-branch reform of labour and product markets and greatly accelerated institutional change, including the issue of joint and severally guaranteed 'eurobonds', a single treasury and finance minister, and the collectivisation of fiscal policy as the final step towards political union.

Getting all this done, or at least getting it done within a timescale that was acceptable to the individual governments and electorates of the member countries, was (and remains) another matter, however.

Where quantitative easing is concerned – despite the burgeoning distortions associated with it, evidence of its diminishing returns and the undoubted complexities associated with exiting from such strategies – I have long been a supporter of the approach embraced by the Federal Reserve and the Bank of England.

The rationalisation for quantitative easing is intricately bound up with the nature of the current business cycle and the assorted constraints acting on orthodox macroeconomic policy in 2007. The major economies have been in the midst of an extended period of financial sector dysfunction and private sector balance sheet adjustment, such that both the supply of credit and the demand for it are severely compromised. In this context, the initial downdraft to real activity was extremely severe and the recovery has proved painfully hesitant and uneven. As a result, six years on there remains considerable excess capacity, not least in labour markets.

After some reluctance, especially in Europe, standard monetary policy tools were used with some aggression to counter this set of circumstances, but they were exhausted as short-term interest rates encroached on the zero bound. More monetary stimulus was required, and this could be applied only by bearing down on the longer end of the yield curve through a combination of the manipulation of short-term interest rate expectations and resort to outright bond purchases to moderate, if not altogether remove, the term premium and directly influence corporate and mortgage spreads over the risk-free rate. The net result was a huge increase in the monetary base and the expansion of central bank balance sheets.

However, such an environment resembles Keynes's famous 'liquidity trap'. If that logic is applied, then, to supplement monetary policy, fiscal policy should also assume a responsibility for sustaining final demand. This occurred in 2009 and 2010 but, of late, public sector debt sustainability issues have intervened and limited the room for budgetary largesse, if not actively encouraged pro-cyclical fiscal restraint. The negative attitude to fiscal policy may, at least in some countries, be an overreaction, but it is nevertheless a reality and it means that the overwhelming burden of supporting final demand falls on the shoulders of monetary policy. Without quantitative easing, the risk would have been of a deflationary spiral.

That said, macroeconomic policy is now close to its limits. Should another negative shock to demand intervene, quantitative easing as currently configured, however aggressively it was pursued, might not be enough. In such circumstances the only alternative might be direct debt monetisation, whether to fund additional tax cuts or public investment programmes.

The primary benefit of direct debt monetisation would be that it breaks the policy logjam produced by a simultaneous requirement for deleveraging in both the private and public sectors. And because it makes no call on private sector savings, it should also prove more expansionary than quantitative easing or orthodox fiscal stimulus on a unit-by-unit basis. Moreover, provided that any programme of direct debt monetisation was confined merely to closing a large output gap, any impact on inflation expectations should be contained.

However, there is no escaping the fact that disengagement from unorthodox macro policies is likely to prove vexed. These strategies have laid central banks open to renewed political interference, if not (so far at least) explicit dilution of their independence. In particular, central banks could require recapitalisation in the face of major losses on their inflated and increasingly diversified asset holdings, while the public may react negatively to the prospect of significant transfers to banks as the interest rate on reserves is raised.

Moreover, before this exit process has started in earnest, and despite central bankers' efforts to avoid it, considerable volatility has already been sparked in asset markets. Even in relatively normal periods the calibration of monetary policy with the business cycle was more art than science. But the challenges of the initiation, sequencing and tempo of the withdrawal of unorthodox stimulus are enormous when there is unfamiliarity with the apparatus employed and with the macroeconomic circumstances being confronted, and when the influence of central banks in financial markets has become so pivotal.

In the limit, quantitative easing and even direct debt monetisation are better than doing nothing to stabilise economies, but we must not be blind to their costs.

Finally, we turn to Australia itself. On leaving Sydney at the end of 2012 I warned my erstwhile colleagues that, in my view, the economy was about to be confronted with an increasingly demanding set of circumstances – and that it was overdue a recession. The past year has done nothing to change my assessment.

The Australian economy has long been an exception to the OECD rule. It has not suffered a major contraction in output since the early nineties, and over the intervening period the annual rate of growth of real GDP has averaged around 3.3%, while underlying CPI inflation has for the most part remained under control. The country also managed to escape the worst ravages of the Great Recession. Aside from a short sharp contraction in the fourth quarter of 2008 following the Lehman Brothers debacle, the economy continued to expand throughout, and it is noticeable that, unlike in many advanced nations, the absolute level of real GDP has not just returned to its pre-crisis peak but has risen significantly above it. Hence, even though it has latterly edged upwards, unemployment remains at a relatively low 5.7% of the workforce.

That part of this impressive performance can be ascribed to good policy is beyond doubt. The eighties and early nineties saw the implementation of a range of successful structural reforms that exerted an enduring positive influence on the supply side of the economy, while important stability-enhancing improvements were also made to the nation's monetary and fiscal policy frameworks. Australia's Reserve Bank has proved one of the more successful practitioners of inflation targeting, while the net public sector debt ratio is now one of the lowest in the developed world and it is one of the few remaining 'triple-A-rated' sovereigns.

However, during the latter half of this twenty-odd year period of economic success, the most important catalyst for Australia's macroeconomic outperformance was a sizeable boom in the nation's resource sector. Australia's economic development has always been significantly influenced by the prices of its natural resource exports, and over the course of its history it has experienced successive periods of boom and bust as a result. Latterly, the economy has become a vital supplier of raw material inputs for the rapidly developing northern Asian economies, and especially for China. Taken as a whole, the Asian region is not particularly resource rich and it is currently going through its most commodity-intensive stage of development, with the demand underpinned by a range of factors from urbanisation to an increasing demand for protein-rich foodstuffs. Australia has thus been a prime beneficiary of the progressive shift in the world's centre of economic gravity from West to East. The last decade has seen the country's terms of trade surge to a 140-year high.

Aside from during periods of serious oil price volatility, the potential for the terms of trade to shape the contours of the business cycle and dictate the path of national income and living standards is often underappreciated in the Northern Hemisphere. But the relative prices of exports and imports are often of overriding importance in a commodity-producing economy, especially when secondary effects on capital flows and the exchange rate are taken into account.

Between 2005 and 2012, for example, the Australian mining industry doubled its share of total output to more than 10% and tripled its share of business investment to more than 40%, while the manufacturing sector's influence declined to less than 8% of total nominal gross value added. Over the same period, exports of coal and iron ore increased by 100% in value terms, and resource exports grew to account for some 60% of the total. Similarly, mining sector employment expanded rapidly, while it fell in other export industries and in some areas of the domestic economy. In aggregate, the RBA estimates that until recently the broadly defined mining-related economy had been growing at an annual rate of around 7.5% since the middle of the last decade, while the rest of the economy grew at an altogether less impressive rate of 2.5%.

All of this is now starting to change. The terms of trade have already corrected by some 15% from their highs and Australia's resource boom is showing every sign of beginning to wind down. Mining-related outlays have peaked and will now trend lower. In the meantime, GDP growth has slipped below trend. Large changes in relative prices are never comfortable experiences, economically, socially or politically, and the latest episode represents a huge test for Australian policymakers, who are now faced with sustaining overall macroeconomic stability at the same time as securing a rotation to the other sources of final demand that have been so subdued over recent periods.

Of course, high export volumes will help the adjustment process. Iron ore volumes are already expanding at an annual rate of about 15% and natural gas shipments will grow strongly from 2015, although prices will probably be lower as alternative sources in the US, Africa and beyond are tapped. Also, a significant part of the resource sector's investment outlays were supplied by imports, and these will be reduced commensurately in future years. But the fact is that macro stability will only be possible if some combination of non-mining business investment, personal consumption, housing investment and government purchases fills the bulk of the gap.

The exchange rate has long proved a vital equilibrator for the Australian economy as it has ridden the international commodity price cycle, and the trade-weighted Australian dollar's recent depreciation of some 15–20% will, especially if it continues, serve as an important mechanism of structural adjustment. However, the task of achieving the necessary degree of recalibration in the economy is complex and should not be underestimated.

Australia's manufacturing sector has been in persistent decline for the last fifty years in terms of both its share of output and its share of employment. Its ability to drive a revival in non-resource capital investment is therefore questionable.

House prices and building approvals have been trending upwards of late, but the Australian housing market appears to be richly priced on any number of commonly touted valuation metrics. Depending on a strong pickup in housing as a means to rebalance the economy would therefore appear to be fraught with danger. The risk is of boom followed by bust, with considerable collateral damage to both financial and non-financial balance sheets.

After a sharp rise in leverage in the nineties and the noughties, the household sector's total debt and debt service ratios remain onerous, at close to 150% and 10% of disposable income, respectively, and one must therefore question the responsiveness of the consumer to official interest rate reductions. The RBA has already delivered 225 basis points of rate cuts since November 2011 and yet the impact to date has been muted.

Macroeconomic theory suggests that a tight fiscal/loose monetary policy mix is the best combination to deliver the necessary exchange rate adjustment that Australia requires to rebalance, and, consistent with this, over the period since 2010 Australia has tightened fiscal policy by some 2.5 percentage points of GDP in total, which is roughly in line with the OECD average.

However, when private sector debt burdens are hampering the effectiveness of monetary policy, it could be argued that a continuation of such an austere bias in fiscal policy will prove excessively burdensome to domestic spending. Existing plans are for a slower pace of underlying fiscal policy adjustment in the years ahead, and the suggestion is that even these may need to be implemented with a degree of flexibility.

Notwithstanding the prospective positive influence of the resource boom on trade performance, the economy's current account balance remains in structural deficit, as it has been for the last fifty years, while its net external debt is equivalent to nearly 100% of GDP. This external financing requirement and accumulation of overseas liabilities could constrict policy flexibility during times of global risk aversion. It also underlines the importance of policy being conducted in such a way as to retain the confidence of overseas investors.

Australia also remains acutely exposed to trauma in the Chinese economy, where various imbalances and disequilibria – not least the excessive credit intensity of growth – continue to cast a shadow over the pace and sustainability of the country's development.

All in all, Australia appears to face a tougher set of circumstances than has been the case for some time, with the requirement for new sources of demand suggesting that growth will struggle to match potential. Indeed, there is a threat that new shocks could cause growth to stall altogether.

This in turn points to a number of overriding conclusions.

- With inflation well contained, the bias in Australian monetary policy looks likely to remain towards ease for some time to come.

- This also points to further weakness in the Australian dollar over the medium term, and it should be remembered that in the past the Australian currency has exhibited a propensity to overshoot both on the upside and the downside.

- Fiscal policy may have to become more supportive of growth.

- There is a strong requirement for new structural, or supply-side, initiatives.

Despite its impressive aggregate growth performance and resilience to the GFC, Australia's recent productivity record has been disappointing, although no doubt this in part reflects temporary effects linked to the mining boom.

Overall, however, in the new, more challenging, environment confronting the country, it will be vital for Australia to retain its flexible markets and to eschew protectionist and interventionist palliatives.

Further tax reforms would also pay dividends. For example, the consumption tax burden remains relatively low in an international context, while it would make sense for the load on the corporate sector, and especially on SMEs, to be reduced.

There are three other areas of structural policy in particular that require attention: infrastructure, foreign direct investment and innovation, with infrastructure the top priority. Good infrastructure can exert a number of longer-term positive influences on an economy's supply-side potential by enhancing competition, encouraging trade and integration, improving access to resources and public services, and fostering the dissemination of ideas and innovation. But establishing top-quality infrastructure is especially important in a geographically expansive country like Australia, where the dispersion of the population and of production centres is so great, and the distance from major markets so extended.

As suggested above, the end of my time in Sydney with Westpac reflected in part that the role I had essentially been hired to play never materialised. But by the latter part of 2012 I had had my fill of working in a bank or investment bank. I had had enough of the mercurial, inconsistent management, the petty politics, the big egos, the travel, the difficult clients and the constant struggle to prove oneself. Despite a continued fascination with macroeconomics and markets, and a keen interest in acting as a mentor, it was getting difficult to get out of bed in the morning. The thrill had gone. It was time to move on to pastures new.

And I was lucky enough to be offered an opportunity to do this. While on one of my intermittent trips back home, I called in on my ex-boss John Llewellyn, who, in the wake of the Lehman Brothers debacle, had set up his own macroeconomic consultancy (based in the City, near St Paul's Cathedral) with his son Preston. Over lunch I told John how fed up I was, while he told me how much he was enjoying being the master of his own destiny and that he loved working with people he wanted to work with. Before I said goodbye he took me up to see his suite of offices and, pointing at a dormant computer, he said: 'You see that desk? That's yours. Just call me when you want to take up residence.' A couple of months later I did just that, and a few months after that, having negotiated a very amicable departure from Westpac, I found myself sitting at that desk. I haven't looked back since.

CHAPTER 17

JUST MACRO...

L ooking back over my career, with all its ebbs and flows, I cannot but conclude that the era and the environment in which I worked will be considered by future historians as an extraordinary aberration that occasionally bordered on the absurd. It is unlikely that the financial sector's position and influence in the global economy will ever be quite so overwhelming again. The banks' modi operandi have changed: they are less profitable, they have cut costs, they have deleveraged, their market capitalisation has declined, their underwriting has shrunk, they employ fewer people and pay them less, they are less opaque and more risk averse, and much of the growth they are enjoying is emanating from retail rather than investment banking.

Meanwhile, the general public continues to vent its anger and frustration over the GFC and its immensely painful aftermath and, unsurprisingly, politicians are happy to swim with the tide. The financial sector and those employed in it remain an easy target and convenient scapegoats. The upshot will be more regulation and more efforts to prevent what (if I can borrow an old phrase from Ted Heath, the former UK prime minister) is widely regarded as 'the unpleasant and unacceptable face of capitalism' ever rearing its ugly head again.[44] This is especially the case if, as seems likely, governments increasingly seek to address the vexed issue of their sovereign debt liabilities through variations on the theme of financial repression.

I have no little sympathy for this punitive response. Broad-based and efficient financial intermediation is no doubt a necessity for a capitalist economy (and in this category I include any reasonable notion of a 'mixed economy') to function well. Indeed, I would go so far as to say that it is a *sine qua non* of such systems. But equally there is no doubt that shortcomings and failings in the basic architecture of financial intermediation can encourage predatory and destructive tendencies, if not grotesque distortions in the allocation of capital and resources, and huge costs for society as a whole when these distortions unwind. The broader tax-paying community paid a huge bill for the excesses of a relatively small number of people.

I would still argue that the global financial system was in need of reform at the time I began my career in the markets in the mid eighties. It was for the most part lacking competition and transparency, it was subject to excessive and often incoherent government intervention, and it was beset by too many rules that had largely outgrown their original purpose. This encouraged a form of sclerosis, constricting risk taking and entrepreneurship and constraining growth. Nowhere was this more obvious than in the City of London. Encouraging a more vibrant financial sector was bound to pay macroeconomic dividends, and not just to those working within it.

However, nourished by the then intellectually dominant free market school of thought, which effectively suggested that a major disaster couldn't happen, the subsequent process of financial liberalisation was allowed to go too far. Too many of the good rules and regulations were thrown out with the bad, while any notion of imposing new controls on the financial sector's rapidly expanding and evolving activities was largely eschewed. Indeed, such interventions were almost seen as taboo. This was especially the case in the US and the UK, where governments of all hues desperately sought the indulgence and seal of approval of the markets and those who bestrode them, not least because they had become increasingly dependent on them as a source of tax revenue.

Lightly regulated and inadequately overseen, invigorated by a period of apparent macroeconomic calm and quiescent inflation, the system ended up obscenely bloated and bent out of shape by a perverse incentive structure. It ran out of control and became a law unto itself. Hubristic, over-leveraged, over-complex, over-correlated, beset by mispriced risk, insufficiently liquid or capitalised, and inadequately understood at all levels from the trading floor to the cabinet room, it was captured by too many of the narrow, the selfish, the egotistical and the inexperienced, whose alternating tendencies towards collective irrational exuberance and unbounded pessimism proved all too powerful – and ultimately cataclysmic. The fact is that not all entrepreneurship and innovation is good: in the wrong hands it can prove extraordinarily malign.

The large multinational multifaceted investment banks and other financial institutions that grew out of this process didn't work. They proved too unwieldy and the risks associated with them were impossible to control, especially as many of those who assumed senior management positions were poorly equipped to do the job and the techniques employed, such as value at risk analysis, were fundamentally flawed. There were also too many traders occupying these roles. Managers with broad skills who built a team ethic, assiduously looked after their clients' interests and eschewed more Machiavellian approaches to profit maximisation were far too thin on the ground. Furthermore, the emphasis placed on internal competition between business units and creative tension between individuals to achieve results often proved self-defeating: a zero sum, if not a negative sum, game.

But the distortions, inadequacies and failings within the system went far deeper than its larger players and their questionable management practices. Over time, the whole edifice became increasingly rotten, inefficient and unstable and it became a source of rising income inequality. In essence, what developed was akin to a crystal. Outwardly impressive to behold, seemingly structurally rigid and unyielding, but if subjected to a particular set of forces, likely to fracture. This is what happened in 2008.

But not everyone who worked in the financial sector should be tarred with the same negative 'wanker banker' brush. Not all were disciples of cold and unrestrained free market capitalism and variations on the theme of raw social Darwinism. Most were just doing their job: pursuing their particular comparative advantage in an industry where the challenges were considerable, but so too could be the rewards. And some, not least my old bosses John Llewellyn and Alan Lewis, rose conspicuously above the regrettable norm, putting their immediate charges and their clients first.

For my part, I always considered myself to be something of an outsider. I felt part of the financial system but not entirely of it. Indeed, I almost considered myself to be above much of it. I liked to think of myself as relatively untainted by my surroundings. In hindsight, this is at least precious and perhaps delusional. The fact is that for more than twenty-five years I rode the tiger. It proffered me a number of wonderful opportunities to live and work in some exotic and captivating parts of the world, and it allowed me to pursue a career doing something that, for all its ups and downs and my own restlessness, for the most part I greatly enjoyed. I found the intense pressure-cooker environment incredibly stimulating. I embraced the tests, the trials, the intensity, the unexpected and the attention and privilege that went along with them. In short, I became addicted to the buzz. In the process I experienced things that few could dream of and it brought my family wealth and comfort.

At the same time, for all my efforts at aloof detachment, it was all too easy to lose perspective. There were undoubtedly occasions when I exhibited some of the traits that I disapproved of and looked down on in others. Working in the industry for that length of time, however much you tried to do the right thing and be true to your morals, ethics and fundamental beliefs, you could not help but be caught up in its customs and habits. In fact, at RBC, at a time of my career when I should have been comfortable in my professional skin, I became so desperate for recognition and to prove myself that I nearly triggered my own downfall.

Although I can never forgive myself for this reckless foolishness, taking my career as a whole, I am for the most part proud of what I achieved. I think that I did a reasonable job, especially during my second spell in Japan and during the GFC and its immediate aftermath. At those moments of extraordinary economic and financial crisis I dug deep into my historical knowledge and my long-cherished Keynesian principles paid dividends. I made errors, of course, both of commission and omission, and sometimes I got things terribly wrong, but that was unavoidable. Being a financial markets economist is a tough gig. Predicting the future is not easy, and nor is understanding the present, or, for that matter, the past. One of the more interesting recent developments in the study of economic history is that academics are now revising their views of the Great Depression in the light of the policy decisions made since 2007. In particular, the long-standing belief among US monetarists that the dramatic downturn in the early thirties would have been avoided had the Federal Reserve been more willing to expand its balance sheet at the time is now being questioned, given the performance of quantitative easing during the latest crisis.[45]

And just as the overall financial business changed, so, over time, did my job description, and I had to evolve with it. The deregulation process no doubt encouraged this, but so too did the two interrelated considerations of technology and globalisation. The pool of available information and the speed and convenience with which it could be delivered have increased dramatically over the time that I have worked in the markets. And as the world became ever more interconnected and the BRICs and other emerging nations took up a larger and larger share of world output, it became increasingly inappropriate to look at individual economies in isolation. This is not to deny that countries retained their own particular social, cultural and institutional idiosyncrasies, or indeed that national policy analysis remained of primary importance – they did. But global themes and forces came increasingly to the fore and had to be woven into one's analysis. Those who ignored this fact did so at their peril.

Along with these three powerful forces came intense competition. There were some incredibly smart people doing what I did, and the average depth of economic analysis provided by these people increased considerably over time, even if the quality of the language in which it was presented tended to move inexorably in the opposite direction. Sometimes when I happened to see some competitor research I would despair that I could ever hope to match it. Indeed, this no doubt fed my own enduring sense of insecurity. Finding a comparative advantage or a unique selling point for one's views became more and more difficult. This tended to encourage some down the road of ever more complex and, for that matter, often spurious empiricism. Given my quantitative shortcomings this was a route that I was never going to follow. Instead, my response was to look to history, to context, to experience, to clarity of exposition and to humility. Actually admitting what one didn't know, why one didn't know it, and presenting the facts in a clear and engaging manner could become a positive. And one thing is clear: although I learned a vast amount during my career, the older I became, the less I was really sure about. Economies and financial markets are incredibly complex and constantly changing beasts.

That said, I am more than content to defend my profession. It's necessary and it's valuable, in both a financial market context and beyond. The world would be a much poorer, less well understood and unstable place without economists. Those that downplayed or dismissed the importance of macroeconomics to market dynamics and the progress of financial institutions (and there were many) were deluded. If there is one dominant example of this, it comes from the mouth of former Lehman Brothers CEO Dick Fuld. When, a few years before the GFC, Chief Economist John Llewellyn sought to bring to the attention of those present at the regular New York Monday morning senior management meeting the burgeoning risks associated with various global macro imbalances and the diminution of risk premia to historically low levels, he was interrupted by Fuld: 'You've said that once before', he growled, 'Don't say it again. That's just macro.'[46] That's right Dick: the same 'macro' that you never understood, did not even know that you did not understand, and that before long would go a long way towards demolishing the firm you built and held so dear.

On the other hand, even for those with a more enlightened view of my profession, today's ever-more-impatient search for answers and instant gratification means that expectations of what an economist can, or should, do are frequently too high. Simple panaceas are few and far between. This leaves us on a hiding to nothing, although the fact that many practitioners of the art all too often go about their business without the necessary humility that such a difficult job warrants doesn't help. Their arrogance just invites criticism and gives the profession a bad name.

Another problem one faces, as I have emphasised on many occasions, is that because economics palpably encroaches on the lives of every human being on the planet, everyone considers himself or herself to be something of an economist. Most people are always ready to quote some 'obvious' economic truth or seemingly blindingly apparent solution to an economic problem from their own personal experience or their application of layman's logic. Even Dick Fuld's crass put-down of John Llewellyn could be construed as his own particular, if perverse, judgement on the immediate importance of global macroeconomic imbalances and compressed risk premia to his firm and how it was managed.

But what Fuld did is what most lay people do, and, for that matter, what some economists and policymakers do too. He looked at an economic issue from an unduly narrow and short-term point of view. He applied what economists would refer to as 'partial equilibrium analysis' rather than 'general equilibrium analysis'. He failed to recognise that, in economics, everything is connected and that, as sure as night follows day, disequilibria will eventually begin to unwind – it just might take a long time to happen. Furthermore, disturbances to the economic system can rarely be contained as easily as people would like to think. Rather, they will reverberate through it, producing a litany of secondary, often unexpected, effects and costs that can cumulate into some very unpleasant consequences. What seems like an irrelevancy one minute can rapidly become the opposite. What seems like a sensible response to a particular situation or problem can just create another potentially bigger set of difficulties. A lot of what economists do is about trying to work out these general equilibrium consequences in an effort to understand what is the least damaging way forward.

Notwithstanding my own burgeoning professional doubts and uncertainties, and the unfortunately polarised views of what economists could and should know and do, certain economic truths have revealed themselves over the course of my career. Moreover, I am relieved to say that a significant number of these truths were consistent with my own initial 'priors' about how the world worked, many of which I was lucky enough to have passed on to me during my initial academic experiences.

First, uncertainty, as opposed to measurable risk, is a fact of life. Indeed, as the Roman philosopher Pliny the Elder astutely put it: 'Only one thing is certain: that nothing is certain.'[47] And make no mistake, uncertainty can become truly radical in nature, dominating all other considerations in decision making and at every level from the individual upwards.

By damping animal spirits, uncertainty can constrain spending and utterly undermine aggregate demand. As a result, economies do not necessarily rapidly self-regulate and self-heal, smoothly returning to some equilibrium. They can become divorced from any notion of full resource utilisation for a protracted period. This happened in the thirties, it happened to devastating effect in Japan in the nineties and beyond, and it has occurred to some degree in any number of economies, not least those in the Eurozone periphery, since 2008. There was for me a 'Eureka moment' when reading the recently released transcripts of the Fed's policy deliberations during the crisis. At one point Ben Bernanke asserts: 'I don't think that this is going to be a self-correcting thing anytime soon. We are going to have to provide support of all kinds to the economy.'[48]

The latest set of worries about the future relate to the possibility of so-called secular stagnation. Such concerns were first raised by Keynes and his US disciples in the late thirties, but they proved unduly pessimistic. Today, they focus on the depressive influence on animal spirits and on the willingness to invest of minimal OECD population growth, slowing productivity growth, widening income inequalities and the possible exhaustion of innovative potential, at least outside the technology sector, which in any case seems to be failing to mobilise savings and expand the overall capital stock in the same way that the great inventions of the late nineteenth and early twentieth centuries did.[49]

Equally incontestable to my mind is that booms and busts, asset market excesses and deep recessions are difficult, if not impossible, to avoid, and that the downturns that follow large financial crises are invariably the most intractable. Experience suggests that such ebbs and flows in economic and financial activity are part and parcel of human nature, or at least part and parcel of the capitalist system. The business cycle cannot therefore be entirely tamed, as was suggested by some right-wing economists in the noughties.

On the other hand, neither should the business cycle be left to its own devices – the effects of doing that can, in extremis, be truly disastrous. Consistent with all this, the 'New Classical' and efficient markets schools of economics, if taken to their logical conclusions, are dangerous abstractions from reality that risk catastrophic social and political instability.

Similarly, the danger with the supposedly magical properties of 'creative destruction' is that it delivers a very low ratio of creation to destruction. On all levels.

In contrast, many of the fundamental tenets of Keynesian and Minskyian analysis hold true, and two of them in particular: there is an unarguable role for policy activism, especially in the wake of financial crises, and this should extend beyond what central banks do to fiscal and macroprudential policy; and periods of relative tranquillity in macroeconomic and financial terms tend to embody the seeds of their own destruction.

Another overriding conclusion is that fiscal consolidation becomes very difficult to achieve when everybody is doing it at the same time and/or when the private sector is also deleveraging. Keynes's notion of the paradox of thrift holds.

Related to this is the fact that so-called expansionary fiscal contractions are very rare, if not entirely mythical, beasts. They only happen in the most opportune of circumstances.

Sovereign debt crises are invariably the result of private sector credit booms turning to bust. The Global Financial Crisis had little to do with public sector profligacy per se, even if historically high levels of public sector debt subsequently acted to compromise the fiscal policy response to it.

Overcoming a sovereign debt crisis requires sustained economic growth and a dose of debt restructuring. It cannot be cured by fiscal austerity alone, and especially within a half-baked currency union.

Finally, demand management, however well it is done, is not enough. As the American lawyer Clarence Darrow is reputed to have said: 'It is not the strongest of species that survive, nor the most intelligent, but the ones most adaptable to change.'[50] To maximise economic performance, governments must persistently pursue structural reform, or policies that encourage, or at least do not hinder, the flow of resources from declining and less productive activities to growing and more productive activities, and which leave economies better equipped to absorb shocks. In short, initiatives that increase the capacity of economies and societies to adapt to change – and indeed a process of change that is never ending, whether it be the result of globalisation, technological development or the impact of rising per capita incomes on consumption patterns. This means appropriate strategies for education and training, research and development, entrepreneurship, infrastructure, trade policy, foreign direct investment, tax and benefit systems, employment protection and active labour market policies.

All this said, economic policymaking, and in particular the achievement of an enduringly positive balance of benefits relative to costs from policy action, is anything but easy. The list of obstacles that have to be confronted in the pursuit of macroeconomic stabilisation is long and diverse. Macroeconomic data, notwithstanding improvements in coverage and accuracy over recent years, remain inexact, are subject to considerable revision and are published with an unfortunate lag. There is the potential for numerous, perhaps conflicting, shocks to hit an economy within a relatively short period. The time available for decision making is usually inadequate, so that what emerges is a partial or suboptimal response to a situation, especially when there is little consensus across those responsible for policy about the underlying causes of a problem. Too much time is spent fire-fighting and too little on attending to longer-term considerations. Moreover, in most countries the democratic process intervenes with persistent, often highly inconvenient, regularity. And, of course, the lags involved in policy are often long and variable, so that calibrating measures with a business cycle that is forever in flux is extremely difficult.

Notwithstanding the remarkable dedication of most of those responsible and the improvements over time in the authorities' communication methods, my years in the markets were littered with evidence of the shortcomings of economic policymaking. And bad policy invariably results in bad outcomes. Indeed, sadly, for practical purposes policy success must often be judged in terms of the relative paucity of outright error rather than tallying the indisputably positive achievements.

My experience brings me to the following conclusions.

- Too often, policymakers have ended up continuing to fight the last battle long after it has been won and some new challenge has emerged.[50] The next crisis is usually very different from the last.

- Monetary and fiscal policies have rarely been adequately coordinated, either within or across countries.

- Fiscal activism, although undeniably useful in certain circumstances, became severely compromised by fifty years of over-optimism about its effects and short-sighted, politically driven, budgetary excess.

- Monetary policy is not always as potent as it might be, or as policymakers would like it to be. It can become overloaded. It works poorly at the zero nominal interest rate bound, when there is balance sheet adjustment across the private sector, and when uncertainty about the future is especially elevated.

- Not enough attention has been paid to macro imbalances or to supply-side considerations, and the latter's relationship with demand management has been poorly understood. Macroprudential initiatives have been used too little and too late.

- Policymakers, like everyone else, have struggled to differentiate the cyclical from the structural. Whatever the immediate evidence to the contrary, major shifts in underlying macroeconomic performance are rare. Influences come and go, but economies are often prisoners of long-term considerations such as demographics, if not of their own history, their own culture, their own institutions and their own politics. To exert an enduring transformational impact on these considerations, policy changes have to be substantial and persistent in nature.

Despite all these considerations, though, I firmly believe that we are better off trying to manage economies than not.

Perhaps all that remains now is for me to offer some concluding words of advice to anyone thinking of following in my footsteps. Working as a financial markets economist can no doubt be a wonderful and fulfilling career. This is certainly how I look back upon my own experience, and I know that many of my contemporaries, despite all the pitfalls involved, feel much the same way. On the other hand, having witnessed first hand the process by which their father sought to come to terms with successive variations on this often bizarre and challenging professional theme, my own, now grown-up, children have striven to avoid my example like the plague.

I can only therefore conclude that it takes a particular type of person to survive and flourish doing what I did. Furthermore, that particular brand of individual may not necessarily be the most technically gifted economist. Indeed, it rarely is. To prosper, I would venture that you will need to combine such skills as an economist as you can boast with a broader knowledge of history, current affairs and other social sciences. You will need to be able to communicate clearly and concisely on several levels. You will need to exhibit confidence, but not to the level of arrogance. You will need to be organised, innovative, thick-skinned, politically astute, a decent manager of people (both upwards and downwards), physically resilient, and, perhaps most importantly of all, adaptable. The enviable pay and perks you receive are in many ways a reward for the vagaries and uncertainties you are constantly subjected to. Oh yes, and a well-developed and self-deprecating sense of humour certainly doesn't hurt either.

Finally, whatever you were taught at university, you could do a lot worse than to go back and study some of Keynes's original writings.

ENDNOTES

1. John Llewellyn, Stephen Potter and Lee Samuelson. 1986. *Economic Forecasting and Policy: The International Dimension*. Routledge.

2. Some of the more entertaining books on this period are *Strange Days Indeed – the Golden Age of Paranoia* by Francis Wheen (Fourth Estate, 2009) and the two books written by Dominic Sandbrook on the 1970s: *State of Emergency. The Way We Were: Britain 1970–1974* (Allen Lane, 2010) and *Seasons in the Sun. The Battle for Britain, 1974–1979* (Allen Lane, 2012).

3. I have always thought that Keynes was closer to the mark when he suggested that economists should aspire to be closer to dentists or plumbers than physicists: see J. M. Keynes, Economic possibilities for our grandchildren, in *Essays in Persuasion* (Macmillan, 1930).

4. For an excellent summary of what is wrong with a lot of modern economics, see John Cassidy, *Why Markets Fail: The Logic of Economic Calamities* (Allen Lane, 2009).

5. I recall Willem Buiter aptly referring to this as 'the real bollocks theory'.

6. Again John Cassidy does a great job in describing these theories. See also Robert Skidelsky, *Keynes: The Return of the Master* (Allen Lane, 2009), and Willem Buiter's blog of 3 March 2009 at http://blogs.ft.com/marecon/2009/03/the-unfortunate-uselessness-of-most-state-of-the-art-academic-monetary-economics/.

7. J. M. Keynes. 1936. *The General Theory of Employment, Interest and Money*. Cambridge University Press.

8. Robert Skidelsky. 2009. *Keynes: The Return of the Master*. Allen Lane.

9. The article that turned my head was G. C. Peden. 1980. Keynes, the Treasury and unemployment in the later 1930s. Oxford Economic Papers, Volume xxxii. Second Series.

10. Russell Jones. 1983. The Wages Problem in Employment Policy 1936–48. MSc thesis, University of Bristol.

11. These were published after his death and offer a fascinating insight into the policymaking process. See Alec Cairncross (ed.). 1989. *The Robert Hall Diaries, 1947–53*. Allen and Unwin.

12. See, for example, Alec Cairncross. 1985. *Years of Recovery: British Economic Policy 1945–51*. Methuen.

13. Russell Jones. 1987. *Wages and Employment Policy, 1936–85.* Allen and Unwin.

14. Edwin Plowden. 1989. *An Industrialist in the Treasury: The Post-War Years.* Andre Deutsch.

15. For the context relating to this, see David Kynaston. 2001. *The City of London Volume IV: A Club No More, 1945–2000.* Chatto and Windus.

16. John Plender. 2013. Central banks risk sharing too much with investors. *Financial Times*, 17 July.

17. E. C. Brown. 1956. Fiscal policy in the 1930s: a reappraisal. *American Economic Review* 46, 857–879. M. S. Cha. 2003. Did Takahashi Korekiyo rescue Japan from the Great Depression? *Journal of Economic History* 63(1), 127–144.

18. Drexel's fall: the final days. *New York Magazine*, 19 March 1990.

19. Nicholas Crafts. 2013. The economic legacy of Mrs Thatcher. VoxEU, 8 April (www.voxeu.org/article/economic-legacy-mrs-thatcher). Martin Wolf. 2013. Thatcher: the great transformer. *Financial Times*, 8 April. Simon Wren-Lewis. 2013. On the economic achievements and failures of Margaret Thatcher. Available at mainlymacro.blogspot.co.uk/2013/04/on -economic-achievements-and-failures.html.

20. Philip Stephens. 1997. *Politics and the Pound: The Tories, the Economy and Europe.* Papermac.

21. I seem to remember that ours also included a couple of bottles of Scottish malt whisky and a carton of cigarettes. When we left Japan I was given the job of dismantling the kit, only to find that my wife had been intermittently raiding the cash for other purposes such that it was almost all gone!

22. For a detailed description of the time line of events in Japan during the nineties and early noughties, Graham Turner's excellent book *Solutions to a Liquidity Trap* (GFC Economics, 2003) is a superb source.

23. Bill Martin. 1992. Shades of '25. UBS Global Economics.

24. Nicholas Crafts. 2011. *Delivering Growth While Reducing Deficits: Lessons from the 1930s.* Centre Forum.

25. Bank of England. 1995. The bond sell-off of 1994. *Quarterly Bulletin*, Q3 1995.

26. When I eventually got back to Tokyo in the summer of 2005 I asked the head of equity trading at Lehman about this episode in which Leeson undertook unauthorised speculative trades in Japanese stock index futures that went progressively wrong to the tune of $1.4bn. He replied that for some time he and others had had the sense that something was not quite right about the way that the Japanese equity market was trading. He suspected that someone had a huge position that he was desperately trying and failing to manage. He was right.

27. See Liaquat Ahamed. 2009. *Lords of Finance: The Bankers Who Broke the World.* Heinemann.

28.   IMF. 1998. *World Economic Outlook* (May). These policies became known as the 'Washington Consensus' and effectively embodied a competitive exchange rate and some combination of fiscal discipline, improved public spending priorities, tax reform, interest rate liberalisation, privatisation, openness to foreign direct investment and deregulation.

29.   Russell Jones. 2000. A golden age lost. *Asian Wall Street Journal*, June.

30.   Alan Greenspan. 2001. Testimony to Senate Budget Committee, 25 January.

31.   UK Treasury. 2003. UK membership of the single currency. An economic assessment of the five economic tests (June).

32.   Prospects for Iraq: some lessons of history (June 2004). The report is available on John Llewellyn's website at www.llewellyn.co.nz/Prospects forIraq.pdf.

33.   *CIA: The World Factbook*. (See www.cia.gov/library/publications/the-world-factbook/geos/ae.html.)

34.   I would add that I was on many occasions less than impressed with the way that some expatriates, not least those from the UK, would treat the immigrant workers that they hired as domestic helps. Not to put too fine a point on it, some of the worst aspects of nineteenth- and twentieth-century European colonialism still appeared to be flourishing in the UAE in the mid noughties.

35.   Raghuram Rajan. 2005. Has financial development made the world riskier? *Jackson Hole Conference Papers*. Federal Reserve Bank of Kansas.

36.   For example, at one of my first official ADIA excursions to see policy-makers I was lucky enough to be granted an hour-long audience with ECB Chief Economist Otmar Issing. Such a meeting would never have come to pass in any of my previous professional incarnations.

37.   David McWilliams. 2009. *The Generation Game, July 2007: Follow the Money*. Macmillan.

38.   No Canadian financial institution failed or required government support in the form of a capital injection or debt guarantee during the crisis. I therefore have little doubt that, whatever effect it had on my Toronto colleagues, Canada's relative success in maintaining financial stability during the GFC was a major reason why Mark Carney was sought out to replace Mervyn King as governor of the Bank of England, although quite how much this was down to Carney himself is another matter.

39.   See M. Blyth. 2013. *Austerity: The History of a Dangerous Idea*. Oxford University Press.

40.   John Llewellyn *et al.* 2010. Lessons from the financial crisis. *The Business Economist, Society of Business Economists*. (Originally a presentation to HM Treasury Economists' Conference in January 2009.)

41.   See 'The rule of four' (Jan Qvigstad and John Llewellyn, with Nikka Husom Vonen and Bimal Dharmasena) in *The Business Economist, Society of Business Economists* (2012).

42. Herbert Stein. 1999. *What I Think: Essays on Economics, Politics and Life*. AEI Press.

43. In the mid thirties, just as the US's recovery was gathering momentum, the Roosevelt administration threw fiscal policy into reverse at the same time as the Federal Reserve raised reserve requirements. Not only did the nascent upswing fizzle out, the economy suffered a downturn that was on some metrics more precipitous than that which followed the Wall Street Crash.

44. Heath used the phrase in 1973 to describe the so-called Lonrho affair.

45. J. Bradford Delong. 2013. The Great Depression of the 1930s from the perspective of today, and today from the perspective of the Great Depression. NBER (September).

46. Actually, his language was more colourful than that, as was his wont. But that was the gist.

47. Gaius Plinius Secundus. AD 77–79. *Naturalis Historia*.

48. Federal Reserve FOMC transcripts, 28–29 October 2008, page 118 (www .federalreserve.gov/monetarypolicy/fomchistorical2008.htm

49. Gavyn Davies. 2013. The implications of secular stagnation. *Financial Times*, 11 November. Martin Wolf. 2013. Why the future looks sluggish. *Financial Times*, 19 November.

50. See http://artquotes.robertgenn.com/auth_search.php?authid=1572#. UoNNnRqpXVU. I would argue that Germany has effectively been fighting a battle with inflation it lost in 1923 ever since.